Issues in computer-adaptive testing of reading proficiency

STUDIES IN LANGUAGE TESTING...10
Series editor: Michael Milanovic

Also in this series:

Issues in computer-adaptive testing of reading proficiency

Edited by Micheline Chalhoub-Deville

Published by the Press Syndicate of the University of Cambridge
The Pitt Building, Trumpington Street, Cambridge CB2 1RP, UK
40 West 20th Street, New York, NY 10011–4211, USA
10 Stamford Road, Oakleigh, Melbourne 3166, Australia

First published 1999

Printed in Great Britain at the University Press, Cambridge, UK

British Library cataloguing in publication data

University of Cambridge, Local Examinations Syndicate
Issues in computer-adaptive testing of reading proficiency

Edited by Micheline Chalhoub-Deville

1. Education. Assessment 2. Education. Tests. Setting

ISBN   0 521–653002   hardback
        0 521–653800   paperback

To my Mother and Father, Badiha and Badih

Contents

Series Editor's note

The use of computers in language assessment has been a topic of great interest for some years and this volume makes an important contribution to thinking on computer adaptive testing (CAT) and reading comprehension. It considers the issues from a number of angles – reading research, design, development and measurement. The three main sections of the book are usefully reviewed by three discussants, Charles Alderson, Carol Chapelle and Bruno Zumbo who provide valuable insights through their comments, and the volume as a whole is ably edited by Micheline Chalhoub-Deville.

At Cambridge, much resource has gone into the development of both adaptive and linear computer-based tests. Work in this area started in the mid-nineties with a project to develop a CAT specifically for Manpower Europe, part of Manpower Inc. the world's largest employment services company. Linguaskill, as it is known, focuses on language for work purposes but is also notable for the fact that it is a multi-lingual system operating in English, French, German, Spanish and Dutch and reporting on the same measurement scale. Nine item types are used in Linguaskill, up to five of them focussing on reading. Two additional multi-lingual adaptive tests have also been developed in Cambridge - the Computer-based Business Language Testing System (CBBULATS) and CommuniCAT. The International English Language Testing System (IELTS) has also been computerised, though this test is linear rather than adaptive.

The development of all these tests have posed interesting practical and theoretical problems related to the way materials are presented, the interaction between test takers and the computer presentation of materials and how best to exploit the computer's power. The UCLES team has worked closely with the Multimedia Development Unit at Homerton College, Cambridge, which has significant expertise in educational software design.

Attention has also focused on using the computer to investigate the relationship between candidates' background characteristics, learning style, cognitive and metacognitive processes and test performance. This work builds on that done by Jim Purpura, reported in Studies in Language 8 and is intended to provide a resource for both learners and teachers. In addition, work continues in the area of self assessment and linguistic audit where the can-do system of performance descriptors, developed in nine European languages to-date, are being computerised as part of a wider project to develop a multi-lingual performance oriented descriptive framework of competence. The latter project will be reported in a later volume in this series.

Michael Milanovic, Cambridge, December 1999

Preface

Researchers in the second language (L2) field, especially those involved in large-scale assessment, are increasingly directing their attention to the development of computer-adaptive testing (CAT) instruments for assessing learners' L2 ability (e.g. TOEFL 2000 Project). Computer-adaptive refers to the procedure where an item(s) is selected on-line for each test taker based on his/her performance on previous items. As such, assessment is tailored on-line to accommodate the test taker's ability. Perhaps the greatest attraction of CAT is the facility to administer the test on a large scale, and at the same time, the potential to optimize the testing situation by targeting each student's ability level. The prevalent interest in CAT has been aided, on the one hand, by the increasing availability of computers and the familiarity of learners with their use, and on the other, by advances in measurement theory, especially item response theory (IRT).

A number of the chapters included in this volume were presented at the invitational conference, 'Issues in Computer-Adaptive Testing on L2 Reading Proficiency', held in Bloomington, Minnesota in March 1996. The conference, which was supported in part by a grant from the Department of Education, International Research and Studies Program, was hosted by the Centre for Advanced Research on Language Acquisition at the University of Minnesota. The conference was unique as it was the first formal meeting to focus on L2 CAT development and research issues.

The main purpose of the conference was to deal with various issues that have an impact on the research and development of CATs for assessing students' L2 reading proficiency. The topic was of interest to the conference organizers as they were involved in the development of CAT reading instruments in various languages. A diverse group of researchers from both the academic and private sectors were invited to share their knowledge and experience on four interrelated issues: L2 reading construct, L2 CAT practices, measurement issues and testing technology. The present volume deals with the various topics addressed in the conference, except for technology. The constant flux in this area and the corresponding rapid rate of change in technological developments mitigate the timeliness and criticality of these issues from the conference. For recent publications in this area, the reader is encouraged to consult Drasgow and Olson-Buchanan (in press), Sands, Waters and McBride (1997) and Shneiderman (1998).

Papers from the conference and from others working on L2 CATs were gathered together to address a broad range of issues regarding the design, development and research of L2 computer-adaptive reading tests. Those involved in the development of L2 CATs have typically faced the arduous task of examining the literature in the various areas pertinent to the development of such tests and reconciling the diverse findings and recommendations. This volume describes the issues in these various disciplines that have an impact on CAT development, highlights the potential challenges and makes recommendations that will help bridge the gap among the different disciplines in order to develop L2 CAT instruments. The major thrust of these issues is laid out in the following three points:

1. It is always important to remember when dealing with computerized testing, adaptive or not, that the computer serves simply as a tool that will enhance the efficiency of assessment. Our foremost consideration, however, must remain the test construct. In developing computer-adaptive reading tests, therefore, it is critical to address the current theoretical arguments and empirical findings regarding the reading construct.
2. Equally important is to translate the theoretical representations of the construct into an operational framework that can be used for the selection of texts and for the development of items that represent the construct and are viable with a computer-adaptive format. For example, constructivist theory researchers argue strongly in favor of open-ended responses that enable us to examine how readers reconstruct the text they read. Such item types, however, are still not feasible with adaptive testing. Consequently, how can L2 CAT developers deal with the need to construct items whose scores have construct validity?
3. With regard to measurement, the debate in the past on which of the item response theory (IRT) models to use in various assessment applications has been quite spirited and remains controversial to some. In developing computer-adaptive L2 reading tests where the adaptive algorithm is often IRT based, it is necessary to examine the appropriateness of the various IRT models. In addition to selecting the IRT model, test developers must also consider a number of issues regarding the adaptive algorithm, such as CAT entry point, exit point, content sampling, exposure control, etc.

It is important to point out that bringing together the various experts was not intended to provide definitive answers to the issues raised. The issues raised by the various experts engender, even in their own respective fields, heated debates. The purpose of bringing together this group of experts was to uncover the issues and expose the audience to the breadth and complexity of these issues within each field, in particular when examined in the context of developing CAT for L2 reading.

Overview of the volume

As stated earlier, the purpose of the chapters included in this volume is to represent the latest thinking and work on some of the major issues pertaining to the development of computer-adaptive L2 tests with a focus on reading. The present volume is divided into three major sections: L2 reading construct, L2 CAT applications and considerations, and measurement issues. An often heard criticism of edited volumes is the lack of coherence and interconnectedness among the chapters included. In order to help address such criticism, discussion chapters are included in each of the three sections. The discussion chapters highlight and discuss the issues raised by the authors in their respective section as well as those of immediate relevance in the other sections.

The chapters in section one by Bernhardt and Grabe focus on the literature pertaining to the L2 reading construct. In her chapter, Bernhardt provides a critical review of research on L2 reading, maintaining that much of it is inadequate. In her arguments, Bernhardt underscores the interactive nature of the components underlying the reading construct, thus questioning the ability of test developers to write reading test items that focus on the individual components or that can capture the components' interactive dimension. Bernhardt, none the less, acknowledges the need for test developers to proceed in their development of reading assessment despite unresolved theoretical issues. She maintains that 'until practicality catches up with theory', test developers are better served by basing their assessments on clear institutional objectives.

The chapter by Grabe provides an extensive review of the theoretical and empirical work exploring the nature of the L2 reading construct. In this chapter, Grabe also delineates the strong impact reading research has had on instruction and laments the lack of an equivalent influence of such research on assessment. He attributes this lack of influence mainly to the success, according to psychometric criteria, reading assessment has had with traditional approaches to assessment. Grabe calls for those involved in reading assessment to consider several issues and challenges, which establish better links between current conceptualizations of L2 reading, and test (including CAT) design and development.

In his discussion of the two chapters, Alderson addresses the dilemmas and challenges advanced by Bernhardt and Grabe, highlighting the theoretical arguments and empirical work that depict a more positive relationship between L2 reading and test development. With regard to Bernhardt's arguments, Alderson maintains that test developers typically do not focus on individual components of the L2 reading construct, and even if these test developers claim to do so, they tend to report scores globally. As such, scores represent the entirety of the construct and not discrete components. Alderson contends that developing a potentially operational theory that captures the interactive nature of reading is indeed a challenge but is not restricted to reading tests. To circumvent this dilemma in assessment, he calls for test developers to construct L2 reading assessments, including adaptive tests, which incorporate items that 'cover a range of skills and levels of understanding' and to avoid reporting results by subskill.

With regard to Grabe, Alderson asserts the value of psychometric criteria, especially for high-stakes testing, and makes a case that computer-based testing can serve to enhance the validity of the scores. Alderson, none the less, indicates that a computer-based test 'might be held doubly removed from real reading'. He points out, however, that given the ever-increasing use of computers, the assessment of computer-based reading is likely to be important in its own right. Finally, Alderson calls for research to reveal the appropriateness and limitation of this mode of assessment.

The chapters by Larson, Dunkel, Laurier and McNamara in section two focus on L2 CAT design and development. All these chapters address one particular challenge, i.e. the increased interest in CAT has not been matched by a corresponding increase in useful information about actual development of L2 CAT instruments. The chapters explore numerous issues that become important at various phases in the design and development of L2 CAT in diverse contexts. The authors address reading as well as the other modalities in commonly taught and less commonly taught languages. In short, these chapters alert potential users and developers of L2 CATs to the critical considerations in developing such assessments.

In his chapter, Larson outlines the most significant advantages and limitations of CAT and provides an overview of several issues pertaining to L2 reading assessment in general and CAT specifically. In his description, Larson focuses on topics such as item bank content, item type, starting point, item selection algorithm and test termination. The chapter also describes the features of a CAT instrument developed for assessing reading proficiency in Russian. The reading CAT mimics the phases of the oral proficiency interview.

The chapter by Dunkel provides information about the process of developing a CAT to assess listening comprehension proficiency in Hausa. It presents the content and task framework used to construct the listening item bank, the trialing procedures to obtain the IRT item calibrations, and analyses that support the unidimensionality of the item bank. In her chapter, Dunkel explains that, given the relatively low enrolments in African languages such as Hausa, the development of a CAT presents a real challenge in terms of item calibration. Dunkel explains how the project goals and design were adjusted according to the limited resources.

The third chapter in this section deals with the development of a CAT for assessing test takers' general ability in French for placement purposes. In this chapter, Laurier discusses the benefits and usefulness of CAT for placement purposes. He also provides information about the various content, design and statistical decisions that he addressed in the different phases of CAT design and development. He deals with issues pertaining to the L2 construct, the structure of the item banks, the IRT models and the hardware and software technology.

The chapter by McNamara, while it deals with L2 CAT applications, does not report on the design and development of a particular project. The chapter serves to broaden the debate on L2 CAT assessment, critically discussing CAT practices from the point of view of performance assessment. McNamara provides an overview of the distinguishing attributes of performance assessment, focusing on task stimulus, response and processing, and examines the extent to which computer-adaptive reading instruments reflect these attributes. Finally, the chapter raises some questions about CAT method effects and the social and ideological roles of CAT.

The discussion chapter by Chapelle provides the link between the first and second sections. Chapelle acknowledges Grabe's and Bernhardt's point regarding the minimal impact of L2 reading theory on assessment, and points out that, in designing and developing instruments, test developers are concerned with factors considered 'closer to home', such as test use and available resources. She asserts, however, the need to connect the two in order to advance the use of CAT in L2 reading.

Chapelle deftly connects the theoretical and empirical considerations presented by Grabe and Bernhardt to the practices discussed by the authors in the second section by positing inference as the critical element where the link can be established. In her definition of inference, Chapelle maintains that CAT applications tend to operate within the ability (vs. performance) tradition where inferences are defined as abilities such as reading comprehension. Consequently, the role of theory in test design is to define the nature of the inference, i.e. to delineate the L2 reading process components. Chapelle points out, however, that within the currently espoused interactionalist definition of the construct, which includes both ability and the context of use, the delineation of the construct should be considered in conjunction with 'who will interpret the meaning and what use they will make of it'. Chapelle proposes using Bachman and Palmer's (1996) test method facets to identify the contextual variables that are likely to be of relevance when making inferences from a test setting to a non-test setting.

The chapters in section three focus on various technical measurement issues that pertain to CAT development and research. The chapter by Eignor explores three major issues that have recently caught the attention of measurement specialists, and are of increasing importance to adaptive testing researchers and practitioners. First, Eignor addresses issues that arise in situations where test developers are dealing with complex content specifications. He argues for algorithmic approaches that balance the psychometric properties of items with content and other attributes. Second, the chapter deals with the issue of item exposure. Eignor discusses various procedures that attempt to control item exposure when administering CAT. The third major issue that Eignor addresses is the level of IRT modeling of IRT testlets in CAT. He explores various options that help make testlet-level CAT a reality.

The basic premise in the Linacre chapter is summarized in his introductory sentence, '[s]cience advances when complex situations are summarized into simple regularities'. Linacre proposes a measurement approach in which a complex construct, such as reading, is on the one hand simplified for measurement purposes, yet on the other hand still enables the discrimination among different levels of text comprehension. Linacre discusses the value of Stenner's Lexile system for measuring reading comprehension. In addition the Linacre chapter addresses several measurement issues that have an impact on the development of L2 CAT reading instruments, including starting point, ability estimation, item sequencing and stopping rules. Linacre points out the importance of balancing psychometric considerations with psychological ones.

The major focus of the chapter by Luecht is IRT model choice and fit. Luecht employs two simulation studies to explore the practical utility of two IRT models, the Rasch model (RM), and the three-parameter logistic model (3PLM), for computer-adaptive reading tests. Results from these two studies indicate that the RM predicts the observed domain scores for the considered multidimensional item pools and corrects for guessing as well as the 3PLM. Given the robust estimation properties of the RM, Luecht supports the overall usefulness of the parsimonious RM for CAT development. He argues for in-depth understanding of misfit due to multidimensionality and assumed guessing before selecting the more complex models.

While the primary focus of the Zumbo and MacMillan chapter is to discuss the Eignor, Linacre and Luecht measurement papers, Zumbo and MacMillan also address some of the issues raised by the other authors in the book, especially those that relate to measurement. Zumbo and MacMillan point out a problem often observed when specialists from different fields, as in the present volume, are talking to one another, i.e. that the various specialists seem to talk past one another. While Zumbo and MacMillan recognize the inevitability of experts in their respective fields developing their own discourse and emphasizing different issues for discussion and research, they emphasize the importance of maintaining lines of communication among the various specialists so as to advance projects that are interdisciplinary in nature, such as L2 reading CAT. Additionally, Zumbo and MacMillan focus on the Linacre paper to make a case for the overlap, despite the differing discourse and emphasis, among the various specialists regarding *some* aspects of L2 reading CAT.

Another issue that Zumbo and MacMillan explore at great length in their chapter is the debate over the use of the varying logistics models, Rasch versus 1-, 2-, or 3PLM. The discussants describe features (e.g. purposes, types and uses) of various 'models', such as the '(a) mathematical model and (b) model in the wider philosophic sense', in order to clarify the nature of item response models and the issues that have sparked the debate over their use. The differential use of these psychometric models is illustrated in the chapters by Eignor and Linacre. The discussants point out that the Eignor chapter shows preference for the 3PLM and the Linacre chapter promotes the RM. Zumbo and MacMillan note that while the Luecht chapter provides evidence to support the overall usefulness of the RM, the evidence is not likely to persuade adherents of the 3PLM to use the RM. Zumbo and MacMillan attribute this phenomenon to the conceptual difference between 1-, 2-, and 3PLM and RM with regard to modeling of data fit. The discussants point out that while proponents of the former group of models argue for the need to evaluate the appropriateness of the model by how well it fits the data, supporters of the RM contend that it is the data that needs to fit the model. Consequently, while empirical evidence may support a particular model, it is the philosophical argument that will continue to keep researchers divided over which model to use.

Final remarks

More and more academic and non-academic institutions are moving to the computerized delivery of tests. Computerized delivery is not inexpensive in terms of cost or labour, so why computerized testing? Is it worth it? The answer is probably as simple as: computers are the way to the future. The situation is comparable, perhaps, to that when the value of moving away from writing on stone to writing on parchment was being considered. While computers today are an optional model of delivery, in a few decades they will be *the* mode of delivery.

It is hoped that this book will provide educators, especially second language testing researchers and practitioners, with useful information needed to pursue the development of L2 CAT. Also, it is hoped that this volume will bring awareness to some of the issues that need to be addressed in order to encourage a research-based approach to CAT.

I would like to conclude my remarks by, again, cautioning ourselves against thinking that in utilizing computer-adaptive technology we are developing the ultimate test for assessing L2 reading or any construct. There is nothing further from reality than the idea that a particular mode of assessment – be it computer-adaptive or an elaborate performance assessment – is some sort of panacea. Any test must be evaluated with regard to its appropriateness within the specific context of use.

References

Bachman, L. F. and Palmer, A. S. (1996) *Language Testing in Practice.* Oxford University Press.

Drasgow, F. and Olson-Buchanan, J. B. (Eds.) (in press) *Innovations in Computerized Assessment.* Hillsdale, NJ: Lawrence Erlbaum Associates Publishers.

Sands, W. A., Waters, B. K. and McBride, J. R. (Eds.) (1997) *Computerized Adaptive Testing: From Inquiry to Operation.* Washington, DC: American Psychological Association.

Shneiderman, B. (1998) *Designing the User Interface: Strategies for Effective Human–computer Interaction.* Reading, MA: Addison-Wesley.

Acknowledgments

I am indebted to a number of people for helping make this volume a reality. I wish to express my sincerest thanks to the authors and discussants who contributed to this volume. Their work lays out the issues and challenges that need to be addressed to advance computer-adaptive testing research and development as we move into the twenty-first century. I also would like to thank John Watzke for his assistance in preparing this manuscript. Finally, thanks are due to those who have helped in the publishing of the present volume. I would like to thank especially Michael Milanovic for his insightful suggestions regarding the content and organization of this book.

Many of the chapters in this volume were presented at the invitational conference 'Issues in Computer-Adaptive Testing of L2 Reading Proficiency' held in Bloomington, Minnesota in March 1995. The contribution of the conference speakers, therefore, helped serve as the impetus for this book. I would like to extend my warmest gratitude to all those speakers.

I also would like to take the opportunity here to acknowledge several individuals who helped in the various aspects of that conference. I extend my thanks especially to Andrew Cohen, Dale Lange, Ray Wakefield and David Weiss for their strong support of and valuable input in the conference organization. I also would like to thank the various people who attended to the logistical, technological and administrative details of the conference, including Cheryl Alcaya, Angela DeGruccio, Gary Jahn, Karin Larson, Daniel Lindsay, Vashti Lozier and Jenise Rowekamp.

Finally, my heartfelt thanks to my husband, Craig Deville, for his loving support and encouragement.

1 If reading is reader-based, can there be a computer-adaptive test of reading?

Elizabeth Bernhardt
Stanford University

Introduction

The universe of comprehension assessment alternatives is extremely limited. The comprehender either has to *be asked questions* that supposedly target key pieces of information in a given text or has to *demonstrate* those key pieces of information. Admittedly, there are variations within each of these basic frameworks. Issues such as whether *questions* should be asked within multiple-choice, open-ended, or true–false formats and in which language they should be posed, or whether *demonstrations* should be in the form of recall or performance tasks, abound in the formal testing literature. These variations in format are by and large trivial when placed against the backdrop of what comprehension assessment is fundamentally about: getting stable information about the abilities of learners so that their strengths and weaknesses can be identified; ranking and ordering comprehenders in their performance abilities; and, most important, making clear what they can or cannot *do* or *understand*.

Comprehension assessment, like any other form of assessment, is forced to serve multiple masters. Garnering stable information about the comprehension abilities of learners is simply not enough. This information must also model as closely as possible research knowledge about comprehension. And both of these forces must be packaged in a convenient, multi-use, multi-user, cost-effective form. All three of these forces make the testing business, euphemistically speaking, the most challenging area of educational research. This chapter is intended to speak primarily to the issue of what is known about comprehension abilities, specifically, reading comprehension abilities, in relation to issues surrounding proficiency assessment—particularly proficiency assessment that uses an adaptive framework. Any attempt at articulating such a relationship first, must examine the knowledge base surrounding second language reading; second, must discuss the theory that has been generated and influenced by means of that knowledge base; and, third, must consider how this all fits with the structures

1

and strictures of the chosen assessment mechanism. The central argument of the chapter pivots on this nexus. Given the conditions of adaptive testing, and particularly *computer*-adaptive testing, can second language reading be assessed in a construct-valid manner?

The second language reading construct

Reading is the extraction and construction of a message from a written text. To do this in a *second* language presumes the existence of an oral first language. In order to extract and construct one has to have some knowledge of the second language. This knowledge is inevitably influenced during reading by the level of first language literacy, the intention to read, the motivation to read and the reader's knowledge base.

Bernhardt (1991) synthesizes the currently available research evidence and contextualizes and reconciles it against that of others. The synthesis was constructed by taking a set of categories that had been explored in the literature (both in L1 and L2). Work such as Goodman (1968), LaBerge and Samuels (1974), Spiro, *et al.* (1980) and Coady (1979) had isolated features such as word recognition and phonemic and graphemic knowledge, syntax, background knowledge, perceptions about texts built through discourse models, and metacognition throughout the work; all of these features were considered to be critical in painting a full portrait of second language reading.

In the 1991 Bernhardt synthesis, *word recognition* meant knowing or translating a vocabulary item; *phonemic features* referred to the visual or phonological features that interfere with or influence the recognition of a word in reading; *syntax* meant broadly both inflection and word order; *background knowledge* meant the use of knowledge that is relevant or irrelevant for interpreting the passage; *metacognition* meant the overt evidence of cognitive effort made during a reading task. Bernhardt searched for these elements using recall data collected across readers of French, German and Spanish in secondary and university-level settings. After a coding procedure, all of these elements were then examined within the context of the length of time readers had instruction in a second languages and then they were plotted according to error rate (Figure 1.1). The plot indicates that the longer the exposure to instruction, the fewer the errors in vocabulary use (both at the word and graphemic level). This phenomenon is illustrated by the sharp decline in the curve after a relatively short time in instruction. The curve for syntactic errors is radically different from the other curves. As a result of a greater amount of information recalled over time, syntax errors increase as classroom exposure increases and then at later stages of development decrease. This phenomenon might be termed the 'a little knowledge is a dangerous thing' syndrome. It seems to be potentially consistent with the U-shaped behaviour patterns observed in other areas of SLA research (Kellerman 1979).

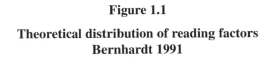

Figure 1.1

**Theoretical distribution of reading factors
Bernhardt 1991**

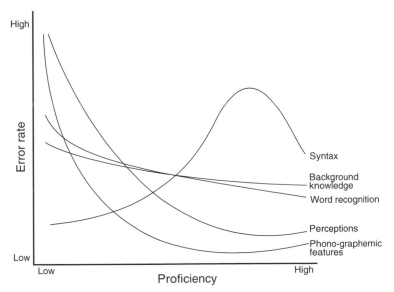

The synthesis also included curves illustrating knowledge variables. These variables include the monitoring processes that bring about readers' perceptions or conceptualizations of the text and the knowledge that readers choose to use during processing. These curves are relatively flat. They are meant to illustrate variables that seem to be distinctly reader-related and not necessarily related to proficiency level or amount of exposure to the language. They are individual differences or language independent predictors.

The question still lingers as to whether Bernhardt's theoretical statement of the distribution of factors involved in reading in a second language is consistent with the entire data base and with evidence generated in the past several years. It still remains, nevertheless, one of the few fully articulated hypotheses about reading in a second language. The model is a multidimensional, multiparameter model. At issue is then, of course, how this fits with assessment models that assume unidimensionality of the data.

Recent research evidence

The classic question in second language reading is whether the emphasis should be placed on second language or on reading. Alderson (1984) articulated the question with whether L2 reading was a language or a reading problem. Recent research has re-opened this question (Bernhardt and Kamil 1995; Bossers 1991; Brisbois 1995; Carrell 1991; Hacquebord 1989). Recent endeavours have analyzed the contribution of first language reading (as well as grammar and vocabulary measures in both L1 and L2) to second language reading. Figure 1.2 illustrates the consistencies across the studies. Hacquebord (1989) and Bossers (1991) each analyzed adolescent speakers of Turkish being schooled in Dutch; Carrell (1991) examined an adult group of Spanish ESL readers and an English-speaking group of Spanish-as-a-foreign language learners; Brisbois (1995) and Bernhardt and Kamil (1995) focused on English speakers reading in English, French and Spanish, respectively.

Figure 1.2

Summary data
The contribution of L1 reading and L2 grammar to L2 reading

Hacquebord (1989) Turkish/Dutch N = 50	L1 reading = 16%	
Bossers (1991) Turkish/Dutch N = 50	L1 reading = 19% L1 reading + L2 grammar	= 62%
Carrell (1991) Spanish/English N = 45	L1 reading + L2 grammar	= 35%
English/Spanish N = 75	L1 reading + L2 grammar	= 53%
Brisbois (1995) French/English N = 126	L1 reading = 14% L1 writing = 7% L2 vocabulary = 35% L2 grammar = 3%	= 59%
Bernhardt/Kamil (1995) Spanish/English N = 187	L1 reading = 16% L2 grammar = 38%	= 54%

The data indicate that second language reading is principally dependent on *grammatical* ability in the second language (meaning how competently learners can place endings on inflected words, whether they can indeed produce past tense forms, and the like). The evidence listed above, generated across users of different ages and language backgrounds and target languages, is fairly consistent and substantial: grammatical ability generally accounts for around 30% of the variance in second language reading scores. A second piece of evidence that is fairly consistent is that *first language literacy* also accounts for another substantial portion of the variance (14-21%) in second language reading scores. First language literacy has been measured in a variety of ways, from researcher-made tests (Hacquebord, Bossers and Carrell) to traditional large-scale MC ways (namely the Nelson Denny which measures both reading and the ability to get through traditional large-scale tests illustrated in Brisbois and in Bernhardt and Kamil), through more time-consuming, less conventional ways (namely through the scoring of holistic reading and writing samples as in Brisbois) with a variety of age groups and different first language literacies, and the story generally comes out the same—around 20% explanatory power. The most sophisticated of the studies, Brisbois, used an array of elaborate measures and was able to specify the difference between vocabulary and grammar which were mixed in Bernhardt and Kamil. The consistencies are remarkable.

As with all research, scepticism about findings is critical. An overwhelmingly convincing factor in the viability and believability of these particular studies is that the evidence was generated across so many different texts, assessment schemes, populations, researchers, and contexts. These studies comprise one of the few areas in the data base in second language reading research that demonstrates a good deal of consistency. What are the implications of these data? Certainly, the data indicate that the shape of the curves of the model in Figure 1.1 would change depending upon first language literacy. To be more explicit, the theory must read: second language reading is a function of *L1 ability*.

The bulk of research evidence

But what of the bulk of second language reading research? The research evidence that currently exists in reading in a second language deserves careful analysis. There is an array of problems with the set of studies that constitute the data base in second language reading. As noted above, that data base may be organized according to the following areas:

1. word recognition;
2. background knowledge;
3. text structure;
4. oral–aural factors;
5. syntactic features;
6. cross-lingual processing;
7. metacognition;
8. testing; and
9. instruction.

While one could do a complete analysis on each study, for purposes of this chapter, only those issues that are most important for assessment will be mentioned.

First, most of the materials used in the studies are researcher generated; i.e. the texts read do not meet the criteria of authentic texts. Often, in fact, the texts used were translations from texts used in 1970s psychology experiments. It is important to realize how data exist from readers performing real reading tasks. Given the current emphasis on authentic assessment tasks, there is not much of a data base from which to work. *Second*, the total number of subjects is usually fairly small in these studies and that number is made even smaller by the fact that many of the groups are of mixed language background. In other words, if part of the data base such as word recognition and cross-lingual studies indicates that there really are differences across languages, then studies that did not or do not acknowledge these differences are problematic. *Third*, from a careful look at any of the studies (and assuming for the moment that they do not contain any of the concerns listed in points one and two above) the observed differences in performance are generally very modest, the means generally separated by a point or two. Considering the current research evidence regarding the impact of grammatical knowledge and literacy knowledge (Figure 1.2), there are few if any studies in second language reading in which an observed statistically significant effect would hold. Effect–size calculations in light of the evidence in Figure 1.2 would render most of the L2 reading studies studies of little value.

The most critical area for any discussion regarding the assessment of second language reading abilities is what is actually known about the development of reading abilities in a second language. This is the most critical issue at hand because if it is unknown *what is better than what* or *which reader is better than which reader* or *which group of people should be placed in X-class versus which group should be placed in Y-class* there is little reason to pursue this area of assessment for anything other than purely theoretical reasons.

There are no published studies available that inform—or even hint at—what proficiency levels might look like within the contexts of *readers*. Of course, there is some work (it cannot be termed research because there is no data base behind it) that describes what some readers can or cannot do with certain kinds of text features and certain kinds of grammatical features. This work has been discussed thoroughly within the context of the 'proficiency literature'. Studies that have tried to make the text-features scheme work have come up wanting. There are generally flat lines observed across college groups and across levels and languages (Allen *et al.* 1988; Lee and Musumeci 1988). These studies have been criticized because of their text selections; i.e. the 'wrong' texts were chosen for analysis. Although the criticism alone underlines the point (different texts, different answers) the point is this: the only 'proficiency-oriented' system that exists tries to fit *readers* to particular text features rather than fitting the *system* to real readers reading.

Some speculations

An argument that can be made is that the only thing that operates with a great deal of consistency within second-language reading is that the more language knowledge a learner has (i.e. higher grammar score or more years), the more total amount of information the learner is able to extract and construct from a text; Figure 1.3 illustrates the point. Learners as groups across time indeed increase their reading abilities. But within groups, individuals do not necessarily always outperform or underperform others based on their time in instruction.

Figure 1.3

A prototype scattergram of comprehension scores across language levels

Isolating particular kinds of features has been attempted a number of times

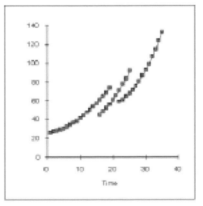

and has come out wanting. There is still hope for this approach particularly with the use of qualitative data programs; the downside of course, is, as in all language research, multiple performances are critical and the coding of these is very costly and time-consuming in research. Some examples might be helpful. For example, in German if one can on-line resolve some of the inflexions, such as identifying the genitive case (which takes an -s ending) as possession rather than as plural (again the -s from English), then one might be demonstrating a high level of grammatical knowledge that is automatic and immediately available. Or assigning subject/object relations (again in German signaled at times by word order, at times by inflexion, at times by both)—if a reader comes away from a text having made rapid assignments accurately, then this might indicate important processing behaviours that are indeed markers of growth and development. Whether this happens within a friendly letter or within a magazine report is irrelevant; when it happens—that is the crucial dimension in assigning proficiency levels.

There is also a mythology that second language reading works from the word to the sentence to the discourse level. In most research studies that have readers reading, it is clear that readers at any grammatical level are able to get information at all informational levels—the word level, the middle level, the top-structure level. The issue is one of quantity rather than of quality. The more language knowledge, the more total amount of information at each level. In other words, a proficiency scheme based on particular kinds of features such as words, then passive structures, then something else, is not based on the reality of second language readers. The model illustrated in Figure 1.1 could potentially help to perpetuate this myth since the model suffers from two-dimensionality: the model is not meant to indicate that the features in reading are independent. Features are embedded in other features and interact with each other on the basis of previously processed features.

Conclusion

The mythology of *particular* features involved in reading and the reality of the *interactivity* of these features are the underpinnings of the fundamental assessment dilemma of the *ask-questions* type of assessment. If features are embedded and interactive, how is it possible to write particular 'items' or to argue that some items are inherently more difficult than others? Hence, how can they be calibrated? It is difficult to conceptualize how a particular question is supposed to capture an interactive dimension of second language reading.

Clearly, certain kinds of assessment mechanism, CAT being one of them, allow access to a virtually unlimited universe of *items*. Having such access affords the opportunity to tap an almost infinite number of performances. This advantage should not be overlooked. Figure 1.4 illustrates the enormous variability that has been observed between and among subjects. Any given text evokes a particular *performance*. Subject 4 is clearly 'more able' on Text 2 than on Text 1. It is only across multiple texts that stability emerges. Clearly, all assessments should provide as many performances as possible. Adaptive testing enables this. The issue remains, however, one of the nexus of good assessment practices with rigorous research and substantive model building.

There is a final consideration behind the issue of second language reading assessment: practicality. Tests need to be useful, convenient and user-friendly as well as valid and reliable. They need to be useful, convenient and friendly to both test takers and to test makers who cannot and should not be paralyzed by theoretical issues revolving around tests. Learners come to a learning environment to gain knowledge and skill; teachers are employed to assist that knowledge acquisition and to provide their best wisdom regarding it. All institutions should be clear about the nature of the knowledge that they intend to impart and equally clear to learners about how much they have or have not gained. Tests that assess performance based on clear objectives are completely defensible. Until practicality catches up with theory, such tests are probably the most reasonable choice.

Figure 1.4

Same subjects at the same proficiency level on different texts

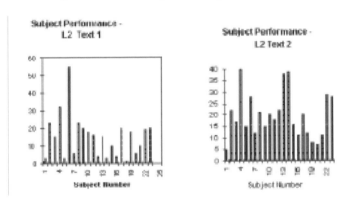

The question posed in the title to this chapter, *If reading is reader-based, can there be a computer-adaptive test of reading?* is embarrassing. The answer is 'Of course.' The real question that should be posed is *Will a computer-adaptive test of reading provide an appropriate general framework for the assessment of second language reading skills?* The answer to this question is unclear in terms of theory and far from answerable in terms of research.

References

Alderson, J. C. (1984) Reading in a foreign language: A reading problem or a language problem? In Alderson, J. C. and Urquhart, A. H. (Eds.) *Reading in a Foreign Language, pp.1–27.* London: Longman.

Allen, E. D., Bernhardt, E. B., Berry, M. T. and Demel, M. (1988) Comprehension and text genre: Analysis of secondary school foreign language readers. *Modern Language Journal* 72: 163–72.

Bernhardt, E. B. (1991) A psycholinguistic perspective on second language literacy. *AILA Review* 8: 31–44.

Bernhardt, E. B. and Kamil, M. (1995) Interpreting relationships between L1 and L2 reading: Consolidating the linguistic threshold and the linguistic interdependence hypotheses. *Applied Linguistics* 16: 15–34.

Bossers, B. (1991) On thresholds, ceilings and short-circuits: The relationship between L1 reading, L2 reading and L2 knowledge. In Hulstijn, J. H. and Matter, J. F. (Eds.) *AILA Review* 8: 45–60.

Brisbois, J. (1995) Connections between first- and second-language reading. *Journal of Reading Behaviour* 27: 565–84.

Carrell, P. L. (1991) Second language reading: Reading ability or language proficiency? *Applied Linguistics* 12: 159–79.

Coady, J. (1979) A psycholinguistic model of the ESL reader. In Mackay, R., Barkman, B. and Jordan, R. R. (Eds.) *Reading in a Second Language*, pp. 5–12. Rowley, MA: Newbury House.

Goodman, K. (Ed.) (1968) *The Psycholinguistic Nature of the Reading Process.* Detroit, MI: Wayne State University Press.

Hacquebord, H. (1989) *Reading Comprehension of Turkish and Dutch Students Attending Secondary Schools.* Groningen: RUG.

Kellerman, E. (1979) Transfer and non-transfer: Where are we now? *Studies in Second Language Acquisition* 2: 37–57.

LaBerge, D. and Samuels, S. J. (1974) Toward a theory of automatic information processing in reading. *Cognitive Psychology*: 293–323.

Lee, J. and Musumeci, D. (1988) On hierarchies of reading skills and text types. *Modern Language Journal* 72: 137–87.

Spiro, R. J., Bruce, B. C. and Brewer, W. F. (Eds.) (1980) *Theoretical Issues in Reading Comprehension.* Hillsdale, NJ: Lawrence Erlbaum Associates, Publishers.

2 Developments in reading research and their implications for computer-adaptive reading assessment

William Grabe
Northern Arizona University

Introduction

Advances in our understanding of reading have expanded considerably in the past 15 years. In particular, research in the areas of cognitive psychology and educational psychology has led to many changes in how reading is described theoretically, and how it is likely to be learned. Research in the past decade has also established better the nature of second language reading: it has become clearer that reading in a second language imposes a number of additional constraints on reading and its development. One strong outcome of this research has been its impact on reading instruction, particularly with respect to greater emphases on word recognition abilities, vocabulary knowledge, strategic processing and awareness of discourse organizing principles. It is probably safe to say, however, that there has not been a similar impact on reading assessment. A major purpose of this chapter will be to explore the possible implications of reading research for assessment purposes. The many potential links to assessment issues will be discussed in terms of dilemmas—issues and questions for rethinking reading assessment so that it might more closely reflect current views on reading abilities.

The present chapter will first outline briefly a view of reading abilities based on research in first language contexts. This overview will describe the reading process and briefly note social and affective influences on reading comprehension. Contexts for second language reading will then be introduced so that the general construct of reading abilities can be reconceptualized with respect to second language reading abilities. Implications of this research for instruction will then be briefly noted since this transfer of research to application illustrates the extensive impact that a theory of reading can have on application. Finally, the relative lack of application of reading research to assessment approaches will be addressed.

The nature of reading

A definition

While one can safely say that reading involves understanding a printed text, this notion does not provide any indication of what specifically must be done in reading, or how it is to be done. A more useful extended definition of reading would provide some indication of the reading process and describe the critical features of this process. The most important defining features of fluent reading include the following:

1. Reading is a rapid process.
2. Reading requires processing efficiency.
3. Reading requires strategic processing.
4. Reading is interactive.
5. Reading is purposeful.
6. Reading requires sufficient knowledge of language.
7. Reading requires sufficient knowledge of the world and of a given topic.

To say reading is a rapid process means that readers typically read most material at between 200 and 300 words per minute. Reading at much slower rates, particularly for L2 students, can cause comprehension problems because working memory capacity is used ineffectively while waiting to assemble clausal information (Carpenter *et al.*1994; Gernsbacher 1990). Slow reading may also indicate minimal processing efficiencies (Biemiller 1994; Perfetti 1994; Breznitz and Share 1992). Good readers are efficient because they recognize words automatically, quickly form meaning propositions, integrate propositional information into a text model rapidly, and restructure the text model to reflect the main ideas of the text being read (van Dijk and Kintsch 1983; Perfetti 1994; Singer 1990).

It is also clear that fluent reading involves goal setting and is purposeful, incorporates interactions among various levels of cognitive processing, and requires combinations of appropriate reading strategies (adjusting reading rates, rethinking goals, previewing texts, predicting discourse organization, monitoring comprehension, etc.). Moreover, reading requires both sufficient knowledge of language and knowledge of the world as basic supporting foundations on which to build comprehension. Finally, while not themselves features of cognitive processing, aspects of social contexts and individual motivation inform and support reading comprehension processes.

These points have been discussed in numerous contexts, so there is little need to review them at length. (See Adams 1990; Barr *et al.* 1991; Carr and Levy 1990; Carver 1990; Gough, Ehri and Treiman 1992; Haenggi and Perfetti 1994; Just and Carpenter 1987; Perfetti 1989, 1991, 1994; Pressley and Woloshyn 1995; Rayner and Pollatsek 1989; Stanovich 1991a, 1992). In the description of the reading process to follow, these issues will also arise in discussions of the various components of reading comprehension abilities.

Components of the reading process

The study of reading components is an important way to understand how fluent readers comprehend texts. The central components of reading processing include the following: orthographic processing, phonological coding, word recognition (lexical access), working memory activation, sentence parsing, propositional integration, propositional text-structure formation, comprehension strategy use, inference making and text model reinterpretation as a situation model (or mental model). Throughout the study of these components, basic issues such as the role of a reader's prior knowledge, the relative importance of each subprocess and the extent of interaction among various subprocesses are important concerns.

Lower-level processing

A central component in all current models of reading is the major role of low-level recognition processes. Low-level processing can be discussed in terms of three subcomponent processes: the recognition of orthographic structure, the recognition of morpheme structure and the processing of phonemic information (Barker *et al.* 1992; Stanovich 1991b; Stanovich *et al.* 1991). *Orthographic structure recognition* involves the recognition of letter forms, various line shapes (as parts of letters), letter groups that typically cluster together (phonotactics) and spelling patterns (Ehri 1991a, 1991b; Templeton 1992). This processing component has a moderate but consistent influence on reading abilities, and it is typically developed from constant exposure to reading itself. Both Ehri (1991b) and Stanovich and West (1989) have argued that orthographic knowledge is a significant source of reading-ability differences.

The role of *morphemic structure* in word recognition has also been recognized as an important component of sub-word level processing, though it is sometimes considered one part of orthographic form knowledge. Recent arguments, however, support a distinct role of morphemic knowledge in that the morphemic structure not only represents aspects of word form (e.g. -ed, -tion, -ize, -able, -ly), but also specific syntactic and semantic information that needs to be incorporated into comprehension (Anderson and Nagy 1991; Guarino and Perkins 1986; Nagy *et al.* 1989; Perfetti 1994; White *et al.* 1989). Morphological forms also create consistent patterns of variation which must be recognized and associated with the same basic meanings (e.g. elect /t/, election /s/; wolf /f/, wolves /v/).

The third and perhaps most important subcomponent is the *phonemic coding* of visual input for assisting in word recognition and for maintaining information in working memory. In fact, some recent research has argued that phonemic coding is an automatic early reflex of word recognition processing. This claim argues that phonemic coding is a central component for all written word processing, even for fluent readers encountering common words, and for readers of non-alphabetic scripts (Bentin and Ibrahim 1996; Berent and Perfetti 1995; Frost 1994, 1995; Lesch and Pollatsek 1993; Lukatela and Turvey 1994a, 1994b, 1995; Perfetti and Zhang 1995). Early phonological activation in word recognition, via phonological coding, now provides a strong alternative to the dual-route theory for word recognition (Perfetti and Zhang, 1995).

In its more reflective form, as *phonemic awareness*, it is also now considered the best early predictor of later reading development (Adams 1990; Stanovich 1992). Evidence from various independent research studies has converged to argue that phonemic awareness—awareness of individual sound segments which match orthographic symbols, notions of syllable and rhyme and ability to manipulate this phonemic information—strongly predicts later reading development for beginning readers (cf. Cunningham *et al.* 1990; Haenggi and Perfetti 1994 for older readers).

The three sub-word processes described above all work together as part of *word recognition*, or *lexical access*. (Some researchers distinguish these terms, some do not.) For second language learning, it is often useful to distinguish between the two. The sub-word-processes illustrate well the interactive processing which occurs during reading. For the purposes of word recognition, all three sub-word-processes begin simultaneously when visual information is perceived. Together they assist word recognition, one of the key processing components for reading (Adams 1990; Biemiller 1994; Perfetti 1991, 1992). While specific aspects of word recognition processes have been debated for over twenty years, all researchers recognize the important role of word recognition in reading. The general consensus is that word recognition abilities are a central process for reading comprehension and one of the most important on-going predictors of reading ability, though it diminishes in importance with fluent readers (van Dijk and Kintsch 1983; Juel 1991; Stanovich 1986, 1991b; Perfetti 1989, 1991, 1994; Rayner and Pollatsek 1989).

Word recognition fluency is critical for reading because readers need to see word forms and access the appropriate meanings both rapidly and accurately. The contributing information from the visual form and from phonological coding allows readers to recognize words and access their lexical entries with minimal cognitive effort. (See also Stanovich 1990 and Perfetti 1994 for discussions of acquired modularity in fluent word recognition processes.) For fluent readers, the process of word recognition takes place very quickly, usually in less than one tenth of a second. Moreover, fluent readers on average recognize four to five words per second as they read for comprehension. (The additional time is used for other processing tasks: Rayner and Pollatsek 1989.) Fluent word recognition, then, provides the building blocks for comprehension of the text as a whole. Slow word recognition, on the other hand, creates serious difficulties for reading comprehension that are not easily overcome.

The ability to recognize words rapidly and automatically may well be the most important early developing ability for reading comprehension skills. Perfetti (1992) argues that this ability requires a large set of automatically recognizable vocabulary. Words must be recognized both quickly and also thoroughly. (See also Ehri 1992; Stanovich 1991b.) One critical implication for reading instruction is that reading development will require a large automatically recognizable store of vocabulary. In fact, vocabulary knowledge is widely recognized as a language resource that is essential for reading comprehension (Adams 1990; Stanovich 1986). Of course, the question of 'how much' vocabulary is needed, or how how elaborate the knowledge of a word should be, is an issue that has yet to be resolved, either for first language or second language contexts.

As words are accessed and information is activated, what is brought together is *working memory*, the metaphorical space in which comprehension processing is carried out. Whether there is a separate space, or whether it is simply an activated configuration within long-term memory with some storage buffers, is an open question (Carpenter *et al.* 1994; Gathercole and Baddeley 1993; Jonides 1995). The positing of some 'place' for activated sets of language knowledge which can be integrated easily is not in question, however. With respect to processing operations in working memory, research is still investigating exactly what is stored, how much is stored, how it is stored and how it is used.

Because of all the processing operations in working memory (word recognition, syntactic parsing, word and structure storage, propositional integration, text model building, etc.), this processing environment is a major source of variation in reading abilities, and, in particular, a source of differences between better and less-skilled readers. Those readers who have less efficient (and perhaps smaller) working memory capacity are not able to store and use as much information as other readers, and at times this bottleneck interferes with text comprehension (Carpenter *et al.* 1994; Daneman 1991; Haenggi and Perfetti 1994; Jonides 1995; Just and Carpenter 1987, 1992; Perfetti 1994). Issues of processing efficiency in working memory also implicate speed of lexical access and speed of proposition integration. As a consequence, reading processes need to be carried out at a reasonably rapid rate to ensure fluent reading (Segalowitz 1986; Segalowitz and Hebert 1990).

As lexical information begins to enter (or become activated in) working memory, the processes of *syntactic parsing* and *propositional integration* are activated (Barsalou 1992; Daneman 1991; Kintsch 1995; Perfetti and Britt 1995; Rayner and Pollatsek 1989). Syntactic parsing involves drawing the syntactic information from the incoming string of lexical forms being activated in working memory: it mentally reconstructs the grammatical structure of the sentence; in a parallel manner, the semantic interpretation of the sentence produces a propositional structure, or network, from the lexical forms and syntactic information. In this way, comprehension processes begin building text structure (Gernsbacher 1990).

The notion of propositional integration, and even the notion that meaning is created in terms of propositions, is sometimes challenged. There is now extensive evidence for proposing meaning propositions as the semantic information extracted from sentences (Barsalou 1992; van Dijk and Kintsch 1983; Garnham 1985, 1994; Kintsch 1994; Fletcher 1994; Singer 1990, 1994). In fact, much recent research in comprehension and discourse processing now assumes the centrality of propositions and propositional networks (Britton and Graesser 1996; Gernsbacher 1994; Lorch and O'Brien 1995; Weaver, Mannes and Fletcher 1995). Syntactic knowledge and semantic integration for reading are well established as major contributors to text comprehension in working memory (Bernhardt, 1991; Gernsbacher 1990, 1996; Haenggi and Perfetti 1994; Kintsch 1994, 1995; Mason 1992; Moravcpik and Kintsch 1995; Perfetti and Britt 1995; Tunmer and Hoover 1992).

The two processes of syntactic parsing and propositional integration begin the change to functioning/working to avoid repetition of operation process immediately as the first one or two words are recognized (Perfetti and Britt 1995). While there are a number of unresolved issues in explaining exactly how these two processes operate, a general account would suggest that, as words are activated, the structure of the clause is constructed and the meanings of individual words are integrated into a larger meaning unit, the proposition. The end product of this processing in working memory is the meaning proposition, or what the sentence means.

Up to this point in the discussion, most reading researchers would be willing to accept the general outlines of the processes discussed, while recognizing that many of these component processes generate various specific disagreements. These specific sources of difference are seen in competing theories which examine evidence from experiments and computer simulations (Balota 1994; Carpenter *et al.* 1994; Garnham 1994; Gough, Ehri and Treiman and Gouth, Jeul and Griffith 1992; Henderson *et al.* 1995; Perfetti 1994). Nevertheless, current research perspectives would all recognize the role of orthographic processing, phonemic coding, word recognition, syntactic parsing, propositional integration and working memory in reading comprehension.

Higher-level processing

As one moves from issues involving lower-level processing to higher-level processing (that is, working with larger units of information and information contributed by the reader), the issues become less clear and more controversial. Up until very recently, many researchers disagreed strongly on the processes that may be involved in higher-level comprehension, and others suggested that there was not enough evidence to make confident assertions about the full range of processing that takes place (Barsalou 1992; van Dijk and Kintsch 1983; Rayner and Pollatsek 1989; Singer 1990). However, more recently, research on discourse processing has converged on a number of central ideas, while still disagreeing on many specifics. The central notions now provide a reasonable general account for discourse processes and the ways that they support text comprehension.

Most researchers now agree that some form of text comprehension network, a text model, is generated by the reader, which reflects the textual information closely. A second textual network, a situation model, includes much more reader background knowledge, affective responses, and individual interpretations of the text information. In addition, most researchers believe that some types of inferencing are necessary while reading, that syntactic and discourse signalling in texts is used to strengthen or restructure the text network, and that the textual context contributes to text interpretation. At the same time, higher-level processing also generates considerable disagreement over the specific processing mechanisms involved in text comprehension. In particular, the roles of inferencing, contextual information, reader background knowledge, discourse structuring knowledge and reading strategies (executive processing) have generated a range of alternative positions. The discussion which follows is somewhat more speculative than that presented in the previous section and involves interpretations of arguments from several sources; nevertheless, the explanation given below for text comprehension processing at the discourse level offers a plausible account.

In the past few years a number of volumes have appeared which provide extensive discussion of higher-level comprehension processing (Britton and Graesser 1996; Gernsbacher 1994; Lorch and O'Brien 1995; Weaver, Mannes and Fletcher 1995). Among the most complete and carefully reasoned general descriptions of higher-level comprehension processing are those proposed by Kintsch (1988, 1994), van Dijk and Kintsch (1983) and Singer (1990). (See also various chapters in Gernsbacher 1994.) In both explanations, text comprehension extends beyond sentence-level propositional integration by incorporating each newly formed propositional unit in working memory into a textual propositional network, *a text model of comprehension*. Such a text model creates a close mental representation of the information given (or intended) by the text up to that point in the reading. The text model has hierarchical structure, with a network of important (e.g. thematic, repeated and widely connected) locally linked propositional ideas being gradually restructured to include higher-level macropropositions that capture the main ideas of the text. Only information that is mentioned in the text, or that is needed to make some connection between the newly integrated proposition and the text model, is typically included in the text model.

As each proposition is entered into the text model network, the network restructuring makes certain propositions more central, strengthens the connections among main themes, sorts thematic information from supporting information, consolidates information in a more summary-like form and adjusts the highest-level proposition, or the macro-proposition (van Dijk and Kintsch 1983; Kintsch 1988, 1994, 1995). At this level of comprehension, the role played by the reader's prior knowledge also increases. When topical information is missing and there are no argument overlaps across propositions, the reader makes the necessary *bridging inferences* to connect the incoming proposition most appropriately into the developing propositional network of the text model. Propositions that undergo restructuring are also likely to be influenced by prior knowledge and reader goals. The output of the propositional network is a text model summary that reflects the semantic structure and content of the text. In a narrow sense, this represents the reader's linguistic comprehension of the text (van Dijk and Kintsch 1983; Fletcher 1994; Garnham 1985; Kintsch 1995; Perfetti 1994; Singer 1990).

The ability to construct a text model of comprehension of this type is sometimes argued to be a third important source of individual variation in reading comprehension. It should be noted that the processing required by the text model is most often associated with expository prose, whereas narrative prose is commonly seen as inducing more elaborative processing that is specifically associated with narrative prose (Graesser *et al.* 1996; Graesser and Britton 1996; Lorch 1995). It is also important to point out that all of the many processes discussed to this point occur simultaneously in working memory as the reader continues to read and add new information through lower-level processing.

At the same time that the text model is being created as a close representation of the text information, a second model is constructed that represents the reader's interpretation of the text information, referred to as a *situation model*. This interpretation of the text is not limited to the information given in the text. Rather, the situation model calls on information that is supplied by reader background knowledge, goals for reading, reader motivation, reader attitudes and reader evaluations of the information given (Kintsch 1995). Such information could include the many related texts that have been read before, the extent of topic-specific knowledge available to the reader in long-term memory, and the on-going evaluations of the text as it is processed. Some of this background information may also be visual in nature so that it will not be stored in long-term memory as verbal propositions. Thus there is a need for a second level of text interpretation which allows for individual goal setting and comprehension interpretation (van Dijk and Kintsch 1983; Fletcher 1994; Garnham 1985; Garnham and Oakhill 1996; Kintsch 1994; Mannes and St George 1996; Weaver and Kintsch 1991; McNamara *et al.* 1991).

One way to understand this two-model approach is to assume that the evolving text model is copied to (or embedded within) a second model in which the information is elaborated/evaluated by a variety of the reader's knowledge resources. Exactly how a situation model is structured or copied is not clearly discussed in current research, but it is an issue for future research. There is some evidence that both levels of text representation exist and are used by readers (Fletcher 1994; Kintsch 1994, 1995; Moravspik and Kintsch 1995).

The situation model may best be seen as the reader's interpretation of the text, the domain of knowledge called up by the text, rather than its simple comprehension. By posing two models of comprehension, it is possible for the reader both to recognize and understand the information in the text, and also to create an interpretation that is unique to the particular reader. Thus, different readers are able to provide similar summaries of texts but also interpret them quite distinctly in terms of their own background knowledge and interests (and also depending on the text genre). This approach to text understanding on two levels allows researchers to argue both for the uniformity of text comprehension and also for its potential variability of interpretation (cf. Oakhill and Garnham 1988; Singer 1990).

The ability of a reader to make appropriate *inferences* is seen as critical for reading comprehension. However, many current theories differ on when inferencing is likely to be used, what types of inferences are made while comprehending a text and how inferences contribute to various levels of processing, particularly the levels of text model and situation model construction. Most researchers agree that sentence-level propositional integration (forming the proposition) may be the first processing component which calls on coherence-building inferences. At lower levels of processing, for word recognition processes or for first efforts to parse the incoming information in working memory, inferencing is seldom likely to play a major role in fluent reading, though inferencing may help confirm appropriate parsing (cf. Perfetti 1994).

Once the reader makes an effort to integrate the semantic information drawn from a clause, however, inferences become necessary to establish an antecedent for the definite use of a noun phrase, for a pronoun, or for an elliptical expression. Inferences are also necessary to interpret certain occurrences of new information in sentences, particularly if the new information appears towards the beginning of the sentence, or if there are multiple sets of new information in a single sentence. Finally, newly processed sentences may not directly connect to any part of the evolving text model and *bridging inferences* are needed to create the overlap between the text model and the newly processed sentence.

Inferencing thus becomes very important in the construction of both the text model and the situation model of text comprehension. In the text model, the bridging inferences allow the new proposition to connect minimally with the network in an appropriate way (McKoon and Ratliff, 1995). Inferences may also connect a new proposition with the more thematic information and even with the macrostructure; thus, it is also possible that inferences may be made to link causal antecedent information (*causal antecedent inferences*) or globally relevant information (*global inferences*) or emotional states of characters (*character emotion inferences*). (See Albrecht and O'Brien 1995; Gernsbacher and Givon 1995; Graesser *et al.* 1995; Graesser *et al.* 1996; Long *et al.* 1996; Lorch 1995; Singer 1995). The status of these latter types of inferences currently is source of much debate, and it may well be the case that these inferences are more important in reading certain genres than others; in particular, work on these latter types of inferences is primarily done with narrative fiction texts. Thus, narrative texts may be more conducive to causal, global and emotional-state inferences by readers (Graesser and Britton 1996; Graesser *et al.* 1996; Lorch 1995; cf. Britton 1994).

Elaborating inferences represent a further type of inferencing typically used to retrieve additional information from long-term memory. These inferences might include 'he had a knife' on the basis of the sentence 'He cut himself.' Elaborating inferences involve the incorporation of extra information which is not explicitly stated in the text being read, and which does not strongly associate with causal, global or character emotion inferences. This information is also not used primarily for connecting new information with the already processed information. Rather, elaborating inferences provide additional information which may be called up for the purposes of individual interpretation of a text; that is, it may help build a unique interpretation of a text, but there is no clear evidence that most types of elaborating inferences actually occur as part of the reading comprehension process itself. These inferences, then, do not seem to be part of the on-line processing of text comprehension. Instead, they often appear to reflect the contribution of background knowledge to the later retrieval of textual information, and they occur primarily when a reader is being asked to recall information that he has already stored in long-term memory (Graesser and Kreuz 1993; Perfetti 1993, 1994; Singer 1990). (Elaborating inferences, however, are commonly assessed on reading comprehension tests.)

It should be noted that efforts to establish inferencing abilities as a source of difference between good and poor readers have yet to be very successful. There is evidence that inferencing skills are important for reading comprehension, that good readers are better at making inferences and that inferencing abilities can be taught to some extent. However, the ways in which inferencing skills assist comprehension are not entirely clear, nor is there a well-established set of inferencing skills that are readily identifiable for the improvement of comprehension, or for testing purposes. These limitations for reading assessment have been raised in articles by Alderson (Alderson and Lukmani 1989; Alderson 1990a, 1990b). At present, we know that reasoning about the text is important, but it is not clear what sub-aspects of inferencing are critical.

Aside from inferencing, *discourse structuring principles* also appear to be important both for text model construction and for situation model building, though there is much less research on this topic than on inferencing. These principles include:

1. presenting given information before new information;
2. foregrounding main information and backgrounding supporting information;
3. placing important information in first-mention position;
4. marking thematic information by repetition, pronoun forms or unusual structures; and
5. signalling relations between local propositions as well as their relations to the macroproposition.

Discourse processing researchers argue that these discourse structuring principles contribute to the coherence of a text, giving the reader sufficient textual resources to construct a comprehensible text model and an interpretable situation model (Beck *et al.* 1991; van Dijk and Kintsch 1983; Lorch and O'Brien 1995; Singer 1990). It is also important to recognize that the notion of grammatical structure as signalling mechanisms for discourse processing is gaining greater influence. This perspective is most convincingly presented by Gernsbacher's (1990) Structure Building Framework. (See also Britton 1994; Givon 1995a, 1995b; Kintsch 1995.)

The role of *strategies* in reading comprehension processes has been a source of much discussion in the past ten years, though more so among educational psychologists than cognitive psychologists (cf. Brown *et al.* 1996; Oakhill 1994; Pressley and Woloshyn 1995; Weaver, Bryant and Burns 1995). On a general level, strategies for a model of reading processes could include a full range of inferencing skills, the restructuring of information within a text model of comprehension or a situation model of text interpretation, the adaptation of goals and purposes for reading (for a variety of reasons) and the application of metacognitive processing to clarify comprehension and repair mis-comprehension. As a theoretical concept, then, the notion of reading strategies is protean, and thus not very appealing as a component for a theory of reading comprehension processes (cf. Block 1986, 1992; Hosenfeld 1984; Cohen 1990 for L2 discussion). Nevertheless, the role of reading strategies in reading comprehension is well recognized, and many training studies have demonstrated that strategy instruction can improve reading abilities, and strategic efficiency in reading distinguishes good readers from poor readers.

At one level, the role of comprehension strategies in text comprehension represents an educational response to the issue of explaining how reading comprehension actually works, and why reading comprehension is more than word recognition. A number of researchers have argued that higher-level reading-strategy use is the essence of comprehension, suggesting a problem-solving perspective on comprehension (Pearson and Fielding 1991). It should also be noted, in contrast, that many other researchers feel that the essence of reading comprehension is lexical access and propositional integration. In some respects, both views are right (and this is captured nicely in 'the simple view of reading': Gough, Juel and Griffith 1992; Hoover and Gough 1990; Perfetti 1994; Tunmer and Hoover 1992).

The notion that strategies would be a major source of comprehension derives from instructional research (rather than experimental laboratory research) which explores how to improve comprehension instructionally. A large set of results have shown that word identification without appropriate strategies does not guarantee comprehension. Moreover, many students who have been trained to be more strategic readers have shown clear improvements in reading comprehension (Brown *et al.* 1996; Pressley and Woloshyn 1995; Lysynchuk *et al.* 1990; Slavin 1995). The notion of reading strategies, however, is not a simple issue.

Researchers have, in fact, identified a wide variety of reading strategies; while some are important for lower level processes, others are crucial for higher-level comprehension processes. Thus, the issue of what represents a reading strategy is not well controlled in the psychological experimental sense. However, the use of strategies for good reading comprehension is readily apparent. The issue, then, is how to incorprate these notions of strategies, or more generally—the strategic reader, into psychological processing accounts of reading comprehension.

To illustrate, reading strategies are typically used for the following purposes:

1. recognizing affixes and root forms of words;
2. sounding out of words to assist recognition;
3. determining the subject and main verb of a complex sentence;
4. interpreting and learning new vocabulary;
5. recognizing miscomprehension;
6. recognizing discourse organization;
7. locating the main idea of the text;
8. questioning information and predicting upcoming information;
9. repairing non-comprehension.

Certain of these strategic processes require lower-level processing, others require higher-level processing, so the relation between reading strategies and higher-level processing is not entirely straightforward.

In short, the notion of reading strategies may be applicable at many levels of comprehension processing and its functioning in cognitive processing accounts of reading is not clear. Nevertheless, the idea that fluent readers are strategic readers is well established. There needs to be a greater effort to incorporate these issues into the cognitive processing research on reading comprehension. There needs to be much more research on the various types of strategies that are used, when they are used, how they are used, why they are used, who uses them and in what combinations they are used. Thus, it is possible to say that reading strategies are important for comprehension, but also admit that it is an area of research which is not easy to categorize as a component process in any neat way, nor is it an area of reading research which has been well defined with respect to most of the issues discussed to this point.

On the level of theoretical research, perhaps the best characterization of strategic processing is found in recent discussion of working memory, particularly the work of Gathercole and Baddeley 1993. (See also Baddeley 1992; Jonides 1995.) Their discussion of the roles of central executive processing may provide a locus for strategic processing. Similarly, Van Dijk and Kintsch (1983) argued that their situation model includes control processes and goal setting as influences on working memory. There are, however, few explicit cognitive theories of goal setting, cognitive monitoring and executive processing. This may be due partly to limitations in current research methodologies, and partly due to the protean nature of the issues raised—Many strategies may be of a more general nature than language processing itself (see e.g. Gernsbacher 1990). Having said all this, it is nevertheless true that the good reader is a strategic reader.

Further issues in reading comprehension processing

There has been much written about the impact of context on reading, as well as the roles of schema theory and content knowledge. These topics raise a number of complex issues for theories of reading, and detailed discussion goes beyond the scope of the present paper. However, this section will briefly note positions which are reasonably well supported in general by empirical evidence (as opposed to primarily logical arguments that are potentially flawed).

With respect to *the role of context effects* in reading, there are a number of issues that should be noted. First, context does not usually influence word recognition processes except with unknown words that readers notice and attend to (Perfetti 1992, 1994; Stanovich 1986, 1992). Moreover, context use does not distinguish good readers from poor readers, except in cases when poor readers overuse context resources (Adams 1990; Daneman 1991). Second, there are indeed some context effects which play a role in word recognition, but these typically involve automatic priming of words due to the previous activation of related words in a network. This spreading activation process certainly produces context effects, though not of the sort discussed by Frank Smith (1982), for example. Third, context effects are importance for confirming appropriate meanings of words already active in working memory and for the development of text models and situation models of reading comprehension. (They are, however, less important with the more automatized processes.) Thus context effects will consistently contribute to proposition formation, propositional integration, inferencing and text interpretation.

The concept of *schema theory* has been discussed widely in the past fifteen years, and it has served a useful role in arguing for the important of content knowledge or world knowledge in the interpretation of texts. At the same time, schema theory has been the subject of many serious criticisms which require that the term be used cautiously. It has taken on many different interpretations and it often generates as much ambiguity as it does clarity. While it is a useful metaphor for the role of background knowledge in reading, it should perhaps be used far less than it is when referring to components of reading comprehension. In fact, there is relatively little empirical theory attached to schema theory, and the concept of a schema is too vague to help research specify the nature and specific contribution of content knowledge. (Serious criticisms of schema theory may be found in Alexander *et al.* 1991; Carver 1992; Daneman 1991; Rayner and Pollatsek 1989; Sadoski *et al.* 1991.)

The importance of *world knowledge* or *content knowledge* in reading abilities has been widely discussed and debated for the past 20 years (Alexander *et al.* 1994; van Dijk and Kintsch 1983). Once again, there are a number of issues that need to be disentangled. The first issue is the distinction between the role played by general background knowledge, or knowledge of the world, and the role of specific and often detailed knowledge of topical domains (such as engineering knowledge, or English literature knowledge). Specific domain (or topical) knowledge does seem to play an important role in reading comprehension (Alexander *et al.* 1994). Readers with more detailed or even specialist knowledge of a topic will generally comprehend texts better and offer more detailed interpretations of texts. In contrast, when reading material does not make strong demands on topical knowledge, the supportive effects of topical knowledge on comprehension decrease. A number of studies have shown that background knowledge has a minimal influence on individual differences in L1 reading comprehension more generally, assuming a non-specialist text (Baldwin *et al.* 1985; Long *et al.* 1996; Schiefele 1992). Similarly, Bernhardt (1991) found no supportive effects for background knowledge in second language German students on reading texts that were not strongly biased to a student's major.

Second, in testing contexts, Hale (1988) has demonstrated that students' majors had a minimal impact on TOEFL reading scores even when they read texts completely in line with their major fields or completely aside from their major fields. These readings were not heavily specialized and the effect of domain knowledge in these cases was minimal.

Despite a general observation about learning that students learn best when new information fits with student prior knowledge, there is sufficient evidence in the reading research literature to treat this generalization with some caution. The role of prior knowledge in learning is likely to be generally supportive, but its impact may not be very robust in certain circumstances, one of which may involve the context of standardized reading comprehension tests using general texts without specialist knowledge assumptions.

The review of context effect, schema theory and content knowledge illustrates the more general issue facing reading researchers. Once efforts go beyond well-established components of reading comprehension processing, the nature of the comprehension mechanisms becomes less clear. Aside from the vague, though still real, contributions of background knowledge, there are also ambiguous results with research in inferencing, strategy use and metacognitive processing. In almost all cases, training studies indicate some role for these factors, but research results to date do not converge on a clear set of processes or principles that promote comprehension.

Perhaps the most interesting set of problems for a model of reading is how to establish the role of *reading strategies* in comprehension processes. As noted above, there are now numerous studies which demonstrate the positive role that certain reading strategies play in developing reading comprehension. At the same time, it is not exactly clear how various aspects of reading strategies should be treated in a model of reading. For example, six features of the strategic reader, listed below, would need to be accounted for in some way ...

1. ability to determine main ideas of a text;
2. ability to extract and use information, to synthesize information, to infer information;
3. ability to read critically and evaluate text information;
4. ability to use reading strategies in combination as strategic readers (important identifiable strategies include paraphrase, summarization, prediction, forming questions, visualizing information, skimming, scanning, monitoring comprehension, clarifying comprehension);
5. ability to concentrate on reading extended texts and
6. ability to use reading to learn new information.

Yet how these features will be addressed is not entirely clear.

Finally, a model of reading processes needs to account for *motivation and affective factors* which influence reading comprehension and the development of reading abilities. There are a number of recent efforts to develop the role of affective factors in reading comprehension (e.g. the roles of interest, involvement, attitude, goal setting, attributions of success, self-regulation). Both Mathewson (1994) and McKenna (1994) have developed recent models of affective influences on reading. In addition, a number of reviews and research studies have demonstrated the importance of affective factors for reading development (Borkowski *et al.* 1990; Dweck 1989; Pressley *et al.* 1992; Schiefele 1992; Turner 1993; Wade 1992). Further exploration of specific issues related to motivation and affective factors would require a separate article, however.

A model of reading

Having reviewed in the previous section (Components of the reading process) the many real and possible components of reading ability, we are left with the issue of their assembly for on-line processing during reading. In order to make clearer sense of the operations and interrelationships among components of reading, models become very useful. Models indicate descriptive decisions about the relationships between processes, the possible sequencing of processes and the competition for processing resources at any moment. As a result, it is possible to suggest constraints on reading processes, and hypothesize the relative contributions of various components in future reading contexts.

Four models of reading that are particularly useful for general descriptions of reading are those proposed by Bruer (1993), van Dijk and Kintsch (1983), Just and Carpenter (1987), and Rayner and Pollatsek (1989). Comments on these models given here will serve only to acquaint the reader; these models are described in more detail in the references given. The first model, that by Bruer (1993), is a useful though basic synthesis of recent research on reading combined with earlier model descriptions, principally van Dijk and Kintsch (1983) and Just and Carpenter (1987).

In Bruer's model, the reading processes begin with visual input and word recognition processes, followed by syntactic processing and semantic encoding. The integrated propositions are then incorporated into the text modeling and monitored for comprehension. The model indicates that all of these processes occur in working memory and are supported by resources from long-term memory. This set of components matches well with the description of reading components given above in general (see Figure 2.1). It does not mention inferencing, goal setting, strategy uses apart from monitoring or the role of a situation model of text comprehension. Two aspects of this description might appear misleading from Figure 2.1. The first is the seeming linear path of processing indicated in the figure. In fact, Bruer notes that reading is interactive in that these processes need to operate simultaneously rather than sequentially. The second is the question of where the various processes actually occur: do they occur as part of working memory, as separate from working memory, as part of long-term memory? This issue is only noted in his model. Overall, Bruer's descriptive model is a straightforward and accessible account of major features of reading comprehension processes.

Figure 2.1

A sketch of a cognitive model for skilled reading
[Bruer 1993]

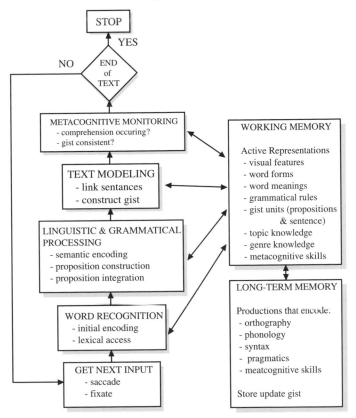

Note - A skilled reader relies on knowledge stored in long-term memory to construct meaning from text and is able to control numerous representations that must be active in working memory. The flow chart on the left indicates the representations and levels of processing involved during each fixation. An average fixation lasts 250 msec.

The earlier model of reading processes by Just and Carpenter appears to have provided a strong foundation for Bruer's synthesis as this earlier model matches quite well with Bruer (see Figure 2.2).

Figure 2.2

The Just and Carpenter (1980) model of reading
[Just and Carpenter 1987]

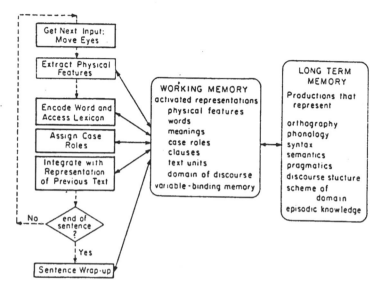

Note - Solid lines denote data-flow paths and dashed lines indicate canonical flow of control. (Reprinted with the permission of the American Psychological Association and the authors.)

The van Dijk and Kintsch (1983) model places a greater emphasis on both propositional formation/integration and on the discourse processing level. In particular, they argued that reading involves three levels of comprehension representation: the verbatim representation which decays rapidly, the text-based representation which follows the meaning of the text and the situation model which brings in much of the reader's prior knowledge and affective states. The unique aspect of their model was the early emphasis on situation modeling as an essential component of reading comprehension (see Figure 2.3). Further development of this model to incorporate lower level processes was introduced by Kintsch in 1988, 1994 as the 'construction-integration' model of discourse comprehension. (See also Mannes and St George 1996; Weaver, Mannes and Fletcher 1995.)

Figure 2.3

**A sketch of the operation of the memory system
in discourse comprehension**

[van Dijk and Kintsch 1983]

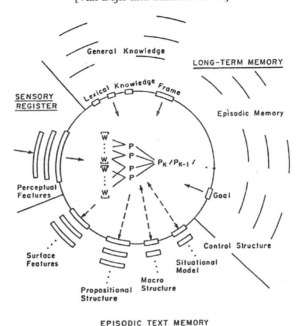

Note - The circle represents working memory, containing words and propositions; P_k is currently under construction while the previous proposition Pk-1 is held in the limited capacity buffer.

In the final model, that of Rayner and Pollatsek (1989), the emphasis is on the word recognition aspects of reading. They present their model in this way because they do not believe that higher-level comprehension processes could yet be reliably modeled. They therefore limit their model to reading processes which demonstrate converging evidence, and which emphasize word recognition and semantic integration processes (see Figure 2.4). While this perspective may strike some as reductionist, it is, in fact, a position that is being taken by more discourse comprehension researchers. This latter position argues that reading comprehension comprizes word recognition abilities and general comprehension abilities. Since comprehension skills are not specific to reading (e.g. Gernsbacher 1990), the only specifically reading-based abilities are the various lower-level visual word recognition skills.

This view is most commonly captured as D x C = R (decoding times comprehension equals reading), and is referred to as 'The simple view of reading'. (See below Gough, Juel and Griffith 1992; Hoover and Gough 1990; Perfetti 1994; Tunmer and Hoover 1992.)

Figure 2.4

Our current model of reading
[Rayner and Pollatsek 1989]

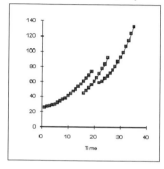

Various other models of reading have been proposed as well over the past fifteen years, and a number of them are influential for research on reading processes, though they have not been schematized as the above models have been. Three currently influential and well-known models include Stanovich's (1980) Interactive-Compensatory model, Perfetti's (1985, 1991, 1992, 1994) Restricted Verbal Efficiency model, and Kintsch's (1988, 1994) Construction-Integration model. Two other models that have been important in research discussions include Seidenberg and McClelland's (1989) Word Recognition Processor, and Hoover and Gough's (1990) 'Simple Model of Reading'. All of these models of reading are interactive and connectionist in their assumptions, though the degrees of constraints on interaction and connectivity strongly distinguish a number of these models. These models provide ways to establish and explore the many processes that are important for reading

Reading in a second language: Adapting a model of reading

For the most part, the component-processes analysis of reading which has been described for L1 reading is also applicable for L2 reading contexts. There are, of course, a number of factors which define L2 reading context and which argue for adaptations in any model of reading that might inform instruction and assessment. Perhaps most important, L2 contexts place a number of processing constraints on reading that are unique. Many of these specific constraints, outlined below, are commonly discussed and do not require extensive rationales. They will, however, require a somewhat different understanding of reading comprehension, particularly at beginning levels of L2 proficiency.

A *first* important difference, and one that typically takes many years to overcome, is the very different ranges of vocabulary knowledge for L1 and L2 reading. First language readers have a large recognition vocabulary, likely to run in the range of 40,000 words (Nagy 1988; cf. Goulden *et al.* 1990; Hazenberg and Hulstijn 1994; Zechmeister *et al.* 1993). First language students at most grade levels read material in which they know 99% of the words on a given page (Carver 1994). Even when students are given reading material three grade levels beyond their school grade, they know 98% of the words on any page.

In L2 reading contexts, minimal word knowledge for *fluent* reading has been estimated at 95% coverage on a given page (Laufer 1989). However, most L2 readers are regularly asked to read L2 text material which includes many more unknown words than the minimal 95% criterion. (And this is a serious dilemma for proponents of only using authentic texts in the classroom.) Second language readers will need years of reading practice to achieve the 95% criterion on a regular basis. Only the best second language readers will experience reading in the way that first language students do, reading texts with 98–99% vocabulary knowledge. Certainly this criterion will mark the early years of second language reading as distinct from L1 reading contexts.

Related to issues of size of vocabulary is the role of the bilingual lexicon in reading processes, particularly in word recognition. Little is known about how the bilingual lexicon might differ from the L1 lexicon, and if it would require distinct processing mechanisms or routes. This issue may be most important in the first years of second language reading.

A *second* major difference for the second language reader is the type of response they may have to difficult 'authentic' texts resources. There is no doubt that second language readers often encounter difficult text materials and are asked to comprehend them. While the language classroom often provides a scaffolding to support this reading activity, it is not clear what sorts of motivational and affective responses these activities generate. Nor is it clear whether such distinct tasks strongly influence attributions for success and failure with second language reading. First language readers who move on to post-secondary education do not typically encounter authentic material that regularly passes beyond their comprehension. We also know what happens to first language readers who consistently encounter very difficult material on a regular basis in primary and secondary education contexts. They typically quit!

A *third* major difference between first language reading and second language reading is the different levels of awareness of language. Second language readers experience a much more conscious awareness of how language works at both the syntactic and discourse levels. Second language readers at beginning levels, in particular, will need to develop syntactic knowledge as well as knowledge of discourse-organizing principles and overt markers of organization (Bernhardt 1991). The distinguishing aspect of this need is that L2 learners will not be able to rely on intuitive knowledge, and they must spend much more time attending to formal aspects of the second language.

One theoretical aspect to formal language awareness that should be noted here is the role of the Orthographic Depth Hypothesis (OHD) for second language reading (Frost 1994; Frost and Katz 1992; Katz and Frost 1992; Segalowitz and Hebert 1990; Shimron and Sivan 1994). The OHD argues that different languages have relatively shallower or deeper orthographies with respect to their transparency with the phonology of the languages. For example, Finnish and Serbo-Croat are seen as the most shallow languages for phonological processing. English, in contrast, is less transparent (thus deeper), Hebrew and Arabic would be deeper still, and Japanese and Chinese may be the deepest. The central issue is whether differing degrees of orthographic depth in a language will lead learners to pursue different strategies for reading at various stages of their development. Learners in English, for example, appear to make use of initial sight word reading until they learn to crack the phonological code. In contrast, learners of Serbo-Croat appear to make early and consistent use of phonological regularities in their early reading. At beginning stages of reading, this issue may have an impact on second language processing.

A further factor related to formal awareness of language is the role of mental translation in second language reading (Kern 1994). While much advice for second language readers has discouraged the use of translating for reading comprehension, this translating ability may represent an important strategic resource of both language awareness and reading comprehension. In fact, translation can be used to provide strong positive mechanisms for noticing formal aspects of the second language and using this knowledge to comprehend texts. This role of translation in various stages of second language reading does not match any comparable strategic resource which could be used by first language readers.

A *fourth* major difference is the very different reading rates and fluency of reading for second language students. Because students have restricted recognition vocabularies, greater 'attending to language' demands, limited practice with word recognition skills and fewer opportunities to read extended texts on a regular basis, they will typically have much lower reading rates and less automaticity in their processing. This bottleneck for reading processing is not easily circumvented and may take many years to overcome, if it ever is overcome (Bernhardt 1991; Haynes and Carr 1990; Segalowitz *et al.* 1991). This issue also implicates differing efficiency in the use of working memory resources for second language readers.

A *fifth* major difference is represented by the different cultural knowledge of the second language and the extent of differences from the first language. This distinction not only applies to cultural knowledge generally but also to specific topical domains of knowledge. While there is considerable evidence that cultural assumptions and cultural knowledge of the L2 will assist language comprehension, it is not clear what such an issue means for reading comprehension processes except that knowing more of the appropriate types of information will improve reading abilities. Again, this is an issue with no direct comparison to most L1 reading contexts.

A *sixth* and final distinction that second language reading must account for is the role of the L2 language threshold for reading. While it is not possible to specify what level of language efficiency and language knowledge any reader needs to have to read fluently, there does appear to be a language threshold that readers must pass through in order to make full use of higher-level comprehension-processing strategies that are available in L1 reading (Bernhardt and Kamil 1995; Bossers 1992; Carrell 1991).

The good reader and implications of instruction

One of the most important outcomes of syntheses of reading research and model building over the past ten years has been the impact of this work on reading instruction, both for L1 and L2 contexts. It is now possible to discuss a converging set of research results which have major implications for how reading instruction should be developed. The extent to which such findings have equal implications for reading assessment is not as straightforward, as will be discussed in the final section of this paper. The list of findings that follows establishes the range of research which informs reading instruction. There are certainly other points, supported by research, which could be added to this list. Moreover, this list, while primarily drawn from L1 reading research, is also compatible with research in second language reading contexts. Additional points specific to second language reading contexts are noted as well.

Abilities of the good reader

Reading research argues strongly that the abilities of the good reader include at least the following:

1. fluent and automatic word recognition skills, ability to recognize word parts (affixes, word stems, common letter combinations);
2. a large recognition vocabulary;
3. ability to recognize common word combinations (collocations);
4. a reasonably rapid reading rate;
5. knowledge of how the world works (and of the L2 culture);
6. ability to recognize anaphoric linkages and lexical linkages;
7. ability to recognize syntactic structures and parts of speech information automatically;
8. ability to recognize text organization and text-structure signalling;
9. ability to use reading strategies in combination as strategic readers (important identifiable strategies include paraphrase, summarization, prediction, forming questions, visualizing information, skimming, scanning, monitoring comprehension, clarifying comprehension);
10. ability to concentrate on reading extended texts;
11. ability to use reading to learn new information;
12. ability to determine main ideas of a test;
13. ability to extract and use information, to synthesize information, to infer information; and
14. ability to read critically and evaluate text information.

There are a number of findings from instructional research which argue, in addition, that readers will improve their reading abilities if they develop the following skills and practices:

1. work with graphic organizers to determine the discourse organization of the text and to restructure text information;
2. metacognitive awareness of strategy use to support reader goals;
3. co-operative learning skills to improve reading and writing abilities; and
4. extensive reading and exposure to print.

Additional abilities of the good second language reader

There are a number of research results which focus specifically on second language reading contexts and which should alter the way that second language reader instruction is carried out:

1. second language readers need to pass through a language threshold in the second language to make full use of L1 reading abilities, particularly higher-level comprehension skills and strategies;
2. second language readers will begin to read in a second language with different strengths depending on what L1 they use and what L2 they are learning (e.g., phonological transparency, morphological differences, orthographic differences, differing cognate relations, different reading experiences);
3. second language learners need to be made aware of the language knowledge that will be useful to them as they learn to read in a second language. They will also need to learn how to make effective use of additional resources that they might possess: these include greater knowledge of the world, skills in attending to language form, the use of cognate knowledge when appropriate, and the use of bilingual dictionaries.

Issues/dilemmas for second language reading assessment (an outsider looking in)

Unlike the impact of research on reading instruction, the impact of research on reading assessment does not seem to have been very prominent. Rather, it would appear that reading assessment has been, and still is, driven by assessment theory more generally, as well as the reasonably strong psychometric qualities of traditional reading comprehension tests. Simple and straightforward measures of main idea and detailed comprehension questions on passages, combined with sections on vocabulary, provide strong reliability and at least arguable validity for these testing approaches. The traditional approaches are also popular because they are easy to administer, to score, and to scale, and they are economical.

Given this historical foundation for reading assessment, it is not easy to see exactly what impact the recent advances in reading research will have on assessment in the future. In the near future, innovations that could be adaptable for reading assessment will most likely have to pass through a similar evaluation in terms of reliability and validity in order to be considered. At issue, however, is whether such a set of criteria should be used in traditional ways to explore future reading assessment procedures. Such criteria may severely impede our abilities to adapt concepts and findings from reading research for new types of reading assessment, assessments which may, in some combination, provide more accurate information for purposes of proficiency measurement, diagnosis and performance skills. In particular, the use of the computer opens up many options for reading assessment that would be cumbersome via paper-and-pencil delivery. For example, a variety of measures of reading rate, word recognition and vocabulary and reading fluency could be developed for computer delivery.

In order to move beyond the limitations of current reading assessment practices, issues which may have an impact on future assessment practices need to be discussed and explored further. One way to suggest issues for discussion is to propose a set of dilemmas for reading assessment. These dilemmas potentially indicate areas to consider in newer approaches to reading assessment. Below are fifteen potential dilemmas for second language reading assessment. The importance of each is perhaps debatable, and that is, in fact, the purpose for including them in the list.

Dilemma 1: Can we assess some concept of 'stages of development' for L2 reading beyond a general proficiency concept? Or beyond some simple rate and accuracy combination? If this is not easy to do, then do we need to know more about the various abilities of L2 readers? Is the notion of 'stages of reading development' important for large-scale reading assessment practices? For example, how does assessment of reading change for beginning readers versus intermediate and advanced readers?

Dilemma 2: Will reading in *different second languages* require different types of reading assessment at different proficiency stages? Particularly at earlier stages of reading development, differences across languages, as well as alternate sets of preferred processing strategies, may be important considerations for test development.

Dilemma 3: How can the computer environment open up new assessment options that may tap into some of the criteria of a good reader noted above? Or are there good reasons to stay within more limited bounds of current reading assessment item types?

Dilemma 4: Will Computer-adaptive Testing (CAT) restrict, in perhaps unforeseen ways, the range of assessment item types that could be explored, and that should be explored?

Dilemma 5: Can tests assess reading abilities as they interact with other language abilities, primarily writing? Should reading tests, in some circumstances, measure certain joint ability levels?

Dilemma 6: Do we want a straight power test or do we want some measure of rate and speed as well, in combination or separately? For example, in power tests of reading comprehension, students have a relatively large amount of time for problem-solving approaches to test questions, yet this emphasis on power may test study skills more than on-line reading comprehension skills.

Dilemma 7: Should some measure of extended reading become part of reading assessment? What can be gained by items based on extended reading? Can new item types be used with extended reading? If assessment items from extended reading are more likely to be linked, how might interdependence of items be handled?

Dilemma 8: Can tests provide reliable measures of word recognition abilities and reading rate levels? What is to be gained from such measures in assessment terms? Can these measures be done quickly and effectively? For which types of students would this information be most informative?

Dilemma 9: Can a test provide, or account for, some useful measure of cultural/world knowledge from the L2 perspective? Is this an issue that should be pursued?

Dilemma 10: How can a test measure the extent to which students are becoming strategic readers in the L2? What are the problems with pursuing this sort of assessment information? What is to be gained? How might this sort of information be at odds with other types of information sought in reading assessment? What would item types look like that could tap into strategic reading abilities? For example, how might items be designed that would measure predictions? question-forming abilities? paraphrase and summary? comprehension monitoring? imagery? Can CAT be useful in developing these types of measures?

Dilemma 11: How can a test measure students' abilities to recognize the structure of text organization? Should a test want to tap into this type of reading ability? If so, what would item types look like? Could CAT items be designed that would be particularly useful for this issue?

Dilemma 12: How can a test measure the extent to which students can extract, synthesize and restructure information from texts? What are the advantages of pursuing this sort of information? What difficulties will be encountered (e.g., testing general problem-solving skills)? How will CAT versions help or hinder this type of measure? What would item types look like?

Dilemma 13: Can CAT versions of reading tests be developed which are still reliable, have equated versions, and are capable of a large item pool, but not be constrained by assumptions of IRT applications? Could CAT versions develop new reading tests which respond to several of the dilemmas posed in this section?

Dilemma 14: Can L2 reading assessment in a CAT environment work with interdependent items? If so, how will reliability be handled? Will sections with interdependent items be scored according to some overall performance assessment criterion?

Dilemma 15: Will different L2s require different types of reading item types and overall text formats? Would this be a problem in university contexts with elementary proficiency students?

Conclusion

This chapter has presented a synthesis of research on the nature of reading. In doing so, it suggests a number of ways in which our understanding of reading has progressed in the past decade. It has also examined issues which create unique aspects of processing for second language reading. From this foundation of research, the chapter then indicated ways in which the findings can influence reading instruction, and have already influenced instruction in a number of cases. It concludes by raising issues that concern second language reading assessment. In particular, it suggests that reading assessment has not made serious efforts to stay abreast of current research in reading, or its implications for reading assessment. The dilemmas proposed are intended to raise issues for the assessment of reading abilities, taking into consideration recent findings on reading research. The issues raised should suggest questions and research agendas for future work in reading assessment.

References

Adams, M. (1990) *Beginning to Read: Thinking and Learning About Print.* Cambridge, MA: MIT Press.

Albrecht, J. and O'Brien, E. (1995) Goal processing and the maintenance of global coherence. In Lorch and O'Brien, pp. 263–78.

Alderson, J. C. (1990a) Testing reading comprehension skills (Part 1). *Reading in a Foreign Language* 6 (2): 425–38.

Alderson, J. C. (1990b) Testing reading comprehension skills (Part 2). *Reading in a Foreign Language* 7 (1): 465–503.

Alderson, J. C. and Lukmani, Y. (1989) Cognition and levels of comprehension as embodied in test questions. *Reading in a Foreign Language* 5 (2): 253–70.

Alexander, P., Kulikowich, J. and Schulze, S. (1994) How subject matter knowledge affects recall and interest. *American Education Research Journal* 31: 313–37.

Alexander, P., Schallert, D. and Hare, V. (1991) Coming to terms: How researchers in learning and literacy talk about knowledge. *Review of Educational Research* 61: 315–43.

Anderson, R. C. and Nagy, W. (1991) Word meaning. In Barr *et al.*, pp. 690-724.

Baddeley, A. (1992) Working memory. *Science* 255: 556–9.

Baldwin, R. S., Peleg-Bruckner, Z. and McClintock, A. (1985) Effects of topic interest and prior knowledge on reading comprehension. *Reading Research Quarterly* 20: 497–504.

Balota, D. (1994) Visual word recognition: The journey from features to meaning. In Gernsbacher Ed. pp. 308-58

Barker, T., Torgeson, J. and Wagner, R. (1992) The role of orthographic processing skills on five different reading tasks. *Reading Research Quarterly* 27: 334–45.

Barr, R., Kamil, M., Mosenthal, P. and Pearson, P. D. (1991) *Handbook of Reading Research.* Volume II. New York, NY: Longman.

Barsalou, L. (1992) *Cognitive Psychology: An Overview for Cognitive Scientists.* Hillsdale, NJ: Lawrence Erlbaum Associates Publishers.

Beck, I., McKeown, M., Sinatra, G. and Loxterman, J. (1991) Revising social studies text from a text-processing perspective: Evidence of improved comprehensibility. *Reading Research Quarterly* 26: 251–76.

Bell, L. and Perfetti, C. (1994). Reading skill: Some adult comparisons. Journal of Educational Psychology, 86:244-255.

Bentin, S. and Ibrahim, R. (1996) New evidence for phonological processing during visual word recognition: The case of Arabic. *Journal of Experimental Psychology: Learning, Memory, and Cognition* 22: 309–23.

Berent, I. and Perfetti, C. (1995) A rose is a REEZ: The two-cycles model of phonology assembly in reading English. *Psychological Review* 102: 146–84.

Bernhardt, E. B. (1991) *Reading Development in a Second Language.* Norwood, NJ: Ablex.

Bernhardt, E. B. and Kamil, M. (1995) Interpreting relationships between L1 and L2 reading: Consolidating the linguistic threshold and the linguistic interdependence hypothesis. *Applied Linguistics* 16: 15–34.

Biemiller, A. (1994) Some observations on beginning reading instruction. *Educational Psychologist* 29: 203–9.

Block, E. (1986) The comprehension strategies of second language readers. *TESOL Quarterly* 20: 463–94.

Block, E. (1992) See how they read: Comprehension monitoring of L1 and L2 readers. *TESOL Quarterly* 26: 319–43.

Borkowski, J., Carr, M., Rellinger, E. and Pressley, M. (1990) Self-regulated cognition: Interdependence of metacognition, attributions, and self-esteem. In Idol, B., and Idol, L. (Eds.) *Dimensions of Thinking and Cognitive Instruction*, pp. 53–92. Hillsdale, NJ: Lawrence Erlbaum Associates Publishers.

Bossers, B. (1992) *Reading in Two Languages: A Study of Reading Comprehension in Dutch as a Second Language and in Turkish as a First Language.* Rotterdam: Drukkerij Van Driel.

Breznitz, Z. and Share, D. (1992) Effects of accelerated reading rate on memory for text. *Journal of Educational Psychology* 84: 193–9.

Britton, B. (1994) Understanding expository text: Building mental structures to induce insights. In Gernsbacher Ed., pp. 641-740.

Britton, B. and Graesser, A. (Eds.) (1996) *Models of Understanding Text.* Mahwah, NJ: Lawrence Erlbaum Associates Publishers.

Brown, R., Pressley, M., Van Meter, P. and Schuder, T. (1996) A quasi-experimental validation of transactional strategy instruction with low-achieving second-grade readers. *Journal of Educational Psychology* 88: 18–37.

Bruer, J. (1993) *Schools for Thought.* Cambridge, MA: MIT Press.

Carpenter, P., Miyake, A. and Just, M. (1994) Working memory constraints in comprehension: Evidence from individual differences, aphasia, and aging. In Gernsbacher.

Carr, T. H. and Levy, B. A. (Eds.) (1990) *Reading and its Development: Component Skills Approaches.* San Diego, CA: Academic Press.

Carrell, P. L. (1991) Second language reading: Reading ability or language proficiency? *Applied Linguistics* 12: 159–79.

Carver, R. P. (1990) *Reading Rate: A Review of Research and Theory.* New York, NY: Academic Press.

Carver, R. P. (1992) Effect of prediction activities, prior knowledge, and text type upon amount compreheded: Using rauding theory to critique schema theory research. *Reading Research Quarterly* 27 (2): 169–74.

Carver, R. P. (1994) Percentage of unknown vocabulary words in text as a function of the relative difficulty of the text: Implications of re-instruction. *Journal of Reading Behaviour* 26: 413–37.

Cohen, A. (1990) *Language Learning*. New York, NY: Newbury House.

Cunningham, A., Stanovich, K. and Wilson, M. (1990) Cognitive variation in adult college students differing in reading ability. In Carr and Levy pp. 129–59.

Daneman, M. (1991) Individual differences in reading skills. In Barr *et al.* pp. 512–38. New York, NY: Longman.

Devine, J. (1993) The role of metacognition in second language reading and writing. In Carson, J. and Leki, I. (Eds.) *Reading in the Composition Classroom*, pp. 105–27. New York, NY: Heinle and Heinle.

van Dijk, T. and Kintsch, W. (1983) *Strategies of Discourse Comprehension*. San Diego, CA: Academic Press.

Dweck, C. (1989) Motivation. In Lesgold, A. and Glaser, R. (Eds.) *Foundations for a Psychology of Education*, pp. 87–136. Hillsdale, NJ: Lawrence Erlbaum Associates Publishers.

Ehri, L. (1991a) Development of the ability to read words. In Barr *et al.* pp. 383–417.

Ehri, L. (1991b) Learning to read and spell words. In Rieben, L. and Perfetti, C. (Eds.) *Learning to Read: Basic Research and its Implications*, pp. 57–73. Hillsdale, NJ: Lawrence Erlbaum Associates Publishers.

Ehri, L. (1992) Reconceptualizing the development of sight word reading and its relationship to recoding. In Gough, Ehri and Treiman. pp. 107–43.

Fletcher, C. (1994) Levels of representation in memory for discourse. In Gernsbacher Ed. 589–601.

Frost, R. (1994) Prelexical and postlexical strategies in reading: Evidence from a deep and a shallow orthography. *Journal of Experimental Psychology: Learning, Memory, and Cognition* 20: 116–29.

Frost, R. (1995) Phonological computation and missing vowels: Mapping lexical involvement in reading. *Journal of Experimental Psychology: Learning, Memory, and Cognition* 21: 398–408.

Frost, R. and Katz, L. (Eds.) (1992) *Orthography, Phonology, Morphology, and Meaning*. Amsterdam: North Holland.

Garnham. A. (1985) *Psycholinguistics: Central Topics*. New York, NY: Methuen.

Garnham, A. (1994) Future directions. In Gernsbacher Ed. pp. 1123–44.

Garnham, A. and Oakhill, J. (1996) The mental models theory of language comprehension. In Britton and Graesser, pp. 313–39.

Gathercole, S. and Baddeley, D. (1993) *Working Memory and Language.*

Gernsbacher, M. A. (1990) *Language Comprehension as Structure Building.* Hillsdale, NJ: Lawrence Erlbaum Associates Publishers.

Gernsbacher, M. A. (Ed.) (1994) *Handbook of psycholinguistsics.* San Diego, CA: L. Lawrence Erlbaum Associates Publishers.

Gernsbacher, M. A. and Givon, T. (Eds.). (1995). *Coherence in spontaneous test.* Philadelphia, T. Benjamin.

Gernsbacher, M. A. (1996) The structure–building framework: What it is, what it might also be, and why. In Britton and Graesser, pp. 289–311.

Givon, T. (1995a) Coherence in text vs. coherence in mind. In Gernsbacher and Givon, pp. 59–115.

Givon, T. (1995b) *Functionalism and Grammar.* Philadelphia, PA: J. Benjamins.

Gough, P., Ehri, L. and Treiman, R. (Eds.) (1992) *Reading Acquisition.* Hillsdale, NJ: Lawrence Erlbaum Associates Publishing.

Gough, P., Juel, C. and Griffith, P. (1992) Reading, spelling, and the orthographic cipher. In Gough, Ehri and Treiman, pp. 35–48.

Goulden, R., Natin, P. and Read, J. (1990) How large can a receptive vocabulary be? *Applied Linguistics* 11: 341–63.

Graesser, A., Bertus, E. and Magliano, J. (1995) Inference generation during the comprehension of narrative text. In Lorch and O'Brien, pp. 295–320.

Graesser, A. and Britton, B. (1996) Five metaphors for text understanding. In Britton and Graesser, pp. 341–51.

Graesser, A. and Kreuz, R. (1993) A theory of inference generation during text comprehension. *Discourse Processes* 16: 145–60.

Graesser, A., Swamer, S., Baggett, W. and Sell, M. (1996) New models of deep comprehension. In Britton and Graesser, pp. 1–32.

Guarino, R. and Perkins, K. (1986) Awareness of form class as a factor in ESL reading comprehension. *Language Learning* 36: 77–82.

Haenggi, D. and Perfetti, C. (1994) Processing components of college-level reading comprehension. *Discourse Processes* 17: 83–104.

Hale, G. (1988) The interaction of student major-field group and text content in TOEFL reading comprehension. *TOEFL Research Report* 25. Princeton, NJ: Educational Testing Service.

Haynes, M. and Carr, T. H. (1990) Writing system background and second language reading: A component skills analysis of English reading by native-speaker readers of Chinese. In Carr and Levy, pp. 375–421.

Hazenberg, S. and Hulstijn, J. (1994) *Defining a minimal receptive second-language vocabulary for non-native university students: An empirical investigation.* Amsterdam: unpublished manuscript.

Henderson, J., Singer, M. and Ferreira, F. (Eds.) (1995) *Reading and Language Processing.* Mahwah, NJ: Lawrence Erlbaum Associates Publishing.

Hoover, W. and Gough, P. (1990) The simple view of reading. *Reading and Writing* 2: 127–60.

Hosenfeld, C. (1984) Case studies of ninth grade readers. In Alderson, J. C. and Urquhart, A. H. (Eds.) *Reading in a Foreign Language*, pp. 231–44. New York, NY: Longman.

Jonides, J. (1995) Working memory and thinking. In Osherson, D. (Ed.) *An Invitation to Cognitive Science. Thinking.* Volume 3 (2nd ed.), pp. 215–65. Cambridge, MA: MIT Press.

Juel, C. (1991) Beginning reading. In Barr *et al.*, pp. 759–88.

Just, M. and Carpenter, P. (1987) *The Psychology of Reading and Language Comprehension.* Boston, MA: Allyn and Bacon.

Just, M. and Carpenter, P. (1992) A capacity theory of comprehension: Individual differences in working memory. *Psychological Review* 99: 122–49.

Katz, L. and Frost, R. (1992) Reading in different orthographies: The orthographic depth hypothesis. In Frost and Katz, pp. 67–84.

Kintsch, W. (1988) The role of knowledge in discourse comprehension: A construction-integration model. *Psychological Review* 95: 163–82.

Kintsch, W. (1994) Psycholinguistics and reading ability. In Gernsbacher (Ed.) pp. 849–94.

Kintsch, W. (1995) How readers construct situation models for stories: The role of syntactic cues and causal inferences. In Gernsbacher and Givon, pp. 139–60.

Laufer, B. (1989) What percentage of text-lexis is essential for comprehension? In Lauren, C. and Nordman, M. (Eds.) *Special Language: From Humans Thinking to Thinking Machines*, pp. 316–23. Philadelphia, PA: Multilingual Matters.

Lesch, M. and Pollatsek, A. (1993) Automatic access of semantic information by phonological codes in visual word recognition. *Journal of Experimental Psychology: Learning, Memory, and Cognition* 19: 285–94.

Levy (Ed.) (199X) *Reading and its Development: Component Skills Approaches*, pp. 375–421. New York, NY: Academic Press.

Long, D., Seely, M., Oppy, B. and Golding, J. (1996) The role of inferential processing in reading ability. In Britton and Graesser, pp. 189–214.

Lorch, J. (1995) Integration of topic information during reading. In Lorch and O'Brien, pp. 279–94.

Lorch, R and O'Brien, E. (Eds.) (1995) *Sources of Coherence in Reading.* Hillsdale, NJ: Lawrence Erlbaum Associates Publishing.

Lukatela, G. and Turvey, M. (1994a) Visual lexical access is initially phonological: 1. Evidence from associative priming by words, homophones, and pseudohomophones. *Journal of Experimental Psychology: General* 123: 107–28.

Lukatela, G. and Turvey, M. (1994b) Visual lexical access is initially phonological: 2. Evidence from phonological priming by homophones and pseudohomophones. *Journal of Experimental Psychology: General* 123: 331–53.

Lukatela, G. and Turvey, M. (1995) Phonological processes in Serbo-Croatian and English. In de Gelder, B. and Morais, J. (Eds.) *Speech and Reading: A Comparative Approach*, pp. 191–206.

Lysynchuk, L., Pressley, M. and Vye, N. (1990) Reciprocal teaching improves standardized reading comprehension performance in poor comprehenders. *Elementary School Journal* 90: 469–84.

Mannes, S. and St. George, M. (1996) Effects of prior knowledge on text comprehension: A simple modeling approach. In Britton and Graesser, pp. 115–39.

Mason, J. (1992) Reading stories to preliterate children: A proposed connection to reading. In Gough, Ehri and Treiman, pp. 215–41.

Mathewson, G. (1994) Model of attitude influence upon reading and learning to read. In Ruddell, R., Ruddell, M. and Singer, H. (Eds.) *Theoretical Models and Processes of Reading* (4th ed.), pp. 1131–61. Newark, DE: IRA.

McKenna, M. (1994) Toward a model of reading attitude acquisition. In Cramer, E. and Castle, M. (Eds.) *Fostering the Love of Reading: The Affective Domain in Reading Education*, pp. 18–40. Newark, DE: IRA.

McKoon, G. and Ratliff, R. (1995) The minimalist hypothesis: Directions for research. In Weaver, Mannes and Fletcher, pp. 97–116.

McNamara, T., Miller, D. and Bransford, J. (1991) Mental models and reading comprehension. In Barr *et al.* pp. 490–511.

Moravcspik, J. and Kintsch, W. (1995) Writing quality, reading skills, and domain knowledge as factors in text comprehension. In Henderson, Singer and Ferreira pp. 232–46.

Nagy, W. (1988) *Teaching Vocabulary to Improve Reading Comprehension*. Urbana, IL: NCTE.

Nagy, W., Anderson, R. C., Schommer, M., Scott, J. and Stallman, A. (1989) Morphological families and word recognition. *Reading Research Quarterly* 24: 262–82.

Oakhill, J. (1994) Individual differences in children's reading comprehension. In Gernsbacher pp. 821–48.

Oakhill, J. and Garnham, A. (1988) *Becoming a Skilled Reader*. New York, (Ed.) NY: Basil Blackwell.

Pearson, P. D. and Fielding, L. (1991). Comprehension instruction. In Barr, R. *et al.* (eds.), *Handbook of reading research*. Volume 2. New York, NY: Longman pp.815-860.

Perfetti, C. (1985) *Reading Ability*. New York ,NY: Oxford University Press.

Perfetti, C. (1989) There are generalized abilities and one of them is reading. In Resnick, L. (Ed.) *Knowing, Learning and Instruction: Essays in Honor of R. Glazer*, pp. 307–34. Hillsdale, NJ: Lawrence Erlbaum Associates Publishing.

Perfetti, C. (1991) Representations and awareness in the acquisition of reading competence. In Rieben, L. and Perfetti, C. (Eds.) *Learning to Read: Basic Research and its Implications*, pp. 33–44. Hillsdale, NJ: Lawrence Erlbaum Associates Publishing.

Perfetti, C. (1992) The representation problem in reading acquisition. In Gough, Ehri and Treiman.

Perfetti, C. (1993) Why inferences might be restricted. *Discourse Processes* 16: 181–92.

Perfetti, C. (1994) Psycholinguistic and reading ability. In Gernsbacher (Ed.) pp. 849–94.

Perfetti, C. and Britt, M. (1995) Where do propositions come from? In Weaver, Mannes and Fletcher, pp. 11–34.

Perfetti, C. and Zhang, S. (1995) Very early phonological activation in Chinese reading. *Journal of Experimental Psychology: Learning, Memory, and Cognition* 21: 24–33.

Pressley, M., El-Dinary, P., Marks, M., Brown, R. and Stein, S. (1992) Good strategy instruction is motivating and interesting. In Renninger, Hidi, and Krapp, pp. 333–58.

Pressley, M. and Woloshyn, V. (1995) *Cognitive Strategy Instruction That Really Improves Children's Academic Performance*. Cambridge, MA: Brookline Books.

Rayner, K. and Pollatsek, A. (1989) *The Psychology of Reading*. Englewood Cliffs, NJ: Prentice Hall.

Reiben L. and Perfetti, C. (Eds.) (1991) *Learning to read: Basic research and its Implications*. Hillsdale, NJ: Lawrence Erlbaum Association Publishers.

Renninger, K., Hidi, S. and Krapp, A. (Eds.) (1992) The Role of interest in learning and Development. Hillsdale, NJ: Lawrence Erlbaum Associates, Publishers.

Sadoski, M., Paivio, A. and Goetz, E. (1991) Commentary: A critique of schema theory in reading and a dual coding alternative. *Reading Research Quarterly* 26: 463–84.

Schiefele, U. (1992) Topic interest and levels of text comprehension. In Renninger, Hidi, and Krapp, (Eds.) pp. 151–82.

Segalowitz, N. (1986) Second Language reading. In Valid, J. (Ed.) *Language Processing in Bilinguals: Psycholinguistics and Neuropsychological Perspectives*, pp. 3–19. Hillsdale, NJ: Lawrence Erlbaum Associates Publishing.

Segalowitz, N. and Hebert, M. (1990) Phonological recoding in the first and second language reading of skilled bilinguals. *Language Learning* 40: 503–38.

Segalowitz, N., Poulson, C. and Komoda, M. (1991) Lower level components of reading skill in higher level bilinguals: Implications for reading instruction. In Hulstijn, J. (Ed.) *Reading in Two Languages. AILA Review* 8: 15–30.

Seidenberg, M. and McClelland, J. (1989) A distributed, developmental model of word recognition and naming. *Psychological Review* 96: 523–68.

Shimron, J. and Sivan, T. (1994) Reading proficiency and orthography: Evidence from Hebrew and English. *Language Learning* 44: 5–27.

Singer, M. (1990) *Psychology of Language*. Hillsdale, NJ: Lawrence Erlbaum Associates Publishing.

Singer, M. (1994) Discourse inference processes. In Gernsbacher, pp. 479–515.

Singer, M. (1995) Causal validation and causal comprehension. In Lorch and O'Brien, pp. 241–61.

Slavin, R. (1995) *Co-operative Learning: Theory, Research, and Practice* (3rd ed.). Englewood Cliffs, NJ: Prentice Hall

Smith, F. (1982) *Understanding Reading* (3rd ed.). New York, NY: Holt, Rinehart and Winston.

Stanovich, K. (1980) Toward an interactive-compensatory model of individual differences in the development of reading fluency. *Reading Research Quarterly* 16: 32–71.

Stanovich, K. (1986) Matthew effects in reading: Some consequences of individual differences in the acquisition of literacy. *Reading Research Quarterly* 21: 360–407.

Stanovich, K. (1990) Concepts of developmental theories of reading skill: Cognitive resources, automaticity, and modularity. *Developmental Review* 10: 72–100.

Stanovich, K. (1991a) Changing models of reading and reading acquisition. In Rieben, and Perfetti, pp. 19–31.

Stanovich, K. (1991b) Word recognition: Changing perspectives. In Barr *et al.*, (Eds.) pp.418–52.

Stanovich, K. (1992) The psychology of reading: Evolutionary and revolutionary developments. In Grabe *et al xxxxxxx*. (Eds.) *Annual Review of Applied Linguistics*, Volume 12, *Literacy*, pp. 3–30. New York NY: Cambridge University Press.

Stanovich, K. and West, R. (1989) Exposure to print and orthographic processing. *Reading Research Quarterly* 24: 402–33.

Stanovich, K. and West, R. and Cunningham, A. (1991) Beyond phonological processes: Print exposure and orthographic processing. In Brady, S. and Shankweiler, D. (Eds.) *Phonological Processes in Reading: A Tribute to Isabelle Y. Liberman*, pp. 219–35. Hillsdale, NJ: Lawrence Erlbaum Associates Publishing.

Templeton, S. (1992) Theory, nature, and pedagogy of higher-order orthographic development in older students. In Templeton, S. and Bear, D. (Eds.) *Development of Orthographic Knowledge and the Foundations of Literacy: A Memorial Festschrift for Edmund H. Henderson*, pp. 253–77. Hillsdale, NJ: Lawrence Erlbaum Associates Publishers.

Tunmer, W. and Hoover, W. (1992) Cognitive and linguistic factors in learning to read. In Gough, Ehri and Treiman, pp. 175–214.

Turner, J. (1993) A motivational perspective on literacy instruction. In Leu, D. and Kinzer, C. (Eds.) *Examining Central Issues in Literacy Research, Theory, and Practice*, pp. 153–61. Chicago, IL: National Reading Conference.

Wade, S. (1992) How interest affects learning from text. In Renninger, Hidi, and Krapp, pp. 255–77.

Weaver III, C., Bryant, D. and Burns, K. (1995) Comprehension monitoring: Extensions of the Kintsch and van Dijk model. In Weaver, Mannes and Fletcher, pp. 177–93.

Weaver III C., Kintsch, W. (1991) Expository text. In Barr *et al.* pp. 230–45.

Weaver III C., Mannes, S. and Fletcher, C. (Eds.) (1995) *Discourse Comprehension: Essays in Honour of Walter Kintsch*. Hillsdale, NJ: Lawrence Erlbaum Associates Publishers.

White, T., Power, M. and White, S. (1989) Morphological analysis: Implications for teaching and understanding vocabulary growth. *Reading Research Quarterly* 24: 283–304.

Zechmeister, E., D'Anna, C., Hall, J., Paus, C. and Smith, J. (1993) Metacognitive and other knowledge about the mental lexicon: Do we know how many words we know? *Applied Linguistics* 14: 188–206.

3 Reading constructs and reading assessment

J. Charles Alderson
Lancaster University

Introduction

In this discussion chapter, I first discuss issues raised by the chapter by Bernhardt entitled *If reading is reader-based, can there be a computer-adaptive test of reading?* and then go on to discuss Grabe's chapter entitled *Developments in reading research and their implications for computer-adaptive reading assessment.* Inevitably there is overlap across the two chapters, and therefore a risk of some duplication in this chapter. However, rather than conflate issues raised by both chapters, I prefer to risk some redundancy and deal with each chapter in its own right.

Discussion of Bernhardt

Bernhardt's chapter ostensibly addresses her title question but, as she confesses in her conclusion, the answer is a clear 'of course': why could there not be a computer-adaptive test of reading? The real question, she says, is: *'Will a computer-adaptive test of reading provide an appropriate general framework for the assessment of second language reading skills?'* and she suggests that the answer to this is far from clear, both in terms of theory and in terms of research results. Unfortunately, at this point I am not sure I understand the question, much less the possible dimensions of the answer, and I am therefore forced to consider in detail what her paper does address, in order to throw light on the question.

Like Grabe, Bernhardt stresses the importance of reading assessment taking account of what she calls 'the knowledge base surrounding second language reading': it must address the resulting theory, and must then fit into the constraints of assessment, in this case of computer-based assessment. Her paper usefully complements Grabe's in that it briefly but critically looks at the research evidence from second language reading, and finds much of it wanting. This is immediately a dilemma for the construct validation of reading tests or assessment procedures, be they computer-adaptive or other. If the research evidence is weak, the theory on which tests might be based is a shaky foundation. So where are reading test developers to go for answers?

One solution, as Bernhardt acknowledges, is practicality and basing tests upon institutional objectives. *'Tests that assess performance based on clear objectives are completely defensible. Until practicality catches up with theory, such tests are probably the most reasonable choice'* (page 9). However, given the paucity of the theory and the lack of research evidence, I would phrase this differently: *'Until theory catches up with practicality, such tests are the only reasonable choice.'*

Bernhardt reports the growing research that has addressed the question I first posed in 1984: Reading in a foreign language: A reading problem or a language problem? (Alderson 1984). The bulk of the evidence is fairly clear by now: namely that reading in a second language is initially a language problem, and only once a threshold of linguistic competence has been reached can first language reading ability transfer or be applied to the second language. However, she overstates the role of what she calls grammatical ability, and given the implicit connection between her Figures 1.1 and 1.2, this needs correction. Figure 1.1 shows syntax to be an important factor in SL reading for quite a large portion of the developmental process. In contrast, word recognition quickly becomes unimportant. However, word recognition is not all there is to lexical knowledge, and Figure 1.1 is misleading in not presenting the continuing importance in SL reading of vocabulary depth and breadth. Bernhardt concludes from Figure 1.2 that 'grammatical ability is more important than L1 reading', but this is only true if grammatical ability includes lexical knowledge. As she reports, Brisbois is the only study to have separated vocabulary and grammatical ability, and the results clearly show the crucial importance of vocabulary knowledge, not grammatical knowledge defined as syntax. Now, I accept that a clear separation of knowledge into lexical and grammatical is virtually impossible to achieve, but the conclusion drawn from Figure 1.1 that grammatical ability is the most important element in SL reading is wrong unless grammatical ability is clearly defined to included lexical knowledge and use.

I also find therefore the conclusion on page 5 that *'second language reading is a function of L1 ability'* to be seriously misleading, even on the basis of the results Bernhardt presents. *'Second language reading is a function of second language proficiency'* is the most obvious conclusion. But even this is inadequate, since it ignores such important factors as text (and especially text topic, but obviously also linguistic features) and the reader's background knowledge. Recent research by Clapham (1996) shows some very interesting results. Below a certain linguistic threshold (not just syntactic ability) SL readers are unable to engage available background knowledge to assist with the comprehension of text. Above a higher linguistic threshold, SL readers can compensate for lack of background knowledge with linguistic proficiency. And none of this appears to relate to first language reading ability, although in Clapham's study it might be assumed that her readers were relatively advanced and homogeneous in their L1 reading abilities.

For the testing of reading generally but computer-adaptive testing in particular, the real issue, as Bernhardt very usefully and concisely points out, is how does second language reading ability develop? There are lots of speculations on this matter, and various reading scales contain statements about what distinguishes a more advanced reader from a less advanced reader. Unfortunately these do not bear much critical inspection — often they refer to increased confidence rather than anything a reader might have learned or developed — which is hardly helpful for assessment purposes. They are clearly speculative, however informed by teaching experience or insightful intuition, and none is based on any empirical research, as I discuss below with respect to Grabe's First Dilemma. The notable exception is Kirsch *et al.*'s work on literacy standards in the USA (Kirsch and Jenkins 1993), as MacNamara points out in his chapter. Sadly though, these refer to first language reading, and a similar massive research effort would be needed to establish equivalent standards for second language reading. And as Bernhardt points out, given the likelihood that one's first language background will influence what one finds easy and difficult at a particular stage of development, especially given the importance of second language proficiency in SL reading, then such standards or scales would need to be developed for each first language background. Something unlikely to happen in the next few years, and something where theory is unlikely to make major contributions either.

So what are poor testers to do? They have little research evidence to guide them, theory is at a level of generality that barely allows any operationalisation, much less relevance in second language contexts, and considerable evidence exists that second language proficiency is what matters most.

Weir (1995) distinguishes three levels of operations in reading, as he calls them, the third of which he says has little to do with general reading ability. These are:

1. skimming: going through a text quickly;
2. reading carefully to understand main ideas and important detail;
3. using a knowledge of more specifically linguistic contributory skills: understanding grammatical notions (like cause, result, purpose), syntactic structure, discourse markers, lexical and or grammatical cohesion, lexis.

This latter 'operation' contributes to operations a) and b), he claims, but admits that the degree to which these are necessary, or indeed can be compensated for, is unknown and probably difficult to quantify. He calls such operations 'microlinguistic' and concludes:

> *The evidence from the literature ... and our own initial investigations throw some doubt on the value of including any items which focus on specific linguistic elements in tests which purport to make direct statements about a candidates reading ability. ... some candidates might be seriously disadvantaged by the inclusion of such discrete linguistic items in tests of reading comprehension.* (page 8).

He warns against any test of reading concentrating on level c) since he asserts this would result in invalid tests of levels a) and b). Intuitively one is obliged to agree with him, of course, but the research evidence that I have gathered shows that even this is not so simple. The relationship between a communicative grammar test designed for the International English Language Testing Systems (IELTS) Revision Project (Alderson 1993) and communicative tests of academic reading ability was so close as to cause us to drop a grammar test from our test battery because it appeared redundant. The alternative would have been to drop the reading tests and concentrate on the grammar test but for face (if not construct) reasons we felt we could not do that. However, the data made us doubt the parallel nature of the various reading tests. We found higher correlations between grammar and reading than between two reading tests supposedly measuring the same trait! Again, we are reminded of Bernhardt's sensible, but theoretically neutral comment on page 8 of this volume that:

> *Any given text evokes a particular performance. ... It is only across multiple texts that stability emerges. Clearly, all assessments should provide as many performances as possible.*

Thus a reading ability estimate should be based on multiple texts, and any view of reading development needs to consider what sort of text can be read by readers at what levels of ability. Most scales do attempt precisely that, but naively and without empirical evidence that their hierarchy of text difficulty is valid, even for groups, but especially not for individuals, about whom, after all, we are making decisions.

Bernhardt rightly attacks the myth that reading develops from ability to understand words to ability to understand sentences to ability to understand paragraphs or texts. She does not directly address the related debate that has raged for some time in second language reading as well as first language reading, namely whether reading can be divided into a number of skills, or whether it is a unitary construct. Most research into tests purporting to test different subksills of reading has failed to verify such claims. The number of separately identifiable skills that have been tested varies, from one — the unitary factor of reading — to five or even eight. However, although there is no consensus, my own view is that the debate is misguided. An item may indeed test one second language subskill for one person, but other subskills for other individuals, depending upon the text, background knowledge and other aspects of linguistic knowledge. Moreover, as Bernhardt also emphasises, skills of reading do not exist or operate in isolation but in interaction with other skills (or what Bernhardt calls features), and this interaction is central to reading.

Thus I find it hard to agree with Bernhardt that 'The mythology of particular features involved in reading and the reality of the interactivity of these features are the underpinnings of the fundamental assessment dilemma of the ask-questions type of assessment.' page 8 Rather, I believe that they are fundamental to the development of any theory of reading that can be operationalised, and are not specifically a dilemma for tests of reading. They only become problems for tests of reading if such tests are based on a multidivisible view of reading, which they need not be. Indeed, most second language reading tests do not depend upon a multidivisibility view of reading: whilst test developers may very well try to write items that appear to test some skills more than others or get at different levels of understanding of text, it does not matter much whether they succeed if scores are not reported by subskill. Usually reading test scores are reported globally, with no claim to be able to identify weaknesses or strengths in particular skills. And this is as true for adaptive tests as it is for paper-and-pencil tests. It is only when we claim to have developed diagnostic tests that this dilemma becomes problematic. All the reading proficiency test developer need do is state that every attempt has been made to include items that cover a range of skills and levels of understanding, in an attempt to be as comprehensive in one's construct coverage as possible. Given that much research shows that expert judges find it hard to agree on what skills are being tested by individual items, it would be hard to contradict or even to verify such test developer claims anyway. But since most second language reading test scores do not claim to show learners' strengths and weaknesses in individual skills, I do not see how this is a dilemma for assessment.

I also find it hard to understand Bernhardt's contention that it is hard '*to argue that some items are inherently more difficult than others*' (page 8), unless by items she means questions claiming to test one particular feature or skill, as discussed above. Certainly the empirical research shows that there is no simple correspondence between item 'type' or 'level' or 'skill', and difficulty, and that should hardly surprise us given the interactivity mentioned above, the difficulty of saying what skill is being tested and the complexity of the variables involved in making any item difficult for any given reader.

But it is clearly the case that items can be calibrated according to difficulty, and have been, even when one might have *a priori* reasons for believing that they do not measure on the same scale: items one might expect not to scale very frequently do, in fact. This is not a problem for most believers in IRT, who distinguish psychometric unidimensionality from psychological unidimensionality, and this distinction may be the source of Bernhardt's confusion. Be that as it may, if we can rank order items in terms of empirical difficulty, we can have an adaptive test. What the difficulty scale is a scale of might be a very difficult question to answer, but it is not relevant as long as we can have a range of difficulties, and we are reporting scores as measures of reading ability. It may be of interest to researchers, and ultimately to those who wish to refine their constructs or the diagnostic capability of our tests. But the test developer can sleep peacefully if she or he can construct an item bank of reading items that cover a range of difficulties. An adaptive test is then possible.

To come back to the question Bernhardt says ought to be asked in preference to the question in her title. '*Will a computer-adaptive test of reading provide an appropriate general framework for the assessment of second language reading skills'?* I am now in a position to address it. A computer-adaptive test can be interpreted to be a bank of items calibrated on a common scale, covering a range of difficulties and person ability estimates. In a sense, then, the item bank is the framework for assessment which Bernhardt's question refers to. But its adequacy as a framework is limited by the item types used. After all, only computer-scorable items are possible, and the process of taking *a test* on *a computer* might be held by some to be doubly removed from real reading—as I discuss below in connection with Grabe's chapter and as McNamara's chapter also discusses. Thus there are reasons for believing that computer-adaptive tests defined as objectively scorable items in a calibrated bank present a necessarily limited view of reading, and therefore of the possibilities for its assessment.

Doubtless further research will throw some light on this matter, and an inspection of the content of items that have been properly calibrated and scaled would reveal the limitations and adequacy of such a framework. However, that also depends upon the extent to which the tests are construct-valid—to what extent they are based on an accepted model of reading. It is Grabe's contention that tests are not based on current models of reading, and so it is to Grabe that I now turn.

Discussion of Grabe

Grabe's chapter is very thorough, thought provoking and usefully iconoclastic. He shows his usual impressive familiarity with recent research in reading, especially within the cognitive psycholinguistic field, and presents a readable and very valuable overview of that research and its implications. Like his 1991 paper, this chapter will become a classic and required reading for anybody wishing to get up to speed with an authoritative synthesis of research, in an area where overviews are notoriously difficult. It might therefore be thought churlish of me to highlight areas where the review is perhaps somewhat weaker. However, given the topic of this volume, at least one of these is relevant, and that is what research has shown about the assessment of reading. Another is a growing concern with the need to take a sociological and not only psychological perspective on reading. In this reaction I address the latter issue, before coming on to the former, and then discuss issues raised by Grabe as well as issues not raised that seem to me to be relevant. I shall discuss the extent to which the issues raised are relevant to computer-adaptive testing, or whether they are simply important considerations for any attempt to mount tests on computer, regardless of adaptivity.

But first one or two comments on Grabe's iconoclasm, and its timeliness. For the past 15 years and more, the psycholinguistic model of reading inspired by Goodman and Smith has held sway in ESL/EFL reading orthodoxy. Readers are said to be top-down, or at best interactive processors, who vary their reading rate, guess and predict meaning, and use context to help them in their construction of meaning. Grabe firmly puts this model in its place by showing how it is not founded upon empirical evidence: worse, that empirical evidence contradicts many of the tenets of the 'theory'. He shows convincingly, for example, that skilled readers do not use context to identify words, and that research has reasonably firmly established under what circumstances such readers do and do not use the context.

Secondly, schema theory has been fashionable in reading research, in both first and second languages, for some time, and many tests and instructional methods are claimed to be based upon schema theoretic approaches. Yet Grabe points out that schema theory is little more than a metaphor, and has proved incapable of precise predictions of the process whereby a reader's knowledge is engaged or modified. Schema theory has proved attractive because of its obvious common sense nature, but neither its empirical basis, nor its relevance to test construction or the design of reading courses, has been adequately established. In fact, careful research has shown that, in most contexts, the presence or absence of background knowledge has relatively small effects, when other variables are controlled. (See Carver 1992, for a critique of schema theory research.) I discuss this further below in relation to Grabe's dilemmas. As Grabe says, many researchers have long been critical of such untested or indeed untestable theories, yet the ESL/EFL profession has ignored them. I wish Grabe well in his attempt to reveal the Emperor's clothes.

Finally, ESL reading research has long been interested in reader strategies: what they are, how they contribute to better reading, how they can be incorporated into instruction. Yet as Grabe shows very clearly, the term is very ill-defined, and his own examples on pages 21 and 22 show a considerable heterogeneity as well as overlap. What exactly *is* the difference between a skill and a strategy? Between a level of processing, and a level of meaning? How are 'inferencing skills' (page 21) different from strategies like 'recognizing miscomprehension' (page 22) or 'ability'—another misused term—*'to extract and use information, to synthesize information, to infer information'?* (page 34) Is *'the ability to extract and use information'* the same strategy (skill?) as *'the ability to synthesize information'?* The field is in a mess, and is in urgent need of terminological clarification and recategorisation, and Grabe's identification of the mess is timely.

Let me now turn to an aspect of Grabe's overview that is perhaps somewhat underdeveloped.

Contexts for literacy

In an overview paper for the TOEFL 2000 Project, Hudson presents a synthesis of recent research findings which covers many of the same topics as Grabe, with an inevitable bias towards reading for academic purposes. It may be this very bias that led Hudson to consider in more detail than Grabe the importance of the uses of literacy, and the extent to which tests can take such contexts into account. Hudson is at pains to stress the need for a model of communicative competence, and the need for views of reading to take cognisance of such models. This leads somewhat inevitably to considerations of language use in context:

> *Reading is motivated by the reader's particular purpose and is propelled along by increasing comprehension of the texts .... Whether we are talking about children reading in school or adults reading university level course material, it seems clear that most comprehension is linked to purpose, and it is thus important to examine reading within the context of that purpose.* (pp. 16–17).

Interestingly however, Hudson does not cite much empirical research showing the effects of purpose, other than one account (Snow and Lohmann 1993) of variation of performance by task.

Indeed, this may be the reason why Grabe has not addressed this issue in any depth: the research findings are sketchy and much less well developed or controlled than the psycholinguistic empirical evidence. The field of literacy, as represented by writings like MacKay (1993) and Hill and Parry (1992), is curiously non-empirical and assertive in its claims for the value of a socially embedded view of reading. However, this may simply be the result of a relatively recently expressed concern with approaches to reading that concentrate, as Hudson says, on strategies, skills and processes to the exclusion of purpose and context: a stake has to be claimed first, a research area identified, before a research agenda can be developed.

Certainly educational psychologists like Royer, Bates (1984), and Fransson and colleagues (Fransson 1984) have investigated motivation and purpose at some length and concluded that reading is indeed affected by such variables (although purpose was often operationally defined as inserted questions, rather than any real-life credible reason for reading texts). There are, however, some researchers who hold a rather controversial view with respect to purpose: Carver (1982, 1983, 1984) maintains that what he calls reading—the normal reading children and adults engage in when understanding text, and distinct from study reading or skimming—is a constant process, which is *not* affected by the reader's purpose. Reading speed is constant across texts and 'purposes'. In fact, he claims that if a reader's purpose does have an effect on reading, that process is no longer 'rauding' but one of the other, less typical and socially valued, types of reading. This may seem like a quibble: if there are different sorts of reading, then by definition purpose has an effect, and so a concentration on rauding is too restrictive. But the fact remains that Carver's empirical results show remarkable stability over replications, and the more socially oriented researchers have failed to deliver convincing empirical evidence to the contrary.

As already suggested, this may be the reason why Grabe's chapter does not address this issue. But it seems to me important to consider what some call the ecological validity of reading tests based on computers–the topic of this book after all—and thus to examine the claims of the literacy advocates to see whether a useful research agenda can be developed.

The most obvious problem for computer-based tests of reading is that the amount of text that can be displayed on screen is limited, and the video monitor is much less flexible in terms of allowing readers to go back and forth through text than the printed page. In addition, screen reading is more tiring, slower, influenced by a number of variables that do not affect normal print (colour combinations, for example, or the need for more white space between words, the need for larger font size and so on). All these variables might be thought to affect the extent to which we are safe to generalise from computer-based reading to print literacy elsewhere.

Now of course it is true that much reading does take place on screen—the increased use of the word processor, the use of e-mail, access to the World Wide Web, computer-based instruction and even computer-based testing are all real and increasingly important elements of literacy, at least in much of the Western world. And it is probably true that future generations will be much more comfortable reading from screen than current generations, who are still adapting to the new media. It is certainly the case that many of my colleagues prefer to print out their e-mails, and read them from paper, to reading long messages on screen. Many who use word processors also print out their drafts and edit them by hand on paper before transferring their amendments back into electronic form.

But it is precisely the need for descriptions of how people use literacy—in this case in interaction with computers—that we need in order to be able to discuss sensibly the validity of computer-based—not merely adaptive—tests of reading. That, then, is clearly one area where a social view of reading can bring a useful perspective. The ethnographic research techniques that many literacy researchers use would be valuable additions not only in investigating computer-based literacy, but also in examining how test takers take adaptive or other tests of reading on computer, and comparing that with other forms of computer literacy.

Research into reading tests and assessments

This brings me to the second aspect of relevant research to which I recommend we give increased attention, and that is research into reading tests. Of course, much reading research does indeed use tests as its elicitation procedure. However, results and conclusions are more often couched in terms of their substantive implications—how they throw light on the reading process, what they contribute to the development of models of reading—than in terms of what they can tell us about reading tests. And often the researchers conveniently ignore the fact that their results are test-based, and therefore potentially biased. After all, test taking is likely to be a very special sort of reading, and conclusions that are drawn from the results of that process may simply be invalid in other contexts. Which makes it even more incumbent on researchers, it seems to me, to explore the instrument effects of their research. We need to understand much better than we do what variables affect test performance, and therefore indirectly our views of the nature of reading.

As might be expected, some research has indeed been conducted in this area, and not surprisingly most of it has investigated test method effects. There is a large literature on the use of the cloze procedure to produce tests of reading, some of it controversial, much of it tedious and simple-minded, but all useful for increasing our understanding of what cloze tests might measure, how they might measure it, and what features need to be taken into account in constructing cloze tests. That literature is too large to review here, but it is sufficiently homogeneous for it to be unforgivable for a researcher to use a cloze test to measure reading without carefully considering both the theoretical and empirical evidence for the validity of the instrument he or she is actually using. All too often, researchers make sweeping statements about cloze tests suggesting that they are in some magic way valid tests. That researchers might wish to believe such nonsense is understandable: cloze tests are quick and easy to produce, and to mark, and the construction of valid and reliable tests is a time-consuming business. However, models of the reading process based upon unvalidated cloze tests are worthless.

The same applies, *mutatis mutandis*, to other test methods. The multiple-choice technique is very commonly used in the construction of reading tests, yet, as Hudson shows, it is quite conceivable that the processes involved in selecting a suitable response from three or four optional completions to a statement might be very different from reading a passage and writing a summary or answering open-ended questions.

> *Tests made up of traditional selected response items present tasks to the reader that are more clearly defined and constrained than most real-world problems. Many real-world tasks are ill defined and allow the reader to make choices in precisely how a problem will be solved.* (p. 19)

The distractors present possible solutions that the reader may not have thought of, or they may lead the reader away from solutions they would have reached without the distractors. Students have been shown in a number of studies to get the answer to multiple choice items wrong whilst having the ability supposedly being measured, and students also make correct responses for the wrong reasons (and not only sheer guessing). Recent testing research has emphasised the importance of understanding the process a student engages in–more likely, the multiple processes they engage in—when answering reading test items, especially multiple choice items. Again it is surely incumbent on reading researchers to demonstrate, not assert, the validity of their measures.

Indeed, one of the reasons why the research into skills, cited by Grabe and others, is so inconclusive might conceivably be for precisely this reason. The test constructors have not established that their test questions do indeed tap the processes they are claimed to, and I have already mentioned that some research shows that judges find it difficult to agree on what skills are being tested by reading items (Alderson 1990). Whilst there is other research (Bachman *et al.* 1996) that shows that judges can be trained to identify item content using a suitably constructed rating instrument, it still does not follow that the processes the test taker engages in reflect those that the reader–judge thinks will be engaged, or that she or he engages in as an expert reader.

It may be possible that carefully constructed reading items can indeed measure one or more claimed skill–for some readers. The problem occurs if some readers do not call upon that supposedly measured skill when responding. In such cases, the 'valid' or intended responses are aggregated to the invalid or unintended ones. It is then not surprising if the analysis of such aggregation shows the lack of a clearly separate skill being tested by an item. In other words, such skill items might be measuring the skill for some readers, but not for others, and so would inevitably not load on a separate factor.

Perhaps we need to rethink the way we design our data collection and aggregation procedures, in order to group responses together in ways that reflect how students have actually processed the items. Mislevy and Verhelst (1990) and Buck and Tatsuoka (1996) have developed different methodologies for exploring this area, which would repay careful analysis.

It may be that the development of diagnostic tests of skills could be facilitated by being delivered by computer, with or without an adaptive mode. Tests can be designed to present clues and hints to test takers, and monitor their use in order not only to understand the test-taking process, but also possibly in order to examine the response validity of the answers. Information would then be used only from those items where the student had indeed engaged in the intended process. And conceivably unintended processing of items, if it could be detected, could be used diagnostically too.

Reading research and the assessment of reading

Grabe is at least implicitly critical of reading assessment for not having been affected by reading research. He suggests that assessment has rather been influenced by traditional psychometric values, and wonders whether progress in reading assessment can be made if such traditional values should continue to dominate assessment. These are strong and interesting statements, worthy of some discussion, as are his 15 dilemmas for second language reading assessment.

Should reading research have an impact on assessment?

My first question is of the relationship between research and assessment. Grabe's assumption is that there should be impact of one on the other (and I have already suggested that the impact might be two-way: much research is based upon the gathering of data from assessment instruments). Construct validation is central to testing concerns, and the identification of a suitable construct or constructs is central to such validation. Therefore it would appear only logical for reading assessment to base itself on the best constructs available. Unfortunately, as Grabe's overview shows, there is no one such construct: there are certainly major disagreements about higher-level processing, about the nature and contribution of inferencing, the role of other cognitive processes and abilities in reading. Even at the lower levels, there are disagreements about what exactly the phenomena to be tested are. So one not unreasonable way for test developers to be influenced by the confusing state of research is to wait and see what consensus emerges.

Nevertheless, I suspect that it is *not* true that reading assessment in general pays no attention to recent research into automaticity, word recognition skills and the like. Indeed, much of first language reading assessment is concerned with the identification of such components, and many test batteries specifically claim to measure diagnostically or otherwise. The problem is, as research consistently shows, that it is difficult to prove the separate existence of such skills. Is that the fault of the test constructors or the model builders? It seems unduly judgmental to blame the test constructors when theory itself is divided. Perhaps the problem is that the model builders are less than explicit about what these skills actually 'look like as Grabe's criticism of the literature on strategies suggests.

Moreover, many test batteries claim to be based explicitly on schema-theoretic approaches to reading—see Johnston (1984). However, researchers like Carver (1992) are highly critical of such practices, as I discuss below with reference to the ninth dilemma. Whilst I acknowledge that schema theory is problematic, it was once considered by many to be 'State of the Art', which is doubtless why reading test developers jumped onto the bandwagon. Should we perhaps rather be critical of them for having been uncritically accepting of and influenced by previously current reading 'research'?

The problem may be greater in the area of second language reading assessment, since the vast volume of reading research takes place in the first language, especially beginning reading, and this may be thought to be of less relevance to second language assessors. Again it is not clear that second language reading research provides satisfactory answers to many questions, as Bernhardt's chapter points out.

However, in the case of the issue discussed earlier as to whether second language reading is a reading problem or a language problem, research fairly consistently shows that second language readers need to pass a language threshold before their first language reading skills can be engaged. But this threshold interacts with background knowledge and text, so that on some texts with some topics, less linguistic proficiency is needed—the threshold is lower—than on other texts and topics. One obvious implication of such research is that low-level second language readers need to improve, and therefore be assessed on, their language proficiency before 'true' reading ability can be estimated.

A further issue, that has little to do with traditional psychometric values, is whether a second language reading test should measure language ability more than reading ability, reading ability more than intelligence, or any other construct which might be implicated in taking a reading test. The answer has to do with equity and justice as much as with reliability, surely: if we say our test measures reading in a second language, then we need to be sure that it does. And that means that we need to know what the difference is between reading in a second language and knowing the language, and reading in a second language and a first language ability. Recent research and recent models do not seem to me to provide adequately clear guidance on this matter, so why should second language reading assessment be influenced?

And that brings me to my second point.

Traditional criteria

Grabe asks whether we should continue to use traditional criteria for assessing test validity and reliability when exploring future reading assessment procedures. Of course, the extent to which such criteria apply depends upon the purpose of the test, and whether it is high stakes or low stakes, a fact not discussed. I cannot imagine candidates for TOEFL being happy with the knowledge that the new techniques used to measure their reading ability on the computer-based TOEFL have low reliability: surely they need to be certain that the assessment of their abilities is accurate? Would candidates be happy to be taking a test that was based on current reading models, even with low reliabilities? Surely not. The point is that many tests are used in high-stakes settings—and for many children, being placed into or out of remedial reading programmes can be very high stakes, or high impact. We need to be sure that it is acceptable for any test or result to have low reliability before we can relax the criteria.

And if we relax these criteria, what will take their place? The literature on alternative assessment is of course full of such complaints and claims—Hill and Parry (1992) are but one example. But there is also a literature that voices serious concern with informal assessment methods—be they portfolio assessment or informal reading inventories—that lack any evidence for their value and consistency. (See for example Fuchs *et al.* 1982.) Unfortunately Grabe does not speculate on what such criteria might be or how the existing criteria '*severely impede our abilities to adapt concepts and findings from reading research for new types of reading assessment, assessments which may, in some combination, provide more accurate information ...*' (page 36)

If the information is more accurate, surely it is more reliable and valid? How else will accuracy be judged? The rhetoric is persuasive but siren-songed. And the suggestion that the use of the computer opens up many possibilities for reading assessment is surely irrelevant to the supposed constraint of traditional criteria of reliability or validity. The use of the computer, I would argue, could enhance validity in some respects, especially if it were able to measure reading rate and automatic word recognition reliably. I believe we have here a false opposition. Computer-based testing does indeed offer new possibilities, not for the removal of psychometric criteria from test evaluation, but for enhanced validity and hopefully for reliability.

The dilemmas

The final list of 15 dilemmas for reading assessment is usefully provocative. Not all are confined to CAT, of course, although they potentially bear on CAT. I will address them one by one, in the hope of pushing the debate and possibly the research and development agenda further.

Dilemma 1: Stages of reading development for L2 reading. This is indeed a difficult area, and what work there is has uneasy empirical foundations, as Bernhardt also comments. Both the ACTFL and the ASLPR contain statements about what L2 readers can do at the various levels. The European ALTE organisation has developed Can-Do statements, including statements of reading attainment, which are in the process of 'validation'. The British National Curriculum for Modern Foreign Languages includes statements of attainment in reading at ten different levels. Brian North, in conjunction with the Council of Europe, has calibrated a number of Can-Do statements about reading ability on the basis of teacher judgements about typical learners.

The IELTS Revision Project attempted to develop Band Scales for reading–Urquhart produced a very interesting paper that looked at the possible dimensions that might be included (Urquhart 1992). So there are scales out there which claim to indicate stages of development.

However, none of these scales has—yet—a basis in longitudinal studies of L2 reading development, or even in cross-sectional studies, and at best they represent informed teacher experience and speculation about how learners might progress. The value of such scales for CAT is the need to be able to place test takers on a common scale, in order for the Rasch scaling model to work, and thus, presumably, an interest if not a requirement to label the points on such a scale, especially for diagnostic and reporting purposes.

The difference between beginning L2 readers and more advanced ones is often held to relate to an increase in the integration of skills at the higher levels. Thus in the earlier stages, readers are thought to have variable mastery of individual skills, but as they progress, these become more automatic and integrated, certainly at the lower levels of processing. This may or may not be reflected in the current scales as worded, and yet again, the empirical support for such beliefs is weak.

Dilemma 2: Differences across languages are almost certainly important: Haynes and Carr's (1990) research with beginning readers of Chinese is indicative of some of the issues. A related issue occasionally discussed in the literature and in Bernhardt's chapter is whether readers of different language backgrounds should be assessed differently, as well as having different expectations of development associated with their test performance. Given the distance between, say, English and Spanish, Arabic and Chinese, it is not surprising that some research shows students with Spanish as their first language to be better readers than those with Arabic or Chinese.

The interesting possibility for computer-based testing is that it might be feasible to allow learners from one language background to take a different test of second language reading from those of another language background, by simple menu selection on entry to the test—the restriction is our ability to identify significant differences and to write items to test for these!

Dilemma 3: The possibilities of the computer environment. I have already suggested above one or two ideas. But it seems to me that there are indeed many such. The possibility of recording response latencies, and time on text or task, opens up a whole new world of exploration of rates of reading, of word recognition and so on, which are closed, or very crude, in the case of paper-based tests: the ability to capture every detail of a learner's progress through a test: which items were consulted first, which answered first, in what sequence, with what result, which help and clue facilities were used, with what effect, and so on. (See Alderson and Windeatt 1991, for a discussion of many of these.) The possibilities are almost endless, and the limitation is more likely to be on our ability to analyse and interpret the data.

In addition, the future availability of tests on the Internet will make available access to a range of media and information sources that can be integrated into the test, thereby allowing the testing of information accessing and processing skills, as well as opening up tests to a variety of different input 'texts'.

However, there are also limitations, one of which was discussed above with respect to the process of reading on a computer screen. Another worry is the effect of test method: all too many computer-based tests use the multiple-choice technique, rather than other more innovative, interesting or simply exploratory test methods. (But see LUCAS and DIALANG for implementations of the Alderson 1990a, and Alderson and Windeatt 1991 ideas for reducing the constraints of computer-based scoring, and see Alderson 1996 for a discussion of the future possibilities of using computer corpora in conjunction with computer-based tests.)

Dilemma 4: Restriction of item types by CAT. I have already touched upon this in my response to the third dilemma above. It is indeed a worry, which has been written about at length in the references given above. However, there is no obvious reason why Computer-adaptive Testing should be more restrictive than other forms of computer testing, unless it is believed that the IRT calibration requires the use of only one test type in order to ensure that items are calibrated on a common scale (an empirical question, I should have thought).

Dilemma 5: Can tests test integrated abilities? The answer to this is clearly yes: see Lewkowicz (1997) for a discussion. The question is whether tests should do this. Weir 1983 designed the TEEP test to integrate reading and writing, and reading, writing and listening, but was careful to separate out scores of the various skills to avoid what he calls muddied measurement. The IELTS test deliberately included input from the reading test in a writing task. Obviously there are problems in doing this, not the least of which is reporting to lay people exactly what is being tested. But insofar as the distinction into four discrete skills is thought to be either invalid, or at least limited and possibly distorting in its view of language use, there is surely no reason why such integrated tests cannot be developed.

Dilemma 6: Do we want power tests or measures of rate and speed? Again the answer is clearly yes, especially in the light of recent research into automaticity and the possibilities of using computers to track rate much more efficiently than was previously possible. Carver, incidentally, has consistently argued that measures of rauding rates are essential to estimates of reading efficiency and has criticised much reading research for ignoring speed.

Dilemma 7: The possibility of testing extended reading. This is indeed an interesting idea, although arguably less so for computer-based tests in light of the doubts expressed above about screen-based reading. Certainly a number of EAP tests—the TEEP, the ELTS and the IELTS, the OTESL—have incorporated tests of the ability to read longer passages, considerably longer than the short texts tested on the TOEFL. But although there is recent interest in extensive reading and its benefits, it is not clear exactly what an extended text is, what the processes are that are engaged during extensive reading and whether a test can measure these. Since most extensive (not extended) reading is for pleasure, it is at least arguable that taking a test will remove the pleasure, and thus make it impossible to simulate the process.

Dilemma 8: Can tests provide reliable measures of word recognition abilities and reading rate? This overlaps with previous dilemmas, and the answer is fairly simple: why not? If reading researchers can measure reading rate and word recognition, why cannot testers? Whether it is worth doing so depends on the purpose of the test and the nature of the results (as well as what will be done with such results).

Dilemma 9: Can a test estimate world or cultural knowledge? This is an interesting issue, because as Johnston (1984) claimed, tests of vocabulary measure world or subject knowledge. He suggests using students' scores on text-related vocabulary tests to adjust their reading comprehension score, so that candidates will not be treated unfairly for lack of knowledge, or so that lack of knowledge can be taken into account in test interpretation.

I have doubts about the meaning of the results of studies like Johnston's. To what extent are vocabulary tests measures of language or knowledge? We know that vocabulary accounts for large proportions of variance in comprehension tests, but we are less sure why: it could be that the tests measure knowledge, or it could be simply that the need for a large vocabulary is essential to fast efficient reading. The answer to the problem probably depends upon why the information is being gathered, what use is made of it, and how believable the test results can be.

It appears that some school boards in the United States have adopted tests based on schema theory, which often include prediction activities, measures of prior knowledge and questions on a single lengthy passage. Attempts have apparently been made to eliminate standardized reading comprehension tests in part because such tests are said to have no theoretical basis in schema theory and because it is thought that the tests are substantially biased because they include no measure of prior knowledge.

Carver (1992) is critical of such practices. First, he criticises many schema-theory based studies for failing to measure general reading ability, the time allowed to read, the 'rauding rate' of the individual and the relative difficulty of the material, since reading speed is known to be an important indicator of reading comprehension. He argues that schema theory in fact applies not to normal reading (rauding) but to study reading and memorising. He claims therefore that schema theory applies only when materials are relatively difficult. Schema theory variables are thus likely to be applicable to college-level students who study relatively hard materials but not to elementary school children because asking them to read relatively hard materials is not recommended.

Carver also criticises school boards for introducing instructional practice that appears to have no effect empirically, simply because it is fashionable.

The direct evidence that activating prior knowledge facilitates comprehension during typical or normal reading is highly questionable. The direct evidence that standardised reading comprehension tests are biased because they contain no measure of prior knowledge is highly questionable. Finally the direct evidence that text type affects comprehension in normal or ordinary reading is highly questionable.

If instructional ideas derived from schema theory are in fact mostly irrelevant in normal reading situations (i.e. not involving relatively hard materials that require studying), then we need to be concerned about the possibility of wasting a great deal of valuable time on instructional techniques that are fashionable but have no more effect than large doses of chicken soup. (Carver 1992: 173).

I am forced to repeat my rhetorical question: should reading assessment really base itself on fashionable models of reading?

Dilemma 10: Can tests measure strategies for reading? This is a very difficult and interesting area. Interesting, because if we could identify strategies we might be able to develop good diagnostic tests, as well as conduct interesting research. Difficult, because we lack adequate definitions of strategies, as Grabe points out. Difficult, secondly, because the test-taking process may inhibit rather than encourage the use of some of the strategies mentioned: would all learners be willing to venture predictions of text content, for example? Third, because testing is prescriptive: responses are typically judged correct or incorrect, or are rated on some scale. And it is very far from clear that one can be prescriptive about strategy use. Good readers are flexible users of strategies. Is it reasonable to clone readers into only using certain strategies on certain questions? Is it at all possible to ensure that only certain strategies have been used? (We find ourselves back with the skills dilemma.) Buck (1991) attempted to measure prediction and comprehension monitoring in his listening tests, and found that he was obliged to accept virtually any answer students gave that bore any relationship with the text (and some that did not). Items that can have any reasonable response are typically very difficult to mark.

Dilemmas 11 and 12: How can we test abilities to recognize text organisation, and to extract and synthesize information? These are surely empirical questions, and it is far from clear that they are confined to CAT, or even to Computer Tests generally. There is nothing inherent in adaptivity that makes it easier or harder to develop such items. Whether they calibrate on the same scale and if they do not, what this might mean, cannot be answered in advance. Some would certainly claim that summary tests test the ability to synthesize and restructure: the problem is how to computerise the scoring, although multiple choice items with different summaries as options are one possibility, and summary completion (see Taylor and Pollitt 1996) is another.

Dilemma 13: Can CAT reading tests not be constrained by IRT assumptions? The answer to this depends on what is meant by an adaptive test. If an adaptive test is defined as a test whose items are calibrated on a common scale for difficulty and person ability, by a method like Rasch, then the answer is by definition negative. If one has a more liberal definition, such as a test whose items adjust in difficulty to ongoing test performance, then the answer is positive. After all, some people criticise oral interviews for varying according to the ability of the candidate: surely an adaptive test by that definition.

It is certainly possible to conceive of learner-adaptive tests: where the candidate decides whether to take an easier or a more difficult next item based on their estimate of their own performance to date (or indeed based upon the immediate feedback that a computer test can provide). Such items need not be constrained by IRT, provided one has some basis for calculating item difficulty.

Dilemma 14: Can reading assessment work with interdependent items? Item dependency is held to be a bad thing in classical test theory. Yet most reading items are passage dependent, and there is usually more than one item per passage, which makes the items linked in some sense. In the sense of one's answer to one item depending on one's answer to another, then such testlets are probably not interdependent. C-tests and possibly some cloze tests contain interdependent items. Yet that does not stop people using such tests. If it is feared that a test contains interdependent items, then it is possible to treat performance on one testlet as a superitem, and not to use the results of the individual items within testlets to calculate reliability. This is incidentally the approach used in calculating C-test reliability.

Dilemma 15: Will different L2s require different types of reading test items? This is an empirical question, which one can only answer once one has an estimate of what it might be about a particular L2 that might interact with item types to provide a different ability estimate. Theory is not so well advanced yet, but this may be a case where the development of reading tests and the examination of differential item functioning might contribute to the development of theory.

With my response to this last dilemma, as well as earlier, I hope to have shown that language testing research can indeed contribute to the development of reading research, and that more progress has been made in thinking about tests than might be apparent from actual samples of tests, or from the nature of the Grabe dilemmas. Indeed, I am uncertain whether these dilemmas really are dilemmas, but simply interesting questions, some of which already have answers, and which are worth exploring in test development and test research, whether that be computer-adaptive, or traditional paper-and-pencil reading tests. Despite their limitations, the advantage of delivering tests by computer is the ease with which data can be collected, analysed and related to test performance. This may well enable us to gain greater insights into what is involved in taking tests of reading, and in its turn this might lead to improvements in test design and the development of other assessment procedures.

References

Alderson, J. C. (1984) Reading in a foreign language: A reading problem or a language problem? In Alderson, and Urquhart, pp.1–27.

Alderson, J. C. (1990a) *Innovation in Language Testing: Can the Microcomputer Help?* Lancaster: Lancaster University.

Alderson, J. C. (1990b) Testing reading comprehension skills (Part 1). *Reading in a Foreign Language* 6 (2): 425–38.

Alderson, J. C. (1993) The relationship between grammar and reading in an English for Academic Purposes Test Battery. In Douglas, D. and Chappelle, C. (Eds.) *A New Decade of Language Testing Research: Selected Papers from the 1990 Language Testing Research Colloquium*, pp. 203–19. Alexandria, VA: TESOL Publishing.

Alderson, J. C. (1996) Do corpora have a role in language assessment? In Thomas, J. A. and Short, M. H. (Eds.) *Using Corpora for Language Research,* pp. 248–59. Harlow: Longman.

Alderson, J. C. and Urquhart, A. H. (1994) (1984) *Reading in a Foreign Language*. London: Longman.

Alderson, J. C. and Windeatt, S. (1991) Computers and innovation in language testing. In Alderson, J. C. and North, B. (Eds.) *Language Testing in the 1990s: The Communicative Legacy*, pp. 226–36. London: Macmillan/Modern English Publications.

Bachman, L. F., Davidson, F. and Milanovic, M. (1996) The use of test method characteristics in the content analysis and design of EFL proficiency tests. *Language Testing* 13 (2): 125–50.

Buck, G. (1991) The testing of listening comprehension: An introspective study. *Language Testing* 8 (1): 67–91.

Buck, G. and Tatsuoka, K. (1996) The subskills of reading: Rule space analysis of a multiple-choice test of second language reading comprehension. *Language Testing Research Colloquium*, Tampere, Finland.

Carr, T. H. and Levey, B. A. (Eds.) (1990) Reading and its Development: Component Skills Approaches. San Diego, CA: Academic Press.

Carver, R. P. (1982) Optimal rate of reading prose. *Reading Research Quarterly* 18 (1): 56–88.

Carver, R. P. (1983) Is reading rate constant or flexible? *Reading Research Quarterly* 18 (2): 190–215.

Carver, R. P. (1984) Rauding theory predictions of amount comprehended under different purposes and speed reading conditions. *Reading Research Quarterly* 19 (2): 205–18.

Carver, R. P. (1992) Effect of prediction activities, prior knowledge, and text type upon amount comprehended: Using rauding theory to critique schema theory research. *Reading Research Quarterly* 27 (2): 164–74.

Clapham, C. (1996) *The Development of IELTS: A Study of the Effect of Background Knowledge on Reading Comprehension*. Cambridge: Cambridge University Press.

DIALANG Diagnostic tests on the Internet for 14 European languages. For information, contact Centre for Applied Language Studies, University of Jyvaskyla, PO Box 35, 40351, Jyvaskyla, Finland.

Fransson, A. (1984) Cramming or understanding? Effects of intrinsic and extrinsic motivation on approach to learning and test performance. In Alderson, and Urquhart

Fuchs, L. S., Fuchs, D. and Deno, S. L. (1982) Reliability and validity of curriculum-based informal reading inventories. *Reading Research Quarterly* 18 (1): 6–25.

Haynes, M. and Carr, T. H. (1990) Writing system background and second language reading: A component skills analysis of English reading by native-speaker readers of Chinese. In Carr, T. H. and Levy, B. A. (Eds.) *Reading and its Development* San Diego, CA: Academic Press, pp. 375–421.

Hill, C. and Parry, K. (1992) The test at the gate: Models of literacy in reading assessment. *TESOL Quarterly* 26 (3): 433–61.

Hudson, T. (no date) *Assessing second language academic reading from a communicative competence perspective: Relevance for TOEFL 2000.* Honolulu: University of Hawaii at Manoa. Unpublished manuscript.

Johnston, P. (1984) Prior knowledge and reading comprehension test bias. *Reading Research Quarterly* 19: 219–39.

Kirsch, I. S. and Jenkins, L. (1993) *Adult Literacy in America.* Washington, ,DC: National Centre for Education Statistics.

Lewkowicz, J. A. (1997) *Investigating authenticity in language testing.* Unpublished PhD dissertation, Department of Linguistics and Modern English Language. Lancaster: Lancaster University.

LUCAS (Lancaster University Computer Assessment System) Mentioned in Alderson (1990a) if more informationis necessary see also: http://www.ling.lancs.ac.uk/groups/ltrg/lucas.htm

McKay, S. L. (1993) *Agendas for Second Language Literacy.* Cambridge: Cambridge University Press.

Mislevy, R. J. and Verhelst, N. (1990) Modelling item responses when different subjects employ different solution strategies. *Psychometrika* 55 (2): 195–215.

Royer, J. M. and Bates, J. A. (1984) Learning from text: Methods of affecting reader intent. In Alderson, and Urquhart pp. 65–81.

Snow, R. E. and Lohman, D. F. (1993) Cognitive psychology, new test design and new test theory: An introduction. In Frederiksen, N., Mislevy, R. J. and Bejar, I. *Test Theory for a New Generation of Tests.*, Hillsdale, NJ: Lawrence Erlbaum Associates Publishers.

Taylor, L. and Pollitt, A. (July 31 to August 3, 1996) the reading process and reading assessment. Paper presented at Eighteenth Annual Language Testing Research Colliquium, Tampere, Finland.

Urquhart, A. H. (1992) *Draft band descriptors for reading.* Unpublished manuscript. Plymouth: College of St Mark and St John.

Weir, C. J. (1983) *Identifying the language problems of overseas students in tertiary education in the UK.* Unpublished PhD thesis, University of London.

Weir, C. J. (1995) *Part 2: Testing reading comprehension(s): Focus on product.* Unpublished manuscript.

4 Considerations for testing reading proficiency via computer-adaptive testing

Jerry Larson
Brigham Young University

Introduction

The concept of computer-adaptive testing has, for the most part, received very positive reviews from testing specialists and test takers alike. The benefits associated with this method of assessing abilities or performance are becoming well documented. Among the most touted advantages are:

1. its potential for reducing the time required for testing without any loss of precision;
2. improved attitudes towards testing because examinees experience less boredom and frustration by not having to answer items that are much too easy or far too difficult for their level of ability;
3. immediate feedback to the examinee and/or curriculum administrators;
4. self-paced testing;
5. flexible test scheduling;
6. enhanced test security;
7. test linking and networking;
8. improved record keeping with less time and expense required for processing test results;
9. fewer test administrators required; and
10. its potential to provide testing research data (Hambleton *et al.* 1991; Henning 1984, 1987; Larson 1989; Madsen 1991).

Although computer-adaptive testing offers significant advantages, some limitations associated with this method of testing also exist. Perhaps the most common objection to computer-adaptive tests is the limited variety of test item types possible. For example, due to the scoring procedures required, CAT instruments are restricted to objectively scored item types. This could have a deleterious effect on the need to test production as well as recognition skills. Another drawback attributed to computer-adaptive testing relates to computer unfamiliarity and anxiety. Some educators claim that although computers are relatively common in education today, there are still a great number of students who are apprehensive or anxious about using computer technology, particularly when it is associated with testing. While this claim may be valid in some cases, studies have shown that this concern is not as serious as once thought, particularly if computer familiarization activities are built into the program (Henning 1991; Larson 1989).

In the following chapter, I will briefly review the types of language tests possible using a CAT format, general concerns in testing reading proficiency, and, finally, issues related specifically to computer-adaptive testing procedures for testing reading proficiency. I will conclude with a brief discussion and overview of a prototype CAT reading proficiency test of Russian developed jointly by the Language Training Division of the Central Intelligence Agency and Brigham Young University.

Computer-adaptive language testing

In addition to the above-mentioned general advantages of computer-adaptive testing, CAT procedures are particularly well suited for various types of language assessment, including achievement and placement testing and the somewhat more complex instruments for diagnostic and proficiency evaluation of language skills.

Achievement tests

The potential for testing achievement of knowledge and language skills acquired in relation to specific concepts presented in a given text or curriculum is well within the capability of CAT tests. Teachers, however, are hesitant to develop such tests for their individual programs because (a) producing a CAT exam requires a tremendous amount of time and preparation, neither of which language teachers have, and (b) the texts in many language programs change every few years, making obsolete tests that were designed specifically for a given text. Therefore, considering the enormous effort one would expend to create a CAT achievement exam for a 'temporary' program, it seems a bit inefficient to invest that kind of time and effort every few years. Because of these circumstances, whatever CAT achievement tests are available, they tend to address a broader content area.

Placement tests

Placement tests are generally less strictly tied to a particular text and have, therefore, received considerably more attention for CAT development. Particularly useful in helping teachers and curriculum administrators know at which level their students should enter their programs, CAT placement exams have been enthusiastically welcomed. CAT placement exams for English have been developed in recent years by The College Board; placements tests for Spanish, French, German, and Russian are available from Brigham Young University.

Diagnostic tests

Diagnostic testing, or identifying, isolating and interpreting the use of specific structures and components of a language, requires a more finely tuned measurement instrument than that generally used for achievement or placement testing. Although the language teaching profession has considerable need for this kind of computerized assessment instrument, relatively little effort has been focused on developing CAT diagnostic measures, perhaps because of the intricacies of test design and programming involved. This area of testing, however, is beginning to gain momentum in CAT development circles. As part of the CAT development project at the Centre for Advanced Research on Language Acquisition in Minneapolis, Minnesota, researchers and test developers are planning to include a diagnostic component in the reading proficiency CAT they are currently developing.

Proficiency tests

Proficiency testing focuses on global language skills. This type of test is necessarily broad, since it has to determine an examinee's communicative ability over a wide range of topics or content areas. Recently, testing specialists have expended considerable effort and resources developing prototype CAT proficiency measures of receptive language skills (i.e. reading and listening) (Dandonoli 1989; Lowe *et al.* 1991), but much work is still to be done in this area. CAT proficiency tests of the productive language skills (i.e. speaking and writing) are still some way away, unfortunately, since the computer is not yet able to evaluate adequately samples of free-form written or spoken language.

General concerns in testing reading proficiency

Before examining issues particular to using CAT approaches to testing reading proficiency, I believe it useful first to consider some of the challenges involved in the assessment of reading proficiency in general; from that point we can look at ways of meeting these challenges via computer-adaptive testing procedures.

Proficiency level descriptors

One of the principal obstacles since the beginning of the proficiency testing movement has been devising appropriate descriptors for each proficiency level. Bachman (1990) asserts that one of the reasons competency testing was not widely used previously is due, in part, to '*the difficulty encountered in defining criterion levels of ability, problems that some language testers view as virtually intractable*' (p. 338).

Level descriptors were first defined by government agencies, in particular the Foreign Service Institute (FSI). The initial level descriptions were stated in fairly broad terms, specifying five levels of proficiency. In a combined effort to make the proficiency scale more discriminating at the lower levels for academic use, the American Council on the Teaching of Foreign Languages (ACTFL) and the Educational Testing Service (ETS) changed the nomenclature for the levels to Novice, Intermediate, Advanced and Superior, adding intra-level descriptors 'low', 'mid' and 'high' for the Novice and Intermediate levels. Descriptors for the receptive skills followed some time thereafter and were based to a large extent on the speaking skill descriptors. However, there is some concern that the descriptors for the reading proficiency scale may require further refining, particularly in the Superior range, in order to assess properly the proficiency of higher-level students. Liskin-Gasparro (1984) explains that the ACTFL/ETS verbal tags (i.e. Novice, Intermediate, Advanced and Superior) '*correlate well with teachers' experience of students' oral proficiency at the various stages of instruction … but this same correlation does not seem to exist for the receptive skills. Most students in intermediate courses … can read at the Advanced level, and the denominations give a false impression of where students are at the various stages of instruction*' (p. 372). Further study needs to be done to determine whether we are really able to discriminate adequately and report meaningfully varying levels of reading proficiency.

Item specifications

Another area in which additional research is needed is that of item specifications. More work is required to determine which item types are best suited for testing the various stages of reading proficiency. Perhaps item types should be classified according to the reading subskill they measure. For example, we should find out what kinds of items are most effective for examining decoding skills, word knowledge, grasping main ideas, or following the author's argument, etc. Additionally, we should determine whether certain types of items are better suited to measure features of reading such as skimming, scanning and gisting (Liskin-Gasparro 1984). Knowing which kinds of items are most effective, and then employing them, will allow us to produce more efficient tests of reading proficiency.

Proficiency test design

As regards test design, Canale (1984) proposes four test design features that are worth considering to improve receptive language testing:

1. thematic organization;
2. four stages in test administration;
3. adaptive testing procedures; and
4. criterion-referenced tests.

Thematic organization

Rather than focusing on linguistic criteria such as vocabulary and sentence structure, a thematically organized reading proficiency test *'would represent and group those tasks that provide a coherent, natural, and motivating structure to the overall test'* (Canale 1984: 354). Liskin-Gasparro (1984) appears to agree with Canale's premise. She believes that most national-level foreign language tests tend to be organized by linguistic criteria, with little or no thematic unity or relationship between one item or stimulus and the next. This, as she says, leads to a series of 'non-sequiturs'. She claims that *'there would be clear improvement in the affective impact of tests, and possibly in their measurement characteristics as well, if language were presented in larger contextual segments'* (Liskin-Gasparro 1984: 370-1).

Not all testing specialists agree whole-heartedly with this point of view, however. Jones (1984) cautions that there are problems with this approach. First, he says, following a thematic organization is generally less efficient than using isolated items. *'Within a passage of natural text there is material for only a limited number of items, i.e. word-for-word, there is a higher ratio of items to text. The examinee must therefore either process more text or respond to fewer items in the same amount of time'* (p. 366). Secondly, he points out that following a thematic organization limits the variety of language samples that can be examined. And, finally, there is the potential problem that a thematic text can result in test contamination, where *'a question that relates to the first portion of the text may be answered unintentionally in a later section of the text or even in another question. ... Because the information is all integrated, it is sometimes difficult to develop items that are not also in some way integrated'* (p. 366). Jones does concede, however, that the text of the test should be 'authentic', which often means being thematically organized.

Another potential problem with total thematic unity is the advantage that may be given to what Lowe (1984b) terms 'hot-house specials', or idiosyncratic speciality topics. He explains that *'we do not want performance in 'speciality fields' or 'semantic feedback' to raise the rating when a general-language assessment is required'* (p. 385).

Four stages in test administration

The four-phase approach to test administration includes first a 'warm-up' to put the examinee at ease, then a 'level check' to determine the approximate proficiency level of the person, followed by a series of 'probes' designed to determine the upper limit of the student's ability, and concluding with a 'wind-down' using medium-difficulty items to ease the examinee out of the testing situation. The four-phase approach for proficiency testing is popular with language testers. Liskin-Gasparro (1984) says the four-phase approach '*makes a great deal of sense. ... It is always good to begin with easy material to counteract students' anxiety in the testing situation. ... It [is] much better to flow from easy to medium difficulty to hard items, and then to end with material in the middle difficulty range*' (p. 371).

Adaptive testing procedures

Because adaptive testing requires fewer items, which should correspond to the examinee's performance level, less boredom and frustration occur and less emphasis is placed on speed. Therefore, '*adaptive testing procedures in general promise more accurate, efficient, and affectively acceptable language tests than do more traditional testing procedures*' (Canale 1984: 354).

Language testing experts recommended using one of three possible procedures for adaptive-test administration:

1. computer delivered;
2. trained test administrators; and
3. multiple nonparallel test forms, '*where mean item difficulty varies from one test booklet to another and examinees select, or have selected for them, only certain booklets*' (Canale *et al.* 1984: 390).

Criterion-referenced tests

A necessary requirement for assessing the proficiency development of an individual is to have an instrument that is capable of evaluating a given student's performance separately and independently from any other student or group of students. This type of assessment matches very well the definition of a criterion-referenced test. Bachman and Clark (1987) have indicated that a criterion-referenced test is ideal as a common metric scale of language proficiency, since '*the interpretation of criterion-referenced test scores is independent of the performance of other individuals on the test*' (p. 28). Canale (1984) recommends the use of criterion-referenced tests for testing receptive language proficiency, emphasizing that this type of test '*is designed to determine the extent to which a given test taker can or cannot perform a target (or criterion) task*' (p. 354), which is an essential feature of proficiency testing.

Test reliability and validity

As with other types of tests, reading proficiency tests must answer satisfactorily questions regarding reliability and validity. Bachman (1990) explains that '*reliability is concerned with answering the question, "How much of an individual's test performance is due to measurement error, or to factors other than the language ability we want to measure?' and with minimizing the effects of these factors on test scores. Validity, on the other hand, is concerned with the question, 'How much of an individual's test performance is due to the language abilities we want to measure?" and with maximizing the effects of these abilities on test scores'* (pp. 160–1). In other words, in order to improve the reliability of our tests, we must find ways to minimize the effects of measurement error and to maximize the effects of the language abilities we want to measure.

Testing specialists point out that tests of reading proficiency are indirect measures of reading ability rather than direct measures, thus raising concerns regarding validity. Canale (1984) warns that *'the type of performance elicited through certain test methods may be qualitatively different from that involved in authentic language use; to the extent that test performance does differ importantly and unpredictably from authentic performance, it is difficult to use a test score to draw firm conclusions about a test taker's true ability to use the language'* (p. 352).

It is important that issues of test reliability and validity be kept in the forefront as we seek to develop appropriate tests of reading proficiency. We must be cognizant of the fact that many factors other than language ability may influence an individual's test performance, including test method, test format, cognitive and affective characteristics of the examinee, real-world knowledge, gender, age, etc. Whatever possible should be done to minimize the effects of these factors.

Test acceptability

In addition to meeting conditions of reliability and validity, reading proficiency tests should be accepted by both test takers and test administrators as *'fair, important, and interesting'* (Canale 1984: 353). Somewhat akin to face validity, test acceptability has a direct impact on examinee attitude, which, in turn, affects test performance. A test considered by either examinees or administrators as being unfair will not be considered by them as an appropriate or effective instrument for evaluating reading ability. Similarly, a test viewed as unimportant will certainly fall short of inspiring test takers to do their best. A test thought to be uninteresting runs the risk of boring the examinees, affecting, in turn, their concentration and test performance. Ideally, according to Canale (1994), tests should be so *'naturally integrated into motivating learning activities that students are not disturbed, and in fact may even forget, that their performance is being assessed'* (p. 353).

Test feedback potential

Tests that are able to assess reading performance in a reliable, valid, and acceptable manner should also provide *'clear, rich, relevant, and generalizable feedback'* (Canale 1984: 353). This feedback should provide understandable information that students, teachers or administrators can interpret easily and utilize reasonably to make appropriate academic or career decisions.

In addition to providing meaningful information, the evaluation report should be issued as promptly as possible. Student attitudes toward testing are much more positive when feedback regarding their performance is readily available. Timely availability of test results is also a tremendous aid to teachers, test administrators and counselors as they try to provide follow-up guidance and assistance to the test takers.

Content sampling

Related to the issue of 'authentic language' in the passages of reading proficiency tests is the need for tests to cover an adequate range of topics or subjects. Items must sample a necessarily broad range of ability in a number of contexts, or content areas. A truly valid reading proficiency measure could not settle for assessment of an examinee's reading comprehension in only one or two content areas, since it is quite possible that an individual could be very familiar with vocabulary pertaining to specific areas of personal interest, yet be absolutely unfamiliar with vocabulary outside this area of expertise or interest. Therefore, it is imperative that reading proficiency tests sample a sufficiently broad range of themes so as to discriminate or distinguish between examinees who are truly proficient and those who are 'skillful' in their areas of interest only.

Using computer-adaptive testing procedures for testing reading proficiency

Testing specialists seem to concur that CAT procedures for testing reading proficiency are suitable and efficient. Lowe (1984) outlines four major factors that impinge on receptive skills testing: correction or scorability, production, content and administration. Each of these factors can be managed well employing computer-adaptive testing procedures.

Scorability

Unfortunately, the computer is not yet able to judge adequately samples of writing, such as translations of reading passages or free-response type answers. Testing specialists (Kaya-Carton *et al.* 1991) have tried to employ a variety of item types (e.g. multiple-choice, multiple-choice cloze, free response cloze, scrambled-order sentences, cloze elide or cloze edit, open-ended, free-response) in a CAT format but found they had to settle with objectively-scored items. Experience has shown, however, that the computer is very proficient and efficient at evaluating binary-choice (i.e. right or wrong) test items. To the extent that valid and reliable objectively-scored items can be created for reading proficiency tests, CAT's potential for properly scoring these items is virtually unsurpassed.

Production

If they are heavily used, reading proficiency tests may become compromised, or, after a short period, they may become outdated, which could create the need to replace them rather often. A CAT reading test has the advantage over traditional paper-and-pencil versions in that each test is virtually unique, generating, as it were, multiple parallel test forms. This feature of CAT reduces dramatically the threat of test compromise. Additionally, it is possible to design the test to allow for 'piloting' new test items during test administration. These new items, if they function properly, can be calibrated automatically and later inserted into the test item bank if desired. Also, other items when outdated or found problematic can be deleted easily from the item bank without affecting the performance of the test.

Item content

The content of test items is, of course, the single most important aspect of any test, including CAT proficiency tests. As discussed above, items in reading proficiency measures must be valid, reliable and acceptable. To the extent that this is possible and feasible, they should contain samples of 'authentic' language, but should be general enough to represent a variety of contexts. Lowe (1984), for example, states that government agencies prefer a *'language-general test, but with the degree of validity conferred by work-related content'* (p. 376). Computer-adaptive tests can be constructed to take into account item content considerations. For example, items should cover a broad range of difficulty within several content areas and should be written to take into account variations in vocabulary, grammar, register, style and cultural diversity at the various proficiency levels.

Local independence of test items is also an important consideration relating to item content. Strict care must be taken to ensure that in the item sequencing no item is dependent upon or related to another within a given test. Failure to do so will seriously affect validation of the test.

Administration

Traditional reading proficiency tests have generally consisted of objectively-scored items presented via paper-and-pencil testing formats. These types of items are just as easily incorporated into a computer-adaptive testing format. As mentioned above, the computer excels in its ability to score an examinee's performance on such items and then branch to an appropriate subsequent item.

Some concern has been expressed about how mode of presentation might affect test validity in a reading test. Since the initial administration and analysis of CAT items was done using paper-and-pencil procedures, some testing specialists feel that subsequent computer administration will have an influence on how items perform. Henning (1991), however, reports that evidence seems to show that '*item difficulty estimates for both verbal and mathematical items are invariant across computer and paper-and-pencil presentation modes*' (p. 214).

Another issue that may have some bearing on test performance regards the time allotted to complete the reading test. It may be that speededness could be a factor in true reading proficiency; that is, we may be able to determine 'nativeness' more accurately if we were to use speeded tests (Lowe 1984). If this is the case, it is possible in CAT tests to program the computer to allow specific amounts of time for completing individual items based on difficulty levels.

A primary concern in reading proficiency tests deals with presenting to the examinee items from a variety of contexts within the various proficiency levels, avoiding the false proficiency rating of 'hot-house specials', or examinees who perform very well in their speciality area but are lacking in other language contexts. In a CAT reading proficiency test, the computer can be instructed to select and present from the item bank items representing a predetermined sampling of contexts and content within a given test taker's range of ability.

Four-phase approach

A four-phase approach (e.g. warm-up, level check, probes, wind-down), as suggested by of a number respected testing specialists for standard reading proficiency testing (Canale *et al.* 1984), makes a lot of sense for CAT language proficiency tests as well. Taking into consideration the normal, high level of test anxiety most students experience, it is advisable to start CAT reading tests with easier items to help counteract this uneasiness and apprehension.

After answering a few relatively easy items, the examinee would then be given items of increasing difficulty from a variety of content areas to determine the upper limits of his or her reading ability. Once the computer has ascertained the examinee's estimated range of ability, a series of questions are given to ensure that he or she is not able to sustain performance at a higher level. Once this ceiling has been certified and recorded, the CAT test ends with a series of easier, 'wind-down' questions, which, hopefully, will allow the students to leave the test with a positive feeling about the testing experience.

Item selection

Decisions regarding item selection routines are crucial to the success of CAT reading proficiency tests. Item selection decisions must take into account several factors. At the beginning of the test it is important to present passages and associated questions that will ease the examinees into the test. Providing the item calibrations are accurate, this is not too difficult: the computer simply selects passages and items with low difficulty indices. At this lower range, it is not as critical to present items from a broad range of contexts. However, as the test progresses, the item selection algorithm necessarily becomes much more complex, having to include passages from a substantial range of settings and circumstances.

Level checking and probing are especially critical to valid assessment of reading proficiency. The test must allow examinees to demonstrate their highest sustained level of reading ability (Liskin-Gasparro 1984); otherwise, the entire test would be fundamentally invalid. In a CAT reading proficiency test, probing, or item selection, is based on the examinee's ability: the computer selects items that contribute the most information to the estimate of the examinee's ability until a desired level of precision is obtained. If an item is answered correctly, a more difficult item is presented. If an item is answered incorrectly, an easier one is given.

Item selection strategies for adaptive testing can be broken down into two types: two-stage strategies and multistage strategies (Hambleton *et al.* 1991). The two-stage strategy could be implemented without the use of a computer. As its name implies, ability estimates are obtained via a two-stage procedure: the examinee completes a 'routing test' and is then directed to another set of several tests that have been *'constructed to provide maximum information at certain points along the ability continuum. Ability estimates are then derived from a combination of scores from the routing test and the optimum test'* (Hambleton *et al.* 1991: 348).

Multistage item selection strategies are much more complex than two-stage strategies, since they involve a branching decision after each item is answered. Multistage strategies include either fixed branching or variable branching decisions. Hambleton *et al.* (1991) explain fixed branching as follows:

> For these multistage fixed-branching models, all examinees start at an item of median difficulty and, based upon a correct or an incorrect response, pass through a set of items that have been arranged in order of item difficulty. After having completed a fixed set of items, either of two scores is used to obtain an estimate of ability: the difficulty of the (hypothetical) item that would have been administered after the nth (last) item, or the average of the item difficulties, excluding the first item and including the hypothetical n + first item. (p. 349)

A second model of fixed branching is referred to by Hambleton *et al.* (1991) as a stratified-adaptive test. This type of test *'has items stratified into levels according to their difficulties. Branching then occurs by difficulty level across strata and can follow any of a number of possible branching schemes'* (p. 348). This fixed-branching model is similar to what Henning (1987) refers to as 'step ladder' tests in which a *'specified number of items are held in the bank at each of a specified number of proficiency or achievement steps'* (p. 138). During such a test, the computer selects an appropriate item at a predetermined number of 'steps' above or below the previous item based on a correct or an incorrect answer to the previous item.

Variable branching item selection routines are based on a maximum likelihood estimation. An example of this type of branching is found in what Henning (1987) calls 'error-controlled' tests. He explains their functioning as follows:

> *Following exposure to a specified set of introductory items, [error-controlled tests] employ a procedure such as unconditional maximum likelihood estimation in order to estimate examinee ability on the ability continuum. They then access and present the item in the bank that is nearest in difficulty to the estimated person ability, provided the item was not previously encountered. After each new item is encountered, a revised estimate of person ability is provided with an associated estimate of measurement standard error. The process continues in an iterative manner until the estimate of measurement error drops to a prespecified level of acceptability. (p. 138)*

A number of branching schemes specifically for selecting passages and items in an adaptive reading test have been suggested. Larson (1987), for example, requires the examinees to answer a single item associated with each reading passage. Each reading passage is relatively short. Madsen (1991) suggests using a 'modified adaptive' format in which the examinee would be required to answer three or four items after branching to a given passage. This he claims is preferable to requiring the examinee to read a lengthy passage, answer a single question, and then repeat the process again. Another approach, he suggests, is to have a relatively large number of items for each passage at varying levels of difficulty and branch within these items before going on to another passage. Kaya-Carton *et al.* (1991) posit the following alternatives for branching in a computer-adaptive reading test:

1. letting the examinee respond to items of a wide range of difficulty;
2. returning the examinee to the passage for another item of different difficulty level;
3. eliminating the passage from further testing; or

4. reducing the range of item difficulty associated with a given passage, letting the subject complete all items associated with that particular passage, and letting the computer calculate a passage mean and branch to another passage with a comparable mean passage score. (p. 268)

The authors say, however, that option number one above could be frustrating to the examinees, because they would be forced to attempt items of a wide range of difficulty, which could defeat the adaptive purpose of the test.

Test termination

Decisions regarding when and how to terminate a test are vital to the success of computer adaptive reading tests. Hambleton *et al.* (1991) outline several possible 'stopping rules'.

- *Several methods and combinations of methods are currently used. In one, testing is continued until some acceptable level of measurement error is achieved. In this way, ability estimates are all at the same level of measurement when testing is terminated (this parallels measurement within a classical test theory framework) though the number of items administered to each examinee will vary. It would also be possible to specify some acceptable but unequal levels of measurement precision for different ability levels. For example, a decision could be made that more precision is needed with middle abilities than for those at the extremes.*
- *Another method involves setting a fixed number (not too large) of test items for the set of examinees. Testing time is (approximately) constant for all examinees, but the standard error of ability estimation will vary from one examinee to the next. In some applications, a minimum number of items which must be administered is specified, and then testing is continued until the measurement error associated with the ability estimate attains some prespecified acceptable level. This method often adds credibility to the testing in the minds of the examinees. Short tests are often viewed suspiciously by examinees. (pp. 249–51)*

As these authors explain, each of the stopping rules has some advantages and some drawbacks. If face validity is a primary concern, which is the case in many government agencies, care must be taken not to terminate the test before the examinees themselves feel they have been given ample opportunity to demonstrate their full level of ability.

Once satisfactory assessment of ability has been achieved, the test should be programmed to present a few 'wind-down' questions of difficulty levels somewhat lower than the estimated ability of the examinee. As Liskin-Gasparro (1984) insists: '*the hardest material is never left for the end of a test, for experience has shown that many students faced with a long or difficult final reading comprehension selection will simply give up and not attempt it, particularly if the test is at all speeded. It works much better to flow from easy to medium difficulty to hard items, and then to end with material in the middle difficulty range'* (p. 371). If administered appropriately, these wind-down questions will hopefully cause the examinees to leave the testing situation with a positive attitude about their performance.

Refining the test item bank

In order to maintain effective, up-to-date items in the item bank, there should be provisions for adding and deleting items. Items in a reading proficiency test must reflect current linguistic and cultural usage. Therefore, it may be necessary at times to change items that do not accurately model prevailing usage. If an item does not perform as anticipated, it must be replaced. With a computerized test it is relatively easy to add or delete items, since it is a fairly simple matter to insert and remove information from data files. The most crucial aspect of this procedure, however, is to ensure that replacement items match the items they replace with respect to difficulty levels so as not to affect adversely the measurement precision of the instrument.

Having sufficient items in reserve can be difficult. It is a labour- and time-intensive task to administer and calibrate new passages and questions periodically. Ideally, it would be advantageous to add a 'field test module' in the testing program that will administer and track the performance of new items as tests are being taken. These items would need to be flagged in such a way that they would not in any way influence the examinee's score.

BYU CAT reading proficiency test prototype

Working with testing specialists Pardee Lowe, Jr. and Danielle Janczewski of the Language Training Division (LTD) of the Central Intelligence Agency, a colleague at Brigham Young University, Kim Smith, and I produced a computer-adaptive reading proficiency exam of Dutch. The testing algorithms and features developed for that test were then used in the creation of a prototype adaptive test of Russian (R-CARPE). The following is a brief explanation of how the prototype test operates and a description of the item contents.

Starting point

In order to minimize the *'invalidating influences'* (Henning 1991: 215) associated with computerized test administration, a computer orientation phase was designed to familiarize the examinees with the computer keyboard layout and necessary keystrokes that would be used during the test. The examinees complete this orientation before the actual test begins. The test was also designed to keep the response requirements as simple as possible, as recommended by Henning (1991). After conducting this brief computer familiarization check, the computer asks for the examinee's identification number, and then a couple of sample test items are presented with on-screen explanations to illustrate to the examinee exactly how to record his or her responses during the test. Once the examinee completes these 'practice' items, the test proper begins.

The first nine items presented to the examinee constitute the 'full range' phase of the test. These items are selected to test the entire range of difficulty of the ILR reading proficiency scale, from Level 1 to Level 5. The purpose of this section of the test is to counter the possible complaint: 'I was never presented an item at levels 4 or 5.'

Adaptive item selection

The items in the test bank have been calibrated and coded according to difficulty estimates arrived at through item response theory Rasch calculations. The difficulty level codes assigned to the items (0 to 4) are in smaller increments than the customary ILR scale references (0 to 5, with pluses at each level except 5, yielding only eleven levels). After completing the 'full range' questions, the adaptive branching of the test begins. The first of these adaptive sequences serves as a 'level check', similar to the procedure used in an Oral Proficiency Interview, during which the test attempts to determine the examinee's approximate level of proficiency. To do this, the computer begins presenting items at a low level (6 on the R-CARPE scale) and advances six levels for each subsequent item if the previous item was answered correctly, or goes back five levels if the previous item was answered incorrectly. This branching continues for seven iterations.

Upon completion of the level check, the test seeks to find the 'ceiling' of the examinee's reading ability; this is done by branching up or down one R-CARPE level, depending upon correct or incorrect responses, until the examinee cannot sustain performance at a given level. The ceiling level is defined as one level below the highest level at which the examinee misses four separate attempts. When the examinee completes this phase of the test, the computer records his or her level score and also computes a logit ability score and standard error, which will all appear on the examinee's performance report after the final phases of the test are completed.

Wind-down

Although theoretically the test could terminate at the point of achieving an ability estimate with a reasonably low standard error, it was decided to extend the test in order to satisfy the concern that might be expressed by some examinees that they had not been given a sufficient number of items to determine accurately their true performance. Therefore, once the examinee's ceiling ability estimate has been determined, the computer administers two additional sets of items five and then six levels above the ability estimate level. The examinee is then presented items two to three levels below the ability estimate to serve as a 'wind-down' for the test, hopefully allowing the examinee to finish the testing experience with a positive feeling about his or her performance.

Field-test module

The final phase of the test consists of a number of items, fifteen at present, that are being field-tested for possible future inclusion in the test item bank. These items are tagged so that data on their performance can be compiled without their contributing to the examinee's ability estimate. (In subsequent versions of the test, we would anticipate 'scattering' these tagged items randomly throughout the test in order not to prolong the test after an ability estimate has been determined.) These items, once they have been validated and calibrated, can be inserted easily into the test item bank.

Item selection algorithms

In an effort to ensure the examinees receive reading passages from a variety of contexts and situations, the original design of the prototype CAT reading proficiency tests included five item selection algorithms originating at the Language Training Division: Content Limitation, Content Distribution, Abstract/Concrete, Exclusivity and Culture Checking.

Content limitation algorithm

Government agency tests are constructed and administered in order to test consistent and sustained performance in general proficiency. These general proficiency skills are stressed by using general language contexts and topics. To accomplish this purpose, the BYU/LTD reading tests were initially designed to allow three questions in a single content area, then the computer would be instructed to select items from other content areas.

Content distribution algorithm

The higher the examinee's proficiency level, the more content areas in which he or she must prove proficient. Therefore, the Content Distribution Algorithm guaranteed that from Level 3 and up the examinee would have to demonstrate ability in an ever-increasing number of contexts.

Abstract/concrete algorithm

The LTD felt is was important that the examinee receive a certain distribution of passages containing 'abstract' as well as 'concrete' vocabulary usage. These decisions were made based on the item as a whole rather than on individual words. For example, the examinee should be able to distinguish between the concrete usage of the word 'house', as in 'He built a new house' and its abstract meaning in the sentence 'The drinks are on the house.'

Exclusivity algorithm

If two or more items in the same test use identical or very similar linguistic structures or information, one can give away the answer to the other. To avoid this possibility, such items were marked as mutually exclusive, and after one such item had been presented to a given examinee, the other(s) could not be administered during that test.

Culture checking algorithm

Because cultural understanding is an integral part of the higher ILR levels, personnel at the LTD also felt it was important that items be presented that reflected various countries or cultures within countries that speak the target language. Therefore, a culture checking algorithm was included that would present an additional item of corresponding difficulty from another culture/country of the target language area if the examinee failed a 'counterpart' item.

A highly complex item coding system was devised to instruct the computer how to accomplish the above-mentioned algorithms and was ready to be activated. However, the algorithms were never fully implemented due primarily to two reasons:

1. after several pilot administrations of the test without the item selection algorithms in place, it was found that the random selection of items seemed for the most part to accomplish the intent for which the algorithms were designed;
2. a change of supervisory personnel at the LTD postponed further development and work on the project.

Item types

Testing specialists at the Language Training Division who were primarily responsible for writing the items for the CAT reading proficiency tests felt it important that a variety of item types be used. Five binary-choice item types were chosen. These item types and their respective instructions are as follows.

1. Best meaning: 'Select the most correct English rendition of the highlighted segment.'

2. Best misfit: 'In the following lists of words or phrases, one item fits less well than the others. Select which one.'
3. Best restatement: 'Select the statement that most accurately restates the information given in the passage.'
4. Best summary: 'Select the statement that best summarizes the situation.'
5. Best logical completion: 'Select the continuation or remark that is most likely to be made in response to the described situation.'

Test report

After an examinee finishes the test, the computer generates a report of his or her performance. Because of security reasons, this report is accessible only to the test proctor. The report lists:

1. the examinee's unique identification number;
2. the date of the test;
3. the time the test began and the time it was completed;
4. the number of items attempted, including their range and number missed;
5. the examinee's reading level (on the R-CARPE scale);
6. the standard error for that test; and
7. the ability estimate (on the logit scale). The report also lists the item selection algorithms implemented for each item. The examinee's ILR proficiency rating (0–5) is determined from the CAT performance score.

Conclusion

Although there are a few limitations in using computer-adaptive tests for assessing reading proficiency, it has been shown to be a viable alternative to traditional methods. CAT has tremendous potential for increasing testing accuracy while reducing testing time and hassles. It provides for flexible scheduling as well as enhanced security and record keeping. Computer-adaptive reading tests can present passages from a number of contexts and cultural situations, using a variety of item types.

Advantages offered through this mode of testing certainly warrant further exploration and development efforts. Former obstacles such as not being able to display 'authentic' reading materials as they appear in their 'natural' environment are not so daunting when we consider the capabilities of some of the new graphical user interface (GUI) computer operating systems being used today. Using these new systems, it is possible to display digitized copies of actual reading materials, ranging from low-level reading texts such as menus, advertisements, recipes, etc., to more difficult texts such as newspaper clippings, journal articles and the like, thus creating a more valid reading experience for test takers. Testing specialists should be encouraged to investigate and experiment with ways to take full advantage of the latest developments in computer technology and testing theory in producing valid and motivating computer-adaptive tests.

References

Bachman, L. F. (1990) *Fundamental Considerations in Language Testing.* Oxford: Oxford University Press.

Bachman, L. F. and Clark, J. L. D. (1987) The measurement of foreign/second language proficiency. *Annals of the American Academy of Political and Social Science* 490: 20–33.

Canale, M. (1984) Considerations in the testing of reading and listening proficiency. *Foreign Language Annals* 17 (4): 349–57.

Canale, M., Child, J., Jones, R., Liskin-Gasparro, J. E. and Lowe Jr., P. (1984) The testing of reading and listening proficiency: A synthesis. *Foreign Language Annals* 17 (4): 389–91.

Dandonoli, P. (1989) The ACTFL computerized adaptive test of foreign language reading proficiency. In Smith, W. F. (Ed.) *Modern Technology in Foreign Language Education: Applications and Projects.* pp. 291–300. Skokie, IL: National Textbook Company.

Dunkel, P. (ed.) (1991) Computer - assisted language and Testing:Research Issues and practice. New York, NY: Newbury House.

Hambleton, R. K., Zaal, J. N. and Pieters, J. P. M. (1991) Computerized adaptive testing: Theory, applications, and standards. In Hambleton, R. K. and Zaal, J. N. (Eds.) *Advances in Educational and Psychological Testing,* pp. 341–66. Boston: Kluwer Academic Publishers.

Henning, G. T. (1984) Advantages in latent trait measurement in language testing. *Language Testing* 1: 123–33.

Henning, G. T. (1987) *A Guide to Language Testing: Development, Evaluation, Research.* Cambridge, MA: Newbury House Publishers.

Henning, G. T. (1991) Validating an item bank in a computer-assisted or computer-adaptive test: Using Item Response Theory for the process of validating CATS. In Dunkel, pp. 209–22.

Jones, R. L. (1984) Testing the receptive skills: Some basic considerations. *Foreign Language Annals* 17 (4): 365–67.

Kaya-Carton, E., Carton, A. S. and Dandonoli, P. Developing a computer-adaptive test of French reading proficiency. In Dunkel 1991, pp. 259-84.

Larson, J. W. (1987) Computerized adaptive language testing: A Spanish placement exam. In Bailey, K. M., Dale, T. L. and Clifford, R. T. (Eds.) *Language Testing Research,* pp. 1–10. Monterey, CA: Defense Language Institute.

Larson, J. W. (1989) S-CAPE: A Spanish computerized adaptive placement exam. In Smith, W. F. (Ed.) *Modern Technology in Foreign Language Education: Applications and Projects,* pp. 277–89. Skokie, IL: National Textbook Company.

Liskin-Gasparro, J. E. (1984) Practical considerations in receptive skills testing. *Foreign Language Annals* 17 (4): 369–73.

Lowe Jr., P. (1984) Setting the stage: Constraints on ILR receptive skills testing. *Foreign Language Annals* 17 (4): 375–9.

Lowe Jr., P., Janczewski, D., Smith, K. and Larson, J. (1991) *Developing a computer-adaptive reading proficiency test: The Russian experience.* Paper presented at the Annual Conference of the American Council on the Teaching of Foreign Languages (ACTFL), San Antonio, Texas.

Madsen, H. S. (1991) Computer-adaptive testing of listening and reading comprehension: The Brigham Young University approach. In Dunkel, pp. 237-57.

5 Research and development of a computer-adaptive test of listening comprehension in the less-commonly taught language Hausa

Patricia Dunkel
Georgia State University

Introduction

In their 1982 survey of materials-development needs for the less-commonly taught languages (LCTLs), Clark and Johnson (1982) decried the fact that no externally-prepared standardized tests of developed language proficiency existed for many of the LCTLs, namely the languages of Sub-Saharan Africa. The situation has not changed appreciably since 1982 with respect to development of assessment instruments designed to measure listening comprehension proficiency in Hausa, the West African language designated one of the highest-priority LCTLs taught in the United States (Dwyer and Hiple 1987). A primary objective of this research and development project was to remedy this situation with the aid of computer technology. The researchers sought to achieve the following objectives:

1. to create a computer-adaptive test (CAT) of listening comprehension proficiency in Hausa that utilizes Item Response Theory (IRT) as the underlying psychometric model for test development and item banking and that utilized aspects of the ACTFL Listening Guidelines (1986) and Lund's (1990) taxonomy of 'real world listening tasks' to create the bank of items;
2. to have the test items reviewed and critiqued by Hausa and testing-and-measurement specialists for the purpose of strengthening the design of the items field-tested; and
3. to field-test (trial) the bank of 144 initial (prototype) test items in paper-and-pencil format (and audiotape) on a sample of American students studying Hausa (as well as a small number of highly proficient and native speakers of the language) for the purpose of calibrating the test items (see discussion below).

Patricia Dunkel

Computer-adaptive testing and item response theory

Computer-adaptive testing (CAT) is a procedure in which specific test items presented by the computer vary with the estimated ability of the examinee and her or his response to previous items. That is to say, *'the order in which items are presented is a function of the test taker's responses. Thus, if the test taker misses a given item, the next item presented is easier than the previous one. Correct responses call up more difficult items'* (Bachman 1990: 121). In discussing the implications of computer-adaptive testing for language test developers and examinees alike, Tung highlights the tailored-testing and efficiency aspects of CAT. *'The principal feature of CAT is that test takers may receive different sets of test items tailored to the individual's ability so that no one needs to put up with items that are too easy or too difficult. In general, by employing items that correspond to the ability of the test takers as nearly as possible, computerized adaptive tests are shorter than conventional fixed-length test at the same level of measurement precision'* (1986: 13). In highlighting the major differences between traditional, standardized, group-administered tests (e.g., the Test of English as a Foreign Language), Stansfield suggests that CAT represents a major improvement over traditional group-administered tests.

> *Traditional tests are of necessity constructed to be most precise for the student whose ability, or whose knowledge of the construct being measured, is above average. Thus, such tests contain a large number of items that are appropriate for the examinee with average or near-average performance, since these students are the most numerous given the typical normal distribution of scores. The farther a student is above or below average, the less appropriate is a group-administered test. On the other hand, given an adequate database, a computerized adaptive testing program can produce tests that are equally appropriate to all examinees, regardless of their level of ability, achievement, or, in the case of second languages, proficiency* (Stansfield 1986: 4).

The potential benefits of CAT are beginning to be recognized in the field of education in general, and in foreign and second language education in particular. To illustrate, in the fall of 1993, the Educational Testing Service (ETS) introduced a computer-adaptive version of the Graduate Record Examination. In April 1994, all candidates for a nursing license in the United States began taking a computer-adaptive test on the content information, and ETS will be phasing in computer-adaptive tests in the areas of teacher and architect licensing in the future (Winrip 1993). With respect to L2 education, several L2 CATs have been developed: the Computerized Reading Comprehension Proficiency Test sponsored by the American Council on the Teaching of Foreign Languages (Dandonoli 1989: 23), the COMPUTEST:ESL reading-structure test (Madsen 1991), and the 1988 S-CAPE: Spanish Computerized-Adaptive Placement Exam given at Brigham Young University, to name but a few. To date, other than the one described in this report, no computer-adaptive test of proficiency in an African language has been devised. CAT research has focused mainly on creating reading- and grammar-skills assessment instruments. Because the inclusion of a speech component to the CAT complicates the research and development effort, few efforts to develop listening comprehension proficiency CATs have been undertaken.

It was decided to develop and field-test (trial) a computer-adaptive test of listening comprehension proficiency, first to continue previous and early-stage research on computerized testing of nonparticipatory L2 listening comprehension proficiency (Dunkel 1991), and second to utilize the speech-digitizing capabilities of today's multi-megabyte personal computers, such as the Macintosh IIx, the Quadra, and the PowerMacintosh. The decision to develop a listening comprehension IRT-based CAT in the less-commonly taught language (LCTL) of Hausa was made, in part, because none exists. This seems ironic because, as Brecht and Walton (1993) point out, the LCTLs *'stand to benefit perhaps more than the more commonly taught languages from the application of new technologies'*, especially in the area of testing materials development. They note that developing even one standardized test for a LCTL is expensive, time-consuming and problematic as it takes years to norm the test since so few students study the language in any one year and at any one institution. It was, as a result, decided to investigate whether development of a LCTL CAT, and one assessing listening comprehension proficiency, would present a viable solution to the problem of developing standardized tests in the LCTLs. The solution entailed developing a bank of items that could be delivered via computer in a tailored-testing (or adaptive) format.

Finally, for development of the Hausa CAT, it was decided to use Item Response Theory, rather than Classical Test Theory (CTT), as the underlying psychometric model for test development. According to Green *et al.* (1984), classical test theory with its item quality and indices of reliability and validity is relevant when all test takers are given the same set of test items. However, in a CAT situation, test takers often confront a different set of items. As a result, IRT is more useful for a CAT, in their opinion. In addition, Choi (1992) explains that Item Response Theory denotes a family of analytical procedures such as the Rasch one-parameter (*difficulty*) model, the two-parameter (*difficulty* and *discrimination*) model, and the three-parameter (*difficulty*, *discrimination* and *guessing*) model, and several extensions of the original IRT model (Madsen 1991). Tung explains that the IRT models describe *'the probabilistic relationship between the response to a test item and the examinee's latent ability or the trait underlying the response'* (1986: 14). Many psychometricians today, according to Bejar (1980) view IRT (with its family of models) as being superior to CTT for purposes of test development and validation because of the precision of measurement, as well as the utility of the following specific properties of the IRT item parameters: first the invariance of the IRT ability estimates (e.g. it is possible to compare two examinees' ability estimates even though they may have taken different test items); and second the invariance of the three IRT item parameters (e.g., regardless of the distribution of ability of the sample used to calculate the estimates, if some other sample is drawn, the two sets of estimates will be linearly related) (Choi 1992). The Hausa CAT items were calibrated using the *one-parameter* or Rasch Model which provided an estimate of item difficulty, as well as person ability. (See Figure 5.1 for an illustration of these two estimates.)

The systems development approach used to develop the Hausa CAT

The development of the computer-adaptive test of listening comprehension proficiency in Hausa, which contains 144 prototype test items[1], was the product of a team effort on the part of Hausa and African language specialists[2], authorities in the field of testing and measurement[3], computer programmers and instructional designers, students at Penn State and at other participating universities and foreign language pedagogy specialists[4]. The African language and content specialists provided the content of the items in the data banks; the testing and measurement authorities provided guidance on test design and data analysis, in addition to providing critiques of the format of the test and the individual test items; the computer programmers and instructional designers created the computer software, and implemented the test to run on a Macintosh computer; the graduate student assistants supported the development effort by helping with implementation of the test and computer programming and by assisting with the trialing of the item bank; the specialists in foreign language pedagogy reviewed the structure and content of the test and provided feedback on the issues of test design, item format and pedagogical viability and utility.

The operational CAT was created with the support and assistance of Penn State's Computer-Based Educational Laboratory-Learning and Technologies Group, a unit within the University's Centre for Academic Computing. The extensive support offered by CBEL staff infused the project with the considerable expertise of computer programmers, experienced instructional designers and software developers, and graduate students skilled in the design and use of educational technology.

The structure, content and task (listener functions) framework used to create the initial bank of test items

The basic structure of the Hausa CAT is designed to evaluate the listeners ability to understand short utterances (words/phrases), mini-dialogues, and short monologues within the framework of four listener functions identified by Lund (1990)[5]. (See the discussion below.) It is expected that many additional listener functions will be included in any revised and expanded version of the CAT. For example, many of the functions identified in various taxonomies of listening skills/functions are expected and should be included in a refined and expanded version of the test. Relevant taxonomic functions identified by L2 listening comprehension theorists and practitioners such as Hadley (1993), Morley (1991), Petersen (1991), Richards (1983), Rivers (1968), Rost (1990), Ur (1984), and Valette (1977), as well as those listener functions identified by first-language (L1) listening specialists such as Wolvin and Coakley (1988), should also be included in item designs when expansions of the item bank are considered. The taxonomies cited vary in focus and degree of specificity. The challenge for future listening CAT developers will be to attempt an integration of the various taxonomies into a unified and comprehensive table of specifications of listener functions/tasks which can be used to create valid and reliable listening comprehension CAT items. A second challenge is to position these listener functions within a coherent framework that allows test developers to specify '*the person, competence, text, and item domains and components of assessment*'.

Although a number of taxonomies of listener skills have been identified, as mentioned above, for the present development initiative the decision was made to focus initially on the listening tasks identified in Lund's taxonomy which he deems '*available to the listener regardless of the text*' (1990: 107). The operation of the CAT proceeds as follows: after the examinee has completed the orientation to the test, the computer screen presents the answer choices when a question is called for by the examinee, who clicks on the 'Next Question' icon. When ready to listen, the examinee clicks on the 'Listen' icon, which looks like a loudspeaker, and is asked to 'Listen carefully.' The listening alert is given in English. The listening stimulus which is spoken in Hausa (i.e. the stimulus is the Hausa input that is to be comprehended) is the next heard. The stimulus is played when the examinee presses the loudspeaker icon. A comprehension question in English about the input follows immediately after the stimulus ceases, and the question is spoken by the same voice that provided the 'Listen carefully' alert. Statistical analysis of the responses to the paper-and-pencil version (and the limited number of computer-assisted trials) of the test yielded the Rasch difficulty parameters that are being used by the algorithm to drive the computer-adaptive version of the test. In the adaptive version of the test, Henning's (1987) algorithm is used to select the items from the bank in reaction to examinees' responses to previously answered items.[6]

As mentioned above, for purposes of test development and in order to construct the initial pool of 144 items that would later be subjected to field testing, Lund's taxonomy of 'real-world listening tasks' was selected as the conceptual framework for development of the preliminary item pool.[7] The taxonomy's four listener functions include:

(1) *identification/recognition*;
(2) *orientation*;
(3) *main idea comprehension*; and
(4) *detailed comprehension*. (See the discussion below for a fuller description of each of these listener functions.)

Each listener function was related to a listening stimulus involving a word or a phrase at the novice level, or a monologue or dialogue at the novice, intermediate, and advanced levels, and to a listener response involving first, a *text choice* which required selection of one of two limited-response options (at the novice level), one of three options (at the intermediate level), or one of four options (at the advanced level) limited response (text) choices; second, a *graphic choice* requiring selection of one of two pictures or graphics (at the novice and intermediate levels); or third an *element in a graphic choice* requiring selection of the correct response among two or three elements within a unified graphic (at the novice level). (See Table 5.1 for a schematic of the conceptual framework used to create the item bank.)

Items incorporating the four listener functions (*identification, orientation, main idea comprehension* and *detailed comprehension*), the two types of language (monologue vs. dialogue) and the three response formats (text, graphic and element-in-a-graphic choice) were written for each of the nine levels of listening proficiency articulated in the ACTFL *Listening Guidelines* (novice-low, novice-mid, novice-high; intermediate-low, intermediate-mid, intermediate-high; advanced, advanced plus, superior). This approach to development of the item bank (n=144) was taken to ensure that the test developers and potential users would have a clear understanding of which types of language, listener functions and listening tasks were targeted for assessment. The item framework (see Table 5.1) was also used to guide the Hausa specialists with the item writing since they were not specialists trained in testing and measurement theory and practice. The item writers attempted to devise easier items at the novice level (with item difficulty parameters in the range of -4.0 to -2.0) and more difficult items at the advanced level (with difficulty parameters in the range of + 1.0 or greater). Field-testing of the items (see discussion below) provided evidence that the item writers were not always 'on target' in designating items to be 'low, mid, or high' levels within each of the categories of proficiency set a priori (i.e., the categories of novice, intermediate or advanced). Still, it was thought that asking the item writers to follow a clearly defined framework of listener functions, types of languages and examinee response formats as they began construction of the item bank would allow them to adopt a more focused and consistent approach to item writing.

The following discussion elaborates upon the specific listener functions (ergo, the test tasks) contained in the framework that guided construction of the item bank.

1. **Recognition/Identification.** According to Lund, focusing on some aspect of the code itself, rather than on the content of the message, calls for recognition/identification which equates with terms such as recognition and discrimination. Identification 'is particularly associated with the novice level because that is all novices can do with some texts. But identification can be an appropriate function at the highest levels of proficiency if the focus is on form rather than content' (1990: 107). For examples of identification items, refer to the six columns marked 'Recog/Iden.' on the grid in Table 5.1. A comprehensive discussion of the test development project, including presentation of all 144 test items, is presented in the report to the United States Department of Education (Dunkel 1992).

Despite Lund's contention that recognition/identification can be appropriate at the highest levels of proficiency, in reviewing the structure of the test, one of the consultants on the project, a language-testing researcher, questioned the use of recognition/identification terms at the advanced level. He commented that

some types of items are not appropriate/needed at certain levels. For example, recognition/identification items probably are not needed at the advanced level. More focus on main idea comprehension and detailed comprehension would be needed if this type of item distinguishes between intermediate and advanced listeners. On the other hand, recognition/identification would be very appropriate for novice level listeners. At the intermediate levels, more focus might be on orientation and main idea comprehension items as these listening skills might distinguish between novice and intermediate listeners. Some of these decisions could be made now, and some will be better answered after pilot testing the item types.

The initial IRT analysis suggests that *recognition/identification* items written for the advanced levels (advanced, advanced plus and superior) were, on the whole, easy items: the difficulty parameter for advanced-level item

#121 is only 1.04 (a mid-range difficulty); for advanced-plus-level item #122 only 0.26, and for the superior-level item #124 it is 1.38. It appears that Stansfield's suggestion that *recognition/identification* tasks are more appropriate for the lower levels of proficiency (rather than Lund's that they can be devised for the upper levels) has merit.

2.   **Orientation** involves the listeners 'tuning in' or ascertaining the *'essential facts about the text, including such message-externals as participants, their roles, the situation or context, the general topic, the emotional tone, the genre, perhaps even the speaker function'* (Lund 1990: 108). Determining whether one is hearing a news broadcast and that the news involves sports is an example of an orientation task, according to Lund.

3.   **Main idea comprehension** involves *'actual comprehension of the message. Initially understanding main ideas depends heavily on recognition of vocabulary. With live, filmed, or videotaped texts, the visual context may also contribute heavily to understanding'* (Lund 1990: 108). Deciding whether a weather report indicates a nice day for an outing, or determining from a travelogue what countries were being discussed constitute examples of main idea comprehension, according to Lund.

4.   **Detail comprehension** items test the listeners ability to focus on understanding specific information. According to Lund, this function *'may be performed independently of the main idea function, as when one knows in advance what information one is listening for; or the facts can be details in support of main ideas'* (1990: 108). Lund's examples of this listener function include: following a series of precise instructions; getting the departure times and the platform numbers for several trains to a certain city, and so on. Presentation of the entire item bank can be found in Dunkel (1992).

In addition to using Lund's taxonomy of listening functions listed above, the item writers also *attempted* to use the ACTFL (1986) *Listening Guidelines'* generic descriptors for listening when in the process of creating the 144 items.[8] For example, the *Guidelines* describe novice-low listening in the following terms: *'Understanding is limited to occasional words, such as cognates, borrowed words, and high frequency social conventions. Essentially no ability to comprehend even short utterances.'* The item writers attempted to keep this descriptor in mind when creating the initial bank of items. For example, in the novice-low *recognition/identification* item, the listener hears a single word *'ruwa'* (water) spoken and is asked to identify the English equivalent of the word by selecting one of the following two text options: (a) water; (b) food. (This particular item is a text-response item with the two answer option.[9]) Additional words (and cognates) could be included as the item bank is increased in number. The *Guidelines* suggest that the novice-mid listener is able to understand some short learned utterances, particularly where context strongly supports understanding and speech is clearly audible. The novice listener comprehends some words and phrases for simple questions, statements, high-frequency commands and courtesy formulae about topics that refer to basic personal information or the immediate physical setting. Items created with this particular *Guidelines* descriptor in mind required listeners to indicate comprehension of main ideas presented in the monologues or dialogues. (See the discussion below.)

Although the item writers made a concerted effort to keep the *Guidelines* in mind when creating the initial pool of items, they found it difficult, and at times impossible, to implement the *Guidelines* in item format, partly because the level descriptors are vaguely worded and generic in form. The Hausa consultants and item writers commented that the *Guidelines* were far too generic to be of much use in creating the entire prototype bank, and, at the same time, too limiting in terms of the number and kinds of tasks identified in the descriptors.[10] It would be necessary to 'flesh out' and expand the *Guidelines* to a significant degree if they are to be of significant utility to item writers seeking to create listening comprehension tests, computer-delivered or otherwise. The descriptions contained in the ACTFL *Listening Guidelines* must be expanded in scope and contain greater degree of specificity with regard to listening content and task if they are to play any role in helping test developers of the commonly and less-commonly taught languages to formulate nonparticipatory listening comprehension tests, computer-delivered or otherwise. Test developers may need to use a number of different L1 and L2 listening taxonomies to help guide the creation of the item bank (for example, Chastain 1988; Hadley 1993; Morley 1991; Murphy 1991; Petersen 1991; Richards 1983; Rivers 1968; Rost 1990; Wolvin and Coakley 1988, 1993).

The programming environment and basic computer design features of the CAT

Hardware and programming environments

All parts of the test were designed to run on an Apple Macintosh IIsi or later-model computer, running System 7.0 at least, with minimum 5 megabytes RAM and access to a large amount of mass storage. (Neither a local hard-drive or an AppleShare server over ethernet–LocalTalk is fast enough to play the sound files with high levels of fidelity.) Each test is stored in a separate folder containing the test document, a folder named 'Sounds' (which contains the sound files), and a folder named 'Results' (which will contain the student result files). The student taking the test *must* have write-access to the 'Results' folder.

The following hardware configurations were used to create and deliver the test: a Macintosh IIfx with 20 megabytes (MB) of RAM (used for programming); and a Macintosh IIci with 8 megabytes of RAM (used for constructing, demonstrating and field-testing of the CAT) and 160 MB of storage.

Basic design features of the CAT

The digitized speech (i.e. the sound data) is stored as normal Macintosh files, and the sound data base only contains the name of the file. This tactic was adopted to ensure that the start of the sound in a question occurs as quickly as possible. In an early version of the CAT, the sound data themselves were stored in the data base, and the time needed to access a sound proved to be as much as 15 seconds. Use of AIFF files allows for the sound to be retrieved instantaneously.

Initial trialing of the Hausa CAT

Initial reviews of the content and structure of the paper-and-pencil form of the test by external consultants.

The 144 items in the test bank were reviewed by Hausa specialists and experts in testing and measurement, and their critiques provided invaluable feedback concerning the appropriacy of the language, content and cultural information contained in the test items, and concerning the overall structure and framework of the test, as well as item formats. The specialists reviewed a paper-and-pencil form of the test (i.e. they reviewed the items displayed in text and with rough illustrations of the graphics associated with the items) which contained the Hausa stimuli, as well as English translations of the Hausa discourse. Those consultants who field-tested the items heard the audiotaped presentation of the items as they were being presented to the subjects during trialing. Their preliminary feedback was incorporated into the revised version of the test used in the field-testing of the item bank.

Although it was decided to use scripted material for the items rather than 'found text', an attempt was made to ensure that the recordings of the monologues and dialogues were 'authentic sounding', and that the content of the discourse reflected the culture and the communication patterns of the Hausa-speaking peoples of West Africa in appropriate fashion.

The graphics on the Hausa test were scanned in from the illustrations contained in the textbook *Introductory Hausa* (Kraft and Kraft 1973); the authors granted permission to use the graphics in their book for research and development purposes. When illustrations in the textbook were not available for specific items, the CBEL staff and a graduate student created the graphics using the MACDRAW (1989) and HYPERCARD (1991) applications. The graphics are, for the most part, stick figures, and the abstraction contained in the illustrations provides a degree of consistency for the illustrations and, at the same time, eliminates much of the 'extraneous noise' contained in the still photos digitized and imported into the program on a trial basis.[11] The static and abstract nature of the graphics, however, also presented problems, as can be noted in several of the comments provided by the Hausa consultants, some of whom sensed that it might be difficult for some listeners to discern the exact meaning of some of the images and actions depicted in the graphics.

It is imperative that items perceived by the consultants to be problematic (i.e. to contain inappropriate vocabulary and pronunciation, etc., and cultural inaccuracies) undergo revision. It may also be necessary to reconsider the basic structure of the test, to rerecord the stimuli of certain items, to digitize these speech samples and to re-input them into the computer, but this should be done in order to improve the quality of the 144 items in the Hausa preliminary test bank. In addition, many more items need to be created and added to the bank. Using digitized photos and real-time video may prove to be preferable to using static graphics in future revisions of the item pool. However, the static graphics do present a certain degree of consistency and clarity of image that cannot be achieved when photographs or full-motion video are used to represent images conveyed in the dialogues and monologues. (Digitized photos were incorporated into an English as a second language version of the test and were found to add a great deal of 'noise' that was eliminated with the use of still graphic images.) Further research on the use of photos and full-motion video to illustrate activities in the graphics is sorely needed. (It remains, in other words, an empirical question whether and how use of static graphics, full-motion video or digitized photos affects the interpretation of, and performance on, particular types of CAT items.[12])

Field-testing of the paper-and-pencil (P&P) form of the item bank to obtain the item calibrations: Deriving the item difficulty and the person-ability parameters

The Hausa test was mainly field-tested using overhead transparencies of the screen displays and an audiotape of the dialogue and monologue stimuli (in Hausa) and the test questions (in English). One hundred and one subjects took part in the field testing at seven testing sites. However, because of audiotape equipment problems which prevented six of the subjects from completing the test, the sample comprised only 101 subjects: (Americans=96; Africans=4; unknown=1) tested at the following institutions: George Mason University (n=4); Indiana University (n=20); the University of Wisconsin (n=26); Boston College (n=12); UCLA (n=12); The Pennsylvania State University (n=17); University of Kansas (n=6); unknown (n=2). Seventeen former Peace Corps subjects were tested at Penn State. Four former Peace Corps members were tested at George Mason University. The remainder of the students were college students who were studying Hausa or Africans who were native speakers or fluent second-language speakers of Hausa. The students indicated they had studied Hausa for the following number of semesters: one semester (n=29); two semesters (n=22); three semesters (n=2); four semesters (n=9); five semesters (n=5); six semesters (n=1); seven semesters (n=1); ten semesters (n=1); 19 subjects reported they had never studied Hausa on a semester basis, and four were native or near-native speakers of the language. Finally, the subjects reported the following levels of perceived listening skill: novice-low (n=10); novice-mid (n=16); novice-high (n=11); intermediate-low (n=11); intermediate-mid (n=13); intermediate-high (n=4); advanced (n=2); advanced plus (n=1); superior (n=3). Thirty subjects failed to register their perceived level of listening skill.

Trialing procedures and data analysis

The question can and should be raised as to whether it is appropriate to make any analytical narrative use of the Rasch results accrued on a relatively small sample (n=101). The authors can only respond that it is expedient that field-testing be continued so that a larger sample size can be acquired. However, it seemed appropriate, at this point in time, to share with colleagues in the field the process of conceptualizing, item writing and trialing a listening CAT in one of the less-commonly taught languages. This we do while recognizing that much research and development remains before a valid and reliable instrument is realized. (The CAT is presently being trialed in its computerized form at the University of Kansas by Dr. Beverly Mack.)

All 144 items in the bank were administered in linear fashion (all 72 designated by the item writers to be novice-level items were administered first, then the 47 intermediate-level items, and finally the 23 advanced-level items) to intact groups of examinees at the above-mentioned testing sites. The administrator displayed each of the test item's options, which consisted of text or graphics, on an overhead transparency. Students viewed the answer choices, heard the audio stimuli and the test question and then pencilled in their responses on a computer answer sheet. Each transparency, with the exception of the first one, was placed on the overhead projector while the examinees were registering their responses to the previous test item on the answer sheet; when they had finished recording their answers, they could look up and examine the options for the next item before hearing the audio cues. This procedure allowed the subjects the chance to view the answer options before they listened to the audio stimuli. The reading of the test directions and the administration of the item bank took approximately 90 minutes. The test directions were not presented via audiotape but were read by the test administrator who had the opportunity to answer any questions the examinees had about the task, the types of items and the testing procedures.

Calibration of the test items and the goals of the calibration phase of test development

The goals of the item calibration phase of the project were the following:

1. to identify an appropriate IRT model;
2. to check the assumptions of the IRT (Rasch) Model;
3. to evaluate the fit of each item to the Rasch Model; and
4. to determine how well the collection of 144 prototype items supports the estimation of ability at all points along the ability scale. (See Figure 5.1 for the Item by Person Distribution Map.)

The field-testing of the paper-and-pencil test and examination of the results of the analysis will be used to inform the next stage of development of the item pool and will help determine the adequacy of the existing bank of items to support tailored (i.e., CAT) testing.

To identify an appropriate IRT model

The three IRT models frequently used to estimate ability include one that uses only item difficulty (the one-parameter Rasch model), one that uses both item difficulty and discrimination (the two-parameter model), and a third model that uses both these plus an estimate for guessing (the three-parameter model). Since this project involves one of the less-commonly taught languages, data were collected on a relatively small sample (n=101) obtained over a four-year trialing period. As a result of the relatively small sample size, the one-parameter IRT model, often referred to as the Rasch model, was selected as the underlying psychometric model for item calibration. Choi points out that the one-parameter logistic model has both desirable and undesirable characteristics. It can be used when sample size is small. In addition, it has '*many statistically refined properties*' (Choi 1992: 24) and is the simplest among the logistic models. The simple form of this model, however, can constitute its chief weakness when applied to empirical data. Empirical (Item Characteristic Curves) representing real data do not necessarily all have the same slope, nor do they necessarily have lower asymptotes of zero. There is substantial evidence to suggest that the assumption of uniform discrimination indices will be violated unless test items are specifically chosen to have this characteristic, according to psychometricians (Choi 1992: 24). Research reported by Lord (1983) however, supports selection of the Rasch model with a small sample size. Simply selecting a model, however, offers little help or assurance about the feasibility and appropriacy of attempting an item calibration with a sample size of 101. With a small sample, it is possible that the estimates of ability may prove to be unstable and, thus, of limited accuracy and utility. As Hambleton and Cook (1983) note, test length and sample size have an effect on the stability of ability estimates. Reporting on research conducted on the influence of sample size on the stability of ability estimates, they found that although a sample size of 200 was reported as optimal, good and stable results were obtained with samples of 50 and a test length of 80 questions with use of the Rasch model. Therefore, given the sample size of 101 and a test length of 144 questions, we concluded that the use of a one-parameter model with these data was warranted and appropriate. The collection of data on the item bank will continue and will inform future decisions concerning IRT model selection.

To check the assumptions of the IRT (Rasch) model

The application of the IRT model rests on one major assumption—that each item or test question in the analysis has a property of conditional independence (Wainer and Mislevy 1990). Another way of stating this assumption is that the collection of test questions in the item bank is unidimensional. Violation of this assumption makes interpretation of ability estimates questionable in the context of tailored testing, according to Steinberg *et al.* (1990), so an important aspect of the item calibration process is to determine how well the items meet the assumption of unidimensionality (Henning *et al.* 1985). Choi notes that even though no one satisfactory procedure for determining the dimensionality of an item bank exists, factor analytic methods are often employed to test this assumption (Bock *et al.* 1988). However, the item response matrix is indeterminate since the number of items (144) is larger than the number of subjects (n=101) making the factor analysis of the item response data infeasible. Still, a variety of techniques have appeared in the literature recently that do not depend on the factor analysis of item responses. Some of these can be adapted to provide information about the validity of the local independence assumption in the current data set. The method of choice for assessing the dimensionality of sets of test items is the Full Information Factor Analysis (Bock *et al.*1988), but this method also requires that the number of subjects be larger than the number of items. So, while we cannot provide a definitive test of the dimensionality, we can provide some evidence that these data are reasonably close to being unidimensional in item content.

Factors that can affect the dimensionality of any particular set of test questions include factors present within the calibration sample and factors that tend to differentiate between sample members when grouped by variables not part of the design, like sex and ethnic identification (Differential Item Functioning). To be able to argue for the assumption of local independence of the items, both of these factors must be shown to be unimportant in the context of the current study. (For a more complete discussion of these issues, see Steinberg *et al.* 1990.)

Since the sample is relatively small and homogeneous with respect to many demographic ethnic factors, it seems reasonable to assume that unidimensionality of the items is not likely to be affected by factors present between subgroups of the calibration sample.

The factors within the calibration sample that can adversely affect the unidimensionality of the items include the presence of identifiable subscales or dimensions of item content as well as other factors. The set of dimensions in the content framework used to guide the creation of the items constitute one set of factors that could lead to multidimensionality in the items. It will be remembered that this framework includes four conceptual dimensions:

1. Difficulty Level (DL) with nine levels of assumed item difficulty;
2. Listener Function (LF) with four levels: recognition/identification, orientation, main idea comprehension and detailed comprehension;
3. Type of Language (TL) with two levels: dialogue and monologue; and
4. Response Selection (RS) with three levels: answer options presented in text only, options presented in two or three graphic illustrations and options presented within a single graphic illustration.

Since the assumed item difficulty is so tightly linked conceptually with what we are trying to estimate, this dimension of the conceptual framework was not included in the analyses that follow. As a result, the conceptual framework gives a 3 x 2 x 4 (TL x LF x RS) matrix that identifies each of the 144 items by a combination of levels of these dimensions. Using item difficulty as estimated in fitting the Rasch model, we can test the independence of this estimate from the framework dimensions by constructing a General Linear Model with estimated difficulty as the dependent variable and the three framework dimensions as the independent variables. Though using the framework dimensions in this way results in cells that have unequal numbers of items, the GLM accommodates this condition. The GLM procedure in the Statistical Analysis System uses techniques that allow the analysis of ANOVA models where the cell frequencies are unequal. A failure to find a statistically significant relationship between the independent and dependent variables will be taken as evidence for the unidimensionality of the set of item responses with respect to the conceptual item-writing framework variables. We recognize that this test is only suggestive of unidimensionality and does not necessarily confirm it.

The analysis of variance showed the absence of a statistical relationship between the full item-writing model (i.e., the dimensions of the conceptual framework used to create the item bank) and the estimated difficulty of the items $(F, df (23, 142) = 0.55, p = .95)$ allowing us to tentatively reject the notion that the conceptual framework is related to item difficulty13. Since none of the four interaction terms was significant, we conducted another analysis of just the main effects and found the reduced models not to be significant. This finding allowed us to conclude tentatively that the three factors (RS x TL x LF) do not systematically affect the empirical difficulty of the items. Departure from unidimensionality could, of course, still be present, and a test that is different and perhaps more sensitive could detect this condition. We will illustrate one of these methods (i.e. Bejar's procedure for examining the dimensionality of a test-item data set) below. It is beyond the scope of this paper to conduct an exhaustive investigation of even a small number of the different techniques that have appeared in the literature in recent years.

Bejar (1980, 1988) described a procedure for examining the dimensionality of a test-item data set. While not constituting a powerful test in all circumstances (see Choi 1992), Bejar's method can be used in a situation where factor analysis of item responses is not possible. Bejar (1980) based his methods on a three-parameter IRT model. Our choice of a one-parameter model was made because of the small number of respondents. Even though these circumstances can be troubling, we discuss the analysis here to illustrate one approach to the problem of assessing unidimensionality given the constraints imposed by having a small sample of test takers.

Bejar (1980, 1988) constructed subsets of items and estimated item parameters and subject ability for each subset and again for all of the items considered together. The selection of the item subsets can be based on a subjective analysis of the content. The analysis then proceeds in two stages. First, the item parameter estimates for each subset are plotted against the parameter estimates calculated when all items are included. If unidimensionality holds, the estimated difficulty for corresponding items will plot on the diagonal. If some items plot too far from the diagonal, then this is taken as evidence of departure from unidimensionality. A second type of analysis proposed by Bejar (1980, 1988) examines the principal components of the ability estimates calculated for item subsets. If only a single principal component is detected, then this is taken as evidence for unidimensionality in the data.

An analysis was conducted with subsets defined for each level of test taker responses (i.e. answer options presented in text only, options presented in two or three graphic illustrations, and options presented within a single graphic illustration) in the Response Selection dimension of the item writing framework. The number of items in each subset was 70, 47 and 24, respectively. Each of these three sets of estimated item difficulties was plotted against the difficulty for the same items estimated when all 144 items were included in the model. Each of these three plots showed the two estimates of item difficulty to be estimated the same. The Response Selection dimension of the conceptual model was seen as most likely to produce multidimensionality. The plots of item difficulty, however, can be seen as evidence that this multidimensionality either does not exist or if it does exist in some items, this effect is not large.

The second stage of analysis involves the analysis of the principal components of the ability estimates calculated separately for each subset of items. The results of the principal components analysis of the set of these three estimated ability scores was tested for unidimensionality by examining the 'scree' plot of eigenvalues against the factor number. The eigenvalues of roots associated with the second and third factors were essentially zero in numerical value, providing additional evidence that the set of estimated abilities can be considered to be unidimensional with respect to the response selection dimension of the item writing framework.

One shortcoming of the procedure above is that it is essentially descriptive. A procedure is needed where a test statistic is examined in relation to a known distribution. This would provide a clearer determination of whether or not more than one scale or factor is present in a collection of items. Full information factor analysis (*Brock, R. D., Gibbons, R. D. and Muriaki, E. 1998*) solves this problem for large tests for more than a single factor. Having a relatively small number of respondents may limit the usefulness of this procedure, but the nonparametric nature of this procedure makes it attractive. Another approach reported by Rekase *et al.* (1988) suggests a method satisfying the unidimensionality with sets of items that are known to be multidimensional.

To evaluate the fit of each item to the Rasch model

How well the item data fit the IRT Rasch model is determined in the item calibration process. The RASCAL program (Rasch Analysis) was used for the calibration. The model was evaluated at the level of individual items and for the entire collection of items remaining in the analysis. The evaluation of individual items showed two items (#18 and #19) of the 144 were too easy since all or nearly all subjects answered them correctly. Since the Rasch model only estimates item difficulty, items that demonstrate a lack of fit are those that fail to discriminate in expected ways between subjects who score high on the test and those scoring low. Generally, the Rasch model correctly fits items where respondents scoring high on the test answer the question correctly more often than do low scorers. When this condition does not hold, then the responses to the items are poorly fit.

To determine how well the collection of test items supports the estimation of ability at all points along the ability scale

The distribution of estimated item difficulty and estimated respondent ability gives evidence about how useful this collection of items might be in a future implementation of tailored testing. In Figure 5.1, estimated item difficulty and respondent estimated ability are plotted on a common scale. The distribution of items is on the left, and the distribution of respondent estimated ability is on the right of the graph. The estimated difficulty of items is distributed reasonably well across the mid-range of the scale, but relatively few easy items and items of high difficulty are present. Additional items in these areas need to be added to the item banks to improve the accuracy of estimated ability for low and high scorers. It also appears that the calibration sample might be improved if additional test takers at the novice level were added to the calibration sample.

Figure 5.2 shows the test characteristic curve which is the sum of the item characteristic curves (ICCs) of the 142 items remaining in the analysis with the ill-fitting (#18, #19) items deleted. The curve has a slight inflection around the middle of the ability scale, the region where the most accurate estimates of ability can be made. The test information curve can be used to determine the expected ability for any number of questions answered correctly. For example, if we want to know the expected ability for a subject who answers 25 per cent of the questions correctly, we first locate .25 in the estimated proportion correct scale and draw a line parallel to the horizontal scale until it crosses the test characteristic curve. At this point, a line parallel to the vertical axis is drawn down until it intersects the ability scale. The estimated ability for this example would be about -1.5.

Figure 5.3 displays the test information curve for the test. This display is helpful in determining the effectiveness of the test at different points along the ability scale. In general, the standard error of measurement of any estimated ability is inversely related to the height of the information curve at that point. Stated another way, the estimated standard error of measurement is smallest where the information function is highest, and conversely, the estimated standard error of measurement is largest when the value of the information function is lowest. This display, then, reinforces the earlier suggestion that the test needs to increase the precision of ability estimates at the low and high ends of the ability scale. This can be accomplished by adding items with relatively low estimated difficulty as well as items with relatively high estimated difficulty.

Conclusion

The evidence from the initial trialing of the paper-and-pencil form of the test and the feedback provided by the various consultants on the project suggests the need for continued research and development of the Hausa listening comprehension proficiency assessment.

Expanding and validating the model and item bank

Field-testing of the paper-and-pencil form of the original 144 items should be continued, and the item bank should be reviewed by Hausa specialists to see if revision is needed. Examination of the item parameters should also help pinpoint problem items. The items in the present bank that were identified as nonfunctioning by the MicroCAT IRT analysis (items 18 and 19) have been discarded from the item bank since they proved to be too easy or poorly fit by the IRT model, according to the statistical analysis. The Hausa project was so labour intensive that it was not possible to advance beyond creation of the prototype 144 items and initial trialing of the items created, given the limited time frame of the project (i.e. 24 months in total). The number of test questions in the Hausa item bank, however, needs to be increased. In addition, the items need to be trialed using computers. To date, only four Hausa subjects have taken the linear computer-assisted version of the test. Thus far, no students have taken the operational adaptive version of the test since the research and development effort is still in the early stage. An additional 100 respondents, encompassing a range of proficiency from novice-low to superior, need to take all the items in the current bank (to obtain more stable IRT parameters). Test takers' perceptions of the utility and effectiveness of the CAT also need to be tapped. In sum, additional research of the following kinds needs to be conducted.

The bank of listening items needs to be increased in number and quality, and the appropriacy and adequacy of the framework further determined

A pool of 144 prototype items for the Hausa test was created. Many of the items were revised in an early phase of item development in response to consultants' reviews of the Hausa item bank. As a result, although 144 prototype items presently reside in the bank, many more than the original 144 were created if one takes into account the revisions of the initial items in the Hausa bank. Additional field-testing will provide further information about the stability and accuracy of the estimated difficulty parameters derived in the analysis of the responses accrued in the first trialing of the items. It is crucial that larger samples are used to obtain the IRT parameters. Furthermore, more items, similar in form and contents, should be added to the present 144 prototype Hausa items to create a substantially larger bank of items. New types of items and items designed with more current technological approaches (e.g. using full-motion video rather than static graphics) need to be designed. Once it has been established that the framework has worth in terms of second language acquisition theory and psychometric principles, Hausa specialists from UCLA, the University of Wisconsin, Indiana University, Boston University, George Mason University and the University of Kansas could help create the additional items and item types.

The items in the bank need to be trialed in a computer-assisted version before the computer-adaptive version is finalized

It will be necessary to trial all 144 items in the bank in a computer-*assisted* version of the test (in which all the items are presented in a linear fashion as they were in the paper-and-pencil trialing) before the computer-*adaptive* version (in which the items will be selected from the bank based on the test takers' previous response to an item presented). As Green and his colleagues note when creating a CAT, the CAT item parameters may be first determined in paper-and-pencil mode (as has been done in the initial calibration phase of the research project). However, the parameters obtained in the paper-and-pencil trialing must be checked in computer mode, for '*there is no guarantee that item difficulty is indifferent to mode of presentation*' (Green *et al.* 1984: 355). They point out that there could be an overall mean shift when the items are presented on the computer. That is, all items presented on the computer may prove to be easier or harder for the test takers. If all the items are affected, '*a simple scale adjustment may be sufficient to bring the paper-and-pencil scale in line with the CAT scale*' (Green *et al.* 1984: 355). Further trialing of the entire item bank on computer is, as a result, a necessary next step in test development.

Green and his colleagues also point out that there might be an item-by-mode interaction when changing from the paper-and-pencil milieu to the CAT environment. When an item-by-mode interaction occurs, some items become harder, others easier when presented by computer. If this occurs, all the items in the computerized version must be recalibrated before the computer-*adaptive* version is finalized. In sum, item calibration must be checked in computer-*assisted* (and later in computer-*adaptive)* mode in the next stages of research and development.

The use of alternate delivery system should be considered

Research and development of a computer-adaptive test of listening comprehension proficiency in Hausa for the Macintosh platform should be continued. Stored digitized speech can be used to provide the listening cues and test questions as it did for the Macintosh-based Hausa listening CAT although interactive videodisc and/or CD ROM disk should also be considered in future development projects. These two storage systems would allow for greater flexibility of design and provide expanded amounts of storage for the creation of sizeable numbers of items in the test bank.

The extant Hausa bank of items needs to be refined, enhanced, and expanded if a valid, reliable and useful test product is desired, one that can be utilized by the African language teaching community in the United States and elsewhere to assess the listening comprehension proficiency of those students who have studied Hausa in both the academic environment and/or country. This test might serve as a prototype for the development of tests of listening comprehension proficiency in the commonly taught, as well as the less-commonly taught languages in the United States and abroad. The research to create a Hausa CAT has begun, but the process is a long, complicated and time-consuming one that can only be completed with the aid of content specialists, applied linguists, testing and measurement experts, computer professionals and great persistence.

Notes

1. To create the initial bank of test items, each item was designed to fill a cell in the test content model (i.e. the item-writing framework or grid—see Table 5.1) and each item can be viewed as a prototype item. Conceivably, a minibank of items could be developed for each cell in the grid (e.g. item #9 was written as a novice-high, detailed comprehension of a short dialogue, with the test takers selecting the appropriate text response to the question they heard about the information contained in the dialogue). A number of items, varying in vocabulary, structure, content, etc., could be designed for this particular cell, as well as for others, so that a bank of items larger than the 144 prototype items could be designed with just these few functions, types of discourse, item format (a limited-response, text-option item), etc. If, for example, a minibank of ten items was designed for each of the 144 cells (or prototype items), a bank of 1,440 items could be created, trialed, and, if the items functioned well, used in the CAT.

2. Beverly Mack of the University of Kansas has worked with Hausa-speaking informants from Niger, Aissata Niandou, Salif Boukhary and Salif Siddo (graduate students at Penn State at the time of development) to create the 144 prototype test items. The following African language specialists reviewed the test items and provided feedback on the content and language contained in the items: Russell Schuh (University of California at Los Angeles); Linda Hunter (University of Wisconsin); Richard Botne and Paul Newman (Indiana University); and Priscilla Sterratt (Boston University). The items were revised to address the criticisms and to strengthen the format and content of individual items.

3. Charles Stansfield (Centre for Applied Linguistics) commented on the test items and the format of the test. Grant Henning, Edmund Marks and Ralph Locklin (Pennsylvania State University) assisted with creation and implementation of the algorithm that derives the test and with provision of IRT calibration of the items.

4. The following foreign language pedagogy experts provided feedback: Jeannette Bragger (Pennsylvania State University) and David Hiple (American Council on the Teaching of Foreign Languages).

5. The item writers' intuition and pedagogical experience guided the construction of the initial pool of items. IRT statistical analysis was then used to check the level of difficulty (or easiness) associated with each item. Since the sample size providing the item parameters was quite small (n=101), caution needs to be exercised when interpreting the initial set of item parameters. Continued field-testing should help determine whether or not the parameters are indeed stable.

6. An adaptation of Henning's (1987) statistical item selection algorithm works as follows.
   a. The examinee begins the test after completing an orientation to the test.
   b. The examinee responds to the item of median difficulty which is displayed by the program.
   c. The program chooses an appropriate second item. The item will be one logit of difficulty above the first item if the examinee succeeded with the first item. The item will be one logit of difficulty below the first item if the examinee experienced failure with the first item.
   d. Items three and four are selected and presented in the same manner as item two.
   e. Once four items have been encountered, the program routinely estimates ability (b_f) and associated error of estimate (s_f) after each item encountered. To do this, use is made of the following approximation formulas:

$$b_f = h + w(f - .5) + \ln\left(\frac{A}{B}\right)$$

where, h=test height of mean difficulty of item encountered at each point, considered cumulatively—the sum of the difficulty estimates divided by the number of items encountered so far, or

$$\frac{\sum d}{L}$$

w=test width of the span of item difficulties encountered, represented as the following quantity:

$$\frac{d_L + d_{L-1} - d_2 - d_1}{2}\left(\frac{L}{L-2}\right)$$

This formula averages the two highest and two lowest difficulties encountered in deriving test width, in order to provide greater accuracy.

f=proportion correct, or r/L
   A=1 — exp(-wf)
   B=1 — exp[- w(w – f)]
   C=1 — exp(-w)

$$s_f = \left(\frac{w}{L} \cdot \frac{C}{AB} \right)^{1/2}$$

An acceptable level of error of estimation is determined in advance by consideration of the precise needs for accuracy of ability estimation with a given test. Once the error of estimate (sf) diminishes to the prespecified, the test is terminated. With [the UCLA] computer-adaptive test, a standard error of estimate of 0.5 logits can be achieved with as few as 18 items encountered. If this level of accuracy is not attained within 30 items (which has not yet happened), the program can be terminated on the grounds that the respondent is misfitting the measurement model by responding arbitrarily (Henning 1987: 139).

7. The Appendix presents the content framework displaying the grid of listener functions and types of language and the levels of proficiency from novice-low to advanced plus. The framework was used to create the items although it was recognized that the MicroCAT analysis of the test taker responses would help identify difficulty levels of the items in a less subjective fashion.

8. It should be noted that the ACTFL *Guidelines* (1986) were used to help guide creation of the initial bank of items, but no claims are made that the listening CAT is an implementation of the ACTFL *Guidelines* in a test, nor that the *Guidelines* were the sole framework used by the item writers. The *Guidelines* served as one of several frameworks used for development. Lund's (1990) framework was also used, and the Hausa language specialists (Beverly Mack and the Hausa informants who were Teaching Assistants of French and ESL at Penn State) also used their intuition and pedagogical experience when designing the initial bank of items. Novice level items contained two options; intermediate item, three options; and the advanced level items, four options. More items were constructed at the novice and intermediate levels to pedagogical experience when designing the initial bank of items.

9. To offset the problem resulting from the greater probability that subjects would get the answer correct due to guessing, the item-selection algorithm will present more items to the novice and intermediate levels.

10. A *Modern Language Journal* reviewer of an earlier version of the present chapter pointed out that although the author is correct '*in stating that the ACTFL Guidelines themselves are not sufficiently detailed to specify all of the linguistic tasks and item types, that would need to be included in a LC test based on these guidelines. However, the 'surrounding context' for the ACTFL scale, including tester training workshops, workshops and textbooks on proficiency-based instruction, etc., do provide a wealth of relevant information and operational expansion of the guidelines themselves.*'

11. The cannon XAP-SHOT image-digitizing camera was used to test whether digitized still photos should be included in the test. It was decided to use graphics rather than photos for this version of the CAT. Photos were included in an English as a second language version of the CAT which is under development at present.

12. It is also not known first, whether the graphic, photo or full-motion images should be used to set the context of the discourse presented to the listener (e.g. should they be used to furnish needed background information?); second, whether the images, rather than text, should be used to display the response options (especially for novice level listeners); or third, whether they should be used to test co-ordinate skills in listening, possibly for advanced level listeners, (e.g. whether they should be used to test the listeners knowledge of the nonverbal cues contained in the spoken discourse).

13. The item-writing framework in Table 5.1 was used primarily to help the item writers generate a pool of test questions. The framework represents aspects of a current, albeit a noncomprehensive (i.e. Lund's 1990) taxonomy of listening skills. It was a concern that aspects of the framework (e.g. the item types—items with responses with text options, responses with graphic options and responses with options within one graphic) would add elements of multidimensionality to the item pool. IRT item calibration seeks to determine whether the collection of items, even if it contains a variety of item types, all measure a common concept. If the components/dimensions of the item-writing framework bear a statistically significant relationship to item difficulty, then it would be important to organize the questions into subsets (or testlets of items, possibly based on item type) and in the process to develop subscales. The GLM ANOVA provides an omnibus test of the relationship between the item-writing framework dimensions and estimated item difficulty. It does not, *per se*, test for the absence or presence of unidimensionality. Rather, it seeks to help identify unidimensional subsets of questions if, in fact, the statistical relationship is significant and large. (It proved to be neither.) In addition to discussing the GLM ANOVA results, we have added text to the manuscript that demonstrates one descriptive method (Bejar's procedure) that tests the assumption of unidimensionality for the item bank, and we have made references to several other procedures designed specifically to describe the structure of the item responses and, therefore, provide evidence about the unidimensionality of the responses.

Figure 5.1
Item difficulty by person ability distribution map

ITEMS		PERSONS	Numbers of Items	People
##	-4.0		3	0
	-3.8		0	0
#	-3.6		1	0
	-3.4		0	0
	-3.2		0	0
#	-3.0		1	0
####	-2.8		6	0
	-2.6		0	0
	-2.4		0	0
##	-2.2		3	0
#	-2.0	##	2	2
####	-1.8	####	6	4
#	-1.6	#	1	1
######	-1.4		8	0
###	-1.2		4	0
#	-1.0		1	0
##	-0.8		3	0
#####	-0.6		7	0
####	-0.4		6	0
######	-0.2		8	0
######	0.0		9	0
######	0.2	####	9	4
#####	0.4	###############	7	15
#	0.6	###############	2	15
#########	0.8	######	13	6
####	1.0	#####	6	5
##	1.2	####	3	4
########	1.4	####	11	4
####	1.6	#############	5	13
#	1.8	######	2	6
#####	2.0	#####	7	5
#	2.2	####	2	4
##	2.4	##	3	2
#	2.6	#	2	1
#	2.8	#	1	1
	3.0	#	0	1
	3.2	##	0	2
	3.4	#	0	1
	3.6	##	0	2
	3.8		0	0
	4.0	###	0	3

Per cent of Items   Per cent of Examinees

Summary Information:	Average difficulty	S.D. difficulty	Average ability	S.D. ability
Theta Metric	0.00	1.54	1.17	1.27
Scaled Score Metric	100.0	14.0	110.7	11.5

115

Figure 5.2
Test characteristic curve

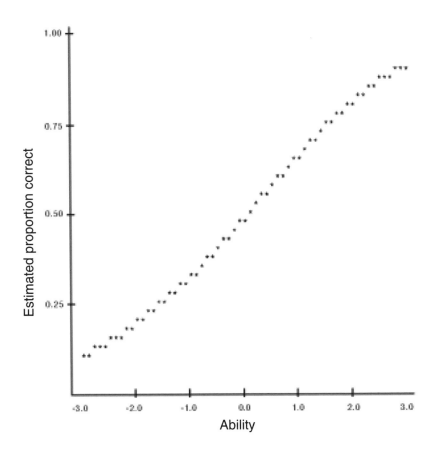

Figure 5.3
Test information curve

Test characteristics:
- Estimated reliability: 0.957
- Expected information: 22.613
- Average information: 18.854

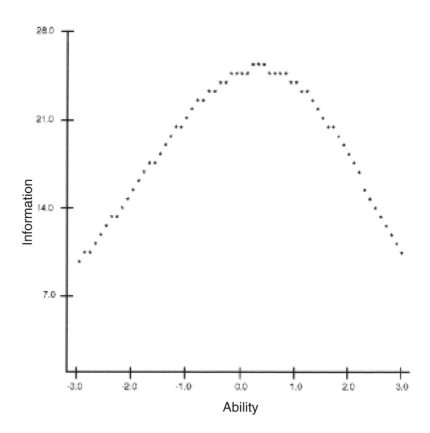

Table 5.1

Schematic of the conceptual item-writing framework used to create the initial bank of 144 Hausa test items

Screen	D2 Text Choice								A1 Graphic Choice								A2 Element in Graphic Choice							
	Dialogue				Monologue				Dialogue				Monologue				Dialogue				Monologue			
	a	b	c	d	e	f	g	h	a	b	c	d	e	f	g	h	a	b	c	d	e	f	g	h
Function / Level	Recog Iden	Orient	Main Idea Comp	Detail Comp	Recog Iden	Orient	Main Idea Comp	Detail Comp	Recog Iden	Orient	Main Idea Comp	Detail Comp	Recog Iden	Orient	Main Idea Comp	Detail Comp	Recog Iden	Orient	Main Idea Comp	Detail Comp	Recog Iden	Orient	Main Idea Comp	Detail Comp
NL	1	4	7	10	13	16	19	22	25	28	31	34	37	40	43	46	49	52	55	58	61	64	67	70
NM	2	5	8	11	14	17	20	23	26	29	32	35	38	41	44	47	50	53	56	59	62	65	68	71
NH	3	6	9	12	15	18	21	24	27	30	33	36	39	42	45	48	51	54	57	60	63	66	69	72
IL	73	76	79	82	85	88	91	94	97	100	103	106	109	112	115	118								
IM	74	77	80	83	86	89	92	95	98	101	104	107	110	113	116	119								
IH	75	78	81	84	87	90	93	96	99	102	105	108	111	114	117	120								
A	121	124	127	130	133	136	139	142																
A Plus	122	125	128	131	134	137	140	143																
S	123	126	129	132	135	138	141	144																

References

American Council on the Teaching of Foreign Languages (1986) *ACTFL Proficiency Guidelines*. Hastings-on-Hudson, NY: ACTFL.

Bachman, L. (1990) *Fundamental Considerations in Language Testing*. Oxford: Oxford University Press.

Bejar, I. (1980) A procedure for investigating the unidimensionality of achievement tests based on item parameter estimates. *Journal of Educational Measurement* 17: 283–96.

Bejar, I. (1988) An approach to assessing unidimensionality revisited. *Applied Psychological Measurement* 12 (3): 377–9.

Bock, R.D., Gibbons, R. and Muraki, E. (1988) Full information factor analysis. *Applied Psychological Measurement* 12 (3): 261–80.

Brecht, R. and Walton, R. (1993) *National Planning in the Less Commonly Taught Languages*. Washington, DC: National Foreign Language Centre.

Celce-Murcia, M. (Ed.) (1991) *Teaching English as a Second or Foreign language* (2nd Ed.). New York, NY: Newbury House.

Chastain, K. (1988) *Developing Second-Language Skills: Theory and Practice* (3rd ed.). New York, NY: Harcourt Brace Jovanovich.

Choi, I. (1992) *An Application of Item Response Theory to Language Testing*. New York, NY: Peter Lang.

Clark, J. and Johnson, D. (1982) *A Survey of Materials Development Needs in the Less Commonly Taught Languages in the United States*. Washington, DC: Centre for Applied Linguistics.

Dandonoli, P., (1989) The ACTFL computerized adaptive test of foreign language reading proficiency. In Smith, W.F. (Ed.) *Modern Technology in Foreign Language Education: Applications and Projects,* pp. 291–300. Skokie, IL: National Textbook Company.

Dunkel, P. (1991) Computerized testing of nonparticipatory L2 listening comprehension proficiency: An ESL prototype development effort. *Modern Language Journal* 75: 64–73.

Dunkel, P. (1992) *The development of a computer-adaptive test of listening comprehension proficiency in Hausa: A final report submitted to the International Research and Studies Program of the United States Department of Education*. Award No. P017A0041. University Park, PA.

Dwyer, D. and Hiple, D. (1987) African language teaching and ACTFL team testing. In Stansfield, C. W. and Harman, C. (Eds.) *ACTFL Proficiency Guidelines for the Less Commonly Taught Languages* (Dept. of Education Program No. G008650634). Washington, DC: Centre for Applied Linguistics and Hastings-on-Hudson, NY: ACTFL.

Green, B., Bock, R. D., Humphreys, L., Linn, R. and Reckase, M. (1984) Technical guidelines for assessing computerized adaptive tests. *Journal of Educational Measurement* 21: 347–60.

Hadley, A. O. (1993) *Teaching Language in Context* (2nd ed.). Boston, MA: Heinle and Heinle.

Hambleton, R. K. and Cook, L. L. (1983) Robustness of item response models and effects of test length and sample size on the precision of ability estimates. In Weiss, D. J. (Ed.) *New Horizons in Testing*. New York, NY: Academic Press.

Henning, G. T. (1987) *A Guide to Language Testing: Development, Evaluation, Research*. Cambridge, CA: Newbury House Publishers.

Henning, G. T., Hudson, T. and Turner, J. (1985) Item response theory and the assumption of unidimensionality for language tests. *Language Testing* 2: 141–54.

HyperCard 2.1 (1991) Cupertino, CA: Apple Computer.

HyperCard Toolbox (1991) Santa Clara, CA: Apple Computer.

Kraft, C. and Kraft, M. (1973) *Introductory Hausa*. Berkeley, CA: University of California Press.

Lord, F. M. (1983) Small N justifies Rasch model. In Weiss, D. J. (Ed.) *New Horizons in Testing*, pp. 51-61. New York, NY: Academic Press.

Lund, R. (1990) A taxonomy for teaching second language listening. *Foreign Language Annals* 23: 105–15.

MACDRAW II 1.1 B2 (1989) Santa Clara, CA: Claris.

Madsen, H. S. (1991) Computer-adaptive testing of listening and reading comprehension: The Brigham Young University approach. In Dunkel, P. (Ed.) *Computer-assisted Language Learning and Testing: Research Issues and Practice,* pp. 237–57. New York, NY: Newbury House.

Morley, J. (1991) Listening comprehension in second/foreign language instruction. In Celce-Murcia, pp. 81–106.

Murphy, J. (1991) Oral communication in TESOL: Integrating speaking, listening, and pronunciation. *TESOL Quarterly* 25: 51–75.

Petersen, P. (1991) A synthesis of methods for interactive listening. In Celce-Murcia, pp. 106–22.

RASCAL RASCH Analysis Program. St. Paul, MN: Assessment Systems Corporation.

Rekase, M. D., Ackerman, T. A. and Carlson, J. E. (1988) Building a unidimensional test using multidimensional items. *Journal of Educational Measurement* 25 (3): 193–203.

Richards, J. C. (1983) Listening comprehension: Approach, design, procedure. *TESOL Quarterly* 17: 219–40.

Rivers, W. (1968) *Teaching Foreign Language Skills*. Chicago, IL: University of Chicago Press.

Rost, M. (1990) *Listening in Language Learning*. New York, NY: Longman.

Stansfield, C. W. (Ed.) (1986) *Technology and Language Testing*. Washington, DC: TESOL Publications.

Steinberg, L., Thissen, D. and Wainer, H. (1990) Validity. In Wainer, pp. 187–231.

Tung, P. (1986) Computerized adaptive testing: Implications for language test developers. In Stansfield, pp. 11–28.

Ur, P. (1984) *Teaching Listening Comprehension*. Cambridge: Cambridge University Press.

Valette, R. (1977) *Modern Language Testing: A Handbook*. New York, NY: Harcourt, Brace, Jovanovich.

Wainer H. (Ed.) (1990) Computerized Adaptive Testing: A foimer. Hillsdale, NJ: Lawrence Erlbaum Associates Publishers.

Wainer, H. and Mislevy, R. (1990) Item response theory, item calibration and proficiency estimation. In Wainer, pp. 65–102.

Winrip, M. (1993) *No. 2 pencil fades as graduate exam moves to computer*. New York Times, November 15, Section B: 9.

Wolvin, A. and Coakley, C. (1988) *Listening* (3rd ed.). Dubuque, IA: Brown.

Wolvin, A. and Coakley, C. (Eds.) (1993) *Perspectives on Listening*. Norwood, NJ: Ablex.

6 The development of an adaptive test for placement in French

Michael Laurier
University of Montreal

Introduction

Many institutions offering language programs at the post-secondary level are faced with the problem of assigning to each student, in a very short period of time, the course that best suits his/her need. In fact, this often means creating homogeneous groups from the point of view of the level of proficiency in the language. This type of group division is based on the assumption that placing a student at the proper level will improve the amount of learning. Although this approach is debatable, it reflects the organization of most language programs that consist of a sequence of courses corresponding to different degrees of language proficiency.

In this context, adaptive testing techniques are particulary interesting for the development of placement tests for several reasons:

1. The use of the computer represents a significant advantage in terms of practicality, when the institution can rely on a large computer lab or when group testing sessions cannot be organized. The computerization accelerates the placement operation and reduces the human resources that are needed for the administration of the test, the marking and the production of student lists.
2. A placement test is typically administered both to very advanced learners who may not be challenged by the test and to absolute beginners who may become frustrated by the difficulty of the tasks. Since it is possible to present items that take into account the learner's level, an adaptive test, as opposed to a conventional test, is a more pleasant experience for the student. It is also a more efficient measurement instrument as it collects relevant information in a short period of time.
3. Although there should be some relation between the competences and abilities that are developed in a program and the content of a placement test, one would expect a placement test to be based on generic competences and abilities; these can be measured with items that generally

fit latent trait models reasonably well. Complex content sampling problems that occur when course objectives must be measured are avoided since the item selection is made on the characteristics of the item with regard to the trait being measured.

4. Open-ended questions are difficult to integrate in an adaptive test. Limitation of cognitive processes or threat to authenticity of discourse are major problems with language tests using multiple choice questions or student ratings. However, these problems do not always affect the predictive validity of a placement test which is not a high-stake test. The number of misclassifications can be reduced if the test is complemented, whenever necessary, with production tasks and if some group changes are allowed at the beginning of the instruction.

As stated by Sawyer (1996: 286) *'decision theory is a useful method for assessing the effectiveness of components of a course placement system'*. The design of the placement test must reflect the predictive value of the instrument and users must understand that it cannot measure achievement in a given course or certify language competence with regard to specific professional needs. Of course the issue of determining the criterion to be used for the evaluation of the predictive validity is not easy to solve. The most common basis for group changes is teachers' judgements. However, since these judgements should be used with caution (Wall *et al.* 1994) it is sometimes difficult to establish the predictive validity of a placement test.

In this chapter, we will present a placement test, the French CAPT. This test has been developed to assign appropriate language courses to English-speaking students enrolled in French programs at the post-secondary level in Canada. Post-secondary institutions are often faced with the problem of quickly placing large numbers of students in groups that correspond to their actual level. Grades obtained in French at high school or at the university are often not reliable because language curriculum and teaching approaches are not comparable and because grades are not based only on judgements about language proficiency. Allowing students to enrol in the course of their choice leads to heterogeneous groups as many students are not sure about their own level of proficiency and know very little about the course they choose. These problems are further amplified by constraints or beliefs that push some students to prefer a course that is too easy or too difficult. In most cases, the institutions must set up large-group testing sessions that are very demanding in terms of resources for administration and marking. An adaptive procedure can be an interesting alternative to these large-group sessions.

The target population is fairly homogeneous in terms of social, cultural and economic background. The students are 17–22 years old, they come from a milieu where higher education is highly valued and affordable, they have a functional knowledge of English (as their mother tongue or as a second language), they show a rather positive atttitude towards the learning of French. However, their levels of proficiency in French are very different: some of them, who did not have French at high school, are still at the beginners' level, whereas others, who are arriving from immersion programs for example, are very advanced. Therefore, the adaptive solution is not only attractive as it allows the test to be tailored to the student level but also feasible because responses from a wide range of abilities can be collected during the development phase.

The remaining discussion will focus on some decisions that have been made during the development of the test. We will consider decisions about the construct of the test, about the general structure, about the prychometric models, about the technology and, finally, about the implementation of the instrument.

Decisions about the construct

Most of the French language study programs in Canada seek to develop the four skills: listening, speaking, reading and writing. Some programs, particularly where there is a large French community, emphasize oral skills and functional competence. Others put more emphasis on written skills and grammatical competence. However, since very few institutions can offer specific courses to develop only one skill (e.g. phonetics, reading strategies or grammar), they all tend to integrate these skills in a series of courses that aim at enabling the learner to use the second language in a variety of situations that are likely to occur in a bilingual environment. Teachers and program co-ordinators expect a placement test to measure abilities which are common to these courses and, consequently, that show some correlation with the assessments which are currently done in the classroom. In addition, because of practical constraints, they also expect a placement test to be easy to score. This is one reason why multiple choice questions are preferred to open-ended questions. The latest version of the test that we devised includes five types of tasks.

1. Short-paragraph reading tasks which are based on approximately 30-word paragraphs that can be encountered in daily life (instructions on a label, excerpts from a film review, statements of a problem ...).
2. Sociolinguistic judgements which consist of selecting the most appropriate French statement in a given situation; as in the test directions, the situation is described in English.
3. 'Fill-the-gap' sentences where the student must select the word that fits best in the blank; approximately half of the items are related to lexical knowledge and half to the application of grammar rules.
4. Listening comprehension based on two-minute 'semi-authentic' passages (radio advertisement, answering machine message, short dialogue ...); each passage is followed by three questions.

5. Self-assessment of oral skills; students are asked to rate their ability to cope with communicative situations where they have to speak (ordering a meal, congratulating, telling a joke ...).

Comprehensive validation studies have been conducted on the first three types of tasks (Laurier 1993; Blais and Laurier, 1993). First, we analysed correlations with other measures: vocabulary, self-assessment of speaking/listening skills and teacher's assessment after about 20 hours of instruction. The most interesting conclusion concerns the role of vocabulary. Students were asked to tell whether they could understand key words used in the items (isolated and in context): high correlations with each type of task (.81< r <.85) confirm the importance of vocabulary in performing these tasks. Second, intercorrelations between the tasks were analysed and revealed that although each of them represented a specific construct, they also shared some common variance so that it would make sense to use an aggregate of these results for a placement decision. Third, we analysed the internal structure of the items related to each task to verify the dimensionality of these groups of items. The short-paragraph reading tasks clearly represent a unidimensional set of items, whereas there are two correlated factors in the 'fill-the-gap' sentences that could be labeled as 'grammar' and 'vocabulary'. The structure of the sociolinguistic judgement items is rather complex as these judgements are based on knowledge that is not always directly related to language competence. As far as the listening comprehension is concerned, preliminary studies have shown that the design of the task must be taken into account: because the three items that verify the comprehension of each passage correlate, the assumption of local independence cannot be met. Finally, in terms of the self-assessment items, a single rating-scale model was used to verify the internal consistency: all the items contributed to increasing the reliability of this set of items. However, further studies of dimensionality are needed.

Decisions about the general structure

Most placement tests incorporate all the items in a single bank. This practice is rather problematic when there are different types of items in the bank because it is very unlikely that these items call for the same skills. In fact, even within the same type of task, more than one factor may be needed to explain the variance—an indication that the set of items may be measuring more than one ability. Of course, in any educational test, the final score is the result of the effects of numerous variables. Unidimensionality should not be considered as a yes/no question but as a matter of degree. Applications of IRT models assume that the object being measured is fairly unidimensional. This may not be a major issue in language testing, because, although unitary models of language competence are generally rejected, language skills tend to be highly correlated (Carroll 1987). Furthermore, many researcher have shown that the estimation of examinees' ability and item parameters are quite robust with regards to departure from unidimensionality (Harrison 1986; Reckase *et al.* 1988; De Ayala 1992). However, the inclusion of different types of tasks or the inclusion of tasks measuring different skills in a single test make the interpretation of the ability estimation somewhat dubious. Inferences regarding the general competence may be questionable and difficulties in different areas of the language cannot be properly diagnosed.

As far as the French CAPT is concerned, we made a conservative decision to ensure that problems of unidimensionality would not affect the quality of the estimation. Therefore, instead of creating a single bank, we created five different banks—each corresponding to a different type of task. An estimate of the ability is calculated at the end of each subtest so that the final result is expressed as a histogram showing the level of proficiency on a 14-level scale (ranging from 'Beginner' to 'Very advanced+') for each of the subtests. With this graphical representation, the learner can visualize, at the end of the test, his/her own profile. Levels on each subtest are also stored in a file so that the teacher or the program administrator can retrieve the information that has been used to build this profile. On the other hand, since the placement decision usually consists in positioning the student on a general competence continuum, a general ability score is reached by a simple average of the five levels. However, should a given institution have specific needs, the weight of the subtests could be changed in the program.

In addition to problems of dimensionality that may arise from the inclusion of all the items in a single bank, the test designer is faced with a problem of content coverage. Because adaptive procedures are usually based on an algorithm that maximizes the information, some items will tend to be over-used because either they discriminate more or they are more informative for a specific portion of the ability range. Various solutions have been proposed to address the problem of content coverage (Kingsbury and Zara 1989 and 1991). Using five different banks to create mini-CATs (Schnipke and Green 1995) is also a solution to the content-coverage problem.

The first three subtests use a selection strategy similar to the 'stradaptive' strategy that has been applied by Bejar and Weiss (1978). A 14 x 10 matrix of items is created. The first axis corresponds to the 14 levels of proficiency that are distinguished along the ability scale ('Beginner', 'Beginner+' ... 'Very Advanced +'). The 10-step axis is a stack where the items are ranked from the most informative at a given level to the tenth most informative. Of course, since the banks are fairly small (approximately 60 items), some items are repeated in the matrix and form clusters of cells in different areas on this information grid.

At the beginning of the test, the learner is asked some questions about his/her background in French, i.e. the number of years of French courses and the number of years spent in a French environment. This information is modulated with respect to the elapsed time since the last course or the last stay. To complement this preliminary information, the learner is asked to rate his/her general level in French choosing from seven levels (Beginner ... Very advanced) which correspond to the main levels of the test scale. As the entry level has always been a major concern, particularly on short tests, the prior information that is collected with these questions is very helpful. Selecting the first item according to an estimation based on this information is a more efficient way to optimize the algorithm than starting with an item in the intermediate range. Once the test has begun, the composite score of the previous subtests is used to determine the entry level in a new subtest.

On the first three subtests, the selection of the second up to the fifth item is based on a simple 'back-and-forth' technique. If the answer is right, the next item is one level more difficult and the ability estimate is adjusted accordingly (with a provision to account for a right answer due to guessing). If the answer is wrong, then the next item is easier and the ability estimate is reduced. After five items, a maximum-likelihood (ML) algorithm (Baker 1992) is applied to estimate the ability. If there is no convergence or if the value is aberrant—a common problem with ML estimation on short tests—then the mid-point between the level of the items answered correctly and the items failed is used. With respect to the general structure, the test designer must also decide what is the termination criterion. In the French CAPT, once the error is acceptable (< .25), the subtest is over. However each of the first three subtests uses a minimum of seven items and a maximum of 12.

The procedure for the fourth subtest, listening comprehension, is different. Three questions are presented on the screen and, once the student has read them, the student listens (only once) to the passage. The passages are ranked from the most difficult to the easiest. Depending on the level, a sequence of three passages (at the extreme ability values) and up to five (in the intermediate range) contiguous passages are presented.

The last subtest is a self-assessment questionnaire to verify oral skills in different real-life situations. The student must rate his/her capability to deal with this situation using a six-step frequency scale (Cannot do at all, rarely ... like a native speaker). This technique has been used successfully for placement purposes using paper-and-pencil version (Leblanc and Painchaud 1985). We believe that the technique is more effective if the questionnaire is administered in an adaptive way. The situations that are submitted to the student are those on which, given the current ability estimate, a 'Half the time' answer is expected.

Grouping the items in five different banks rather than a unique large one is a decision that is debatable. On one hand, as the number of items in a bank increases, the error of measurement of the calibration decreases; yet the error that is produced as a result of the separation of the banks is probably balanced by a better fit. On the other hand, an ability estimate that is computed after the administration of about ten items is probably less reliable than an estimate based on many more items. However, again this may be balanced with a better fit and the calculation of a composite score (an average of the five subtest results) could offset the error. Further research on the data will be required to fully investigate these decisions about the general structure of the test and to determine their impact on test reliability.

Decisions about the psychometric models

One advantage of considering the whole test as a combination of five subtests is certainly the possibility of using different IRT models in each subtest in order to obtain the best possible fit. During the design of the first three parts, we believed that a standard IRT model, among the three models presented by Lord (1980), could be used. All the items were multiple choice items with four options and were dichotomously scored (right/wrong). Each subtest was fairly unidimensional although some techniques that were applied revealed, as stated above, that there may be two dimensions in the 'Fill-the-gap' subtest (vocabulary and grammar) and that a variety of factors affect sociolinguistic judgements in the second part. Given the relative robustness of IRT estimations, these subtests could still be considered as three separate pools, each measuring a different aspect of the general language competence.

The issue was then to determine which one among the three standard IRT models was the most appropriate. The original latent trait model which has been formalized as a logistic function by Birnbaum (1968) involve the estimation, in addition to the examinee's ability (θ), of two item parameters—discrimination (a) and difficulty (b). This model was rejected because it does not take into account the chance factor that is always present in multiple choice items. Therefore the three-parameter model which incorporates 'pseudo-guessing' (c) seemed more appropriate. However, the calibration is more complex and requires a larger sample because the model involves the estimation of an additional value. Fortunately, new estimation algorithms such as the bayesian procedure implemented in the BILOG program (Mislevy and Bock 1990) yields reliable parameter estimates for a 50-item test with samples of only 700 students. Another solution to the estimation of the 'pseudo-guessing' parameter is to fix this parameter at $1/n$, where n stands for the number of options (in our case four). However, since the distractors are not working all the same way, discrepancies can be found between this a priori value and the actual guessing effect.

Like many test developers who are faced with the burden of massive field-testing in a situation where large samples are difficult to gather, we also contemplated the use of the simplest model, the Rasch model. This model has been preferred for the construction of most language adaptive tests. The

Rasch model is a one-parameter model where only difficulty and ability are estimated (on a common scale). Since Lord's (1965) comment, the Rasch model is considered a defensible approach where the sample size is limited (N < 200). However, some researches (Traub 1983; Digvi 1986) have shown that the model fit is often far from perfect on multiple choice items. It is rather bewildering to assume that no guessing occurs or that the item discriminates equally well. Of course, one way to lessen the over-simplication that is inherent to the Rasch model is to rely on a classical item analysis to eliminate items with poor discrimination (as measured by the correlation of the item with the whole test) and make sure that the distractors are attractive. The Rasch model is suitable for paper-and-pencil tests where the score usually corresponds to the number of right answers. However ability estimates on adaptive tests are generally based on procedures that can account for the amount of information that is brought by each item at a given level. In that case, using accurate discrimination and guessing parameters is one way to optimize the adaptive procedure, although this may lead to the over-exposure of the most informative items. With a data set of approximately 700 responses per item for the first three subtests, we finally decided to keep the three-parameter model. The items were calibrated with the BILOG program.

Whereas the unidimensionality and local independence assumptions could be reasonably met in the first three subtests, the fourth one, listening comprehension, posed a particular problem. This problem is common to passage-related tests where the intercorrelations between the questions that refer to a specific passage tend to be higher. This situation precludes the use of standard IRT models which assume local independence of the items. One solution to this problem is the application of the concept of testlet as proposed by Wainer and Kiely (1987). A testlet can be defined as a superordinate item that consists of several content-related items. A 'testlet' is considered as a single item during the calibration and the ability estimation. To circumvent the problems of having three questions related to one passage we decided to consider the fifteen passages that were kept in the fourth subtest as testlets (i.e. as items whose scores could range from 0 to 3). Obviously, standard models which are based on dichotomously scored items could not be applied. We therefore switched to a graded-response model as proposed by Samejima (1978). Using MULTILOG (Thissen 1986), we assigned for each passage, scored 0 to 3, a discrimination index (a) and points on the ability scale where chances of getting the higher and the lower score were equal (b_1, b_2 and b_3). Since we had fewer than 500 examinees, a minimum for an accurate estimation (Reise and Yu 1990), the next versions of the test should include an update of these estimates based on additional data that we intend to gather.

As far as the fifth subtest is concerned, there is so far no evidence of local independence problems. Partial studies on these data indicated that a dominant factor can account for a large portion of the variance. As we mentioned before, this subtest is a self-assessment questionnaire where the student is asked to rate his/her capability to deal with different communicative situations on a Likert-scale. Again, we used the graded-response model to calibrate the 54 statements of the questionnaire. Since there were six points to estimate on the ability scale (b_1 ... b_6) with fewer than 500 examinees, the discrimation parameter (a) was fixed. Although the intervals of confidence are acceptable, we intend to administer the questionnaire to additional subjects in order to improve the quality of the estimates.

Decisions about the technology

Although in the near future one can foresee that most computer programs will work on both platforms, IBM and Mac, at the time we started working on this placement test the decision about the type of machine to be preferred was crucial as conversions were time-consuming and expensive. For practical reasons, we finally chose to work on an IBM platform. The next decision was related to the programing of the adaptive procedure. Two options were contemplated. We could work with an existing software package which allows the user to build an item bank and provides a shell to use the bank for the administration of an adaptive test. At the time we were planning the project, MicroCAT (Assessment Systems Corp. 1988) was the only package that was commercially available. Since then other packages have appeared on the market. Although they incorporate programming facilities, these programs often lack flexibility when one needs to customize the test, for example, to integrate sound, to combine different banks, to modify the item selection procedure and so on. In addition, these programs often require that the institution purchase the program or at least a runtime unit, an expense many small institutions cannot afford. We turned to the second option, the most demanding but the most promising, which led us to use a standard programing language to develop our own testing shell.

The program was developed in Turbo-Pascal (Borland 1990) and comprises three modules. The first one is the item bank manager which includes data base functions to import or create new items, delete or modify existing items and generate information matrices. There are five banks, one for each test. Each item is a record that consists of the following fields:

1. item identification
2. correct answer(s)
3. discrimination: a parameter(s)

4. difficulty: b parameter(s)
5. pseudo-guessing: c parameter
6. information peak: the m value is the ability point where the item is the most informative as calculated according to Birnbaum's (1968) formula
7. prompt: a comprehension question, a paragraph to be read, situation description, a sentence with a missing word, or a 'Can do' statement
8. different possible answers to choose from (or a rating scale)

The second module is an administration module. This is the unit that is distributed to the institutions and used to administer the test to the students. This unit can be installed in a computer lab or on remote stations depending on the resources and the institution's needs. At this point, the test must be installed on every station because it cannot be delivered by a server or via Internet. The student enters the answers by typing the letter that corresponds to his/her choice. The preference for multiple choice is not only due to the problems that are inherent in the psychometric analysis of open-ended questions but also to the limitation of natural language processing techniques with the present technology, and to the importance of minimizing the effect of computer literacy. The administration module includes subroutines to estimate the student level, to select the most appropriate item, to display the instructions and the items and to report the results. The results are stored in an ASCII file that can be used to generate class lists. The final histogram that is shown on the screen is complemented with a short text that can be modified at the institution level to make the correspondence between the levels of the test and course numbers.

The third module is a simulation unit. In fact, it is an expanded version of the administration module. The simulation unit displays a window that works as a tracer which keeps track, after each response, of information such as the number of items administered, the ability estimate, the item parameters, the test information function, the number of steps required by the ML algorithm to converge. This information can be printed to study the evolution of the administration. It was first used as a debugging tool and can now be used for research purposes.

The environment is DOS based. The conversion that is now being done to a Windows environment will certainly help to take full advantage of the computer memory, to present the items in an more attractive way and to simplify the installation procedure. However the DOS version works satisfactorily and can be launched from Windows. Compared to a full Windows version it is fast, simpler to update and portable. A preliminary version of the test which included only the first three subtests could work on a minimal configuration of an IBM machine; the five-subtest present version requires a SoundBlaster card.

Decisions about the implementation

For practical reasons, French CAPT, like many other adaptive tests, has been developed using items previously calibrated from responses obtained on various pencil-and-paper versions. Each new paper-and-pencil version includes anchoring items that have been used on former versions. These old items correspond to approximately 20% to 25% of a new experimental version. This procedure is probably the most convenient way to collect data, particularly in medium-scale testing situations. Mazzeo and Harvey (1988) suggested that, in this situation, a comparability study would be preferable to ensure the parameters are stable across administration modes. We have compared scores on the conventional and the computerized versions but we have not been able yet to conduct this type of study at the item level. An alternative to a comparability study would be to recalibrate the existing items or calibrate new items using responses obtained during the computer administration. However this solution raises practical and theoretical problems that may affect the quality of the data and reduce the efficiency of the adaptive procedure.

Since part of the development of the French CAPT was funded with a grant to explore various aspects of the application of adaptive techniques for language testing, this test is not commercially distributed. Institutions that are using it are not charged any fees, but they have agreed to field-test new items. That means that once in a while they will receive paper-and-pencil versions that will be used to collect additional data. These data needed to improve the parameter estimates for items that were calibrated with samples that were probably too small.

When an institution is sent a copy of the adaptive test, we compile a version with the name of the institution in the source code to prevent unwarranted copies. In addition, the protocol stipulates that the test should be used for placement purposes only and that test security measures should be enforced. However, we realize that some items will eventually have to be replaced or added. In a medium-scale testing situation, the co-operation of participating institutions is needed to collect additional data in order to expand and renew the item banks.

Implementation decisions also concern the generalizibility of the instrument. One advantage of IRT over the classical measurement approach is that the ability and the item parameter estimates are sample free. This property is known as the invariance of subjects and items. Yet invariance does mean that the characteristics of the sample do not affect the estimates. This is the reason why we intend to verify if the test could be used with other populations. As we mentioned before, the test has been calibrated on samples that were drawn from a rather homogeneous population. We wonder if the test would produce comparable results and lead to valid inferences about the general language competence of adults or high school students. We also plan to translate the test to verify if the parameters change when used with different language groups. We are now developing a version for Spanish students and we will use a 'French only' version for a multi-lingual population learning French in France. These data will allow us to determine which items have their psychometric properties modified by the translation and/or by the differences between the original sample and the new sample.

Another problem of IRT which has sometimes been overlooked when presenting the invariance property is the indeterminacy of the zero point. Although the IRT modeling approach compensates for gaps that may be found in the data, the middle point of the ability/difficulty scale is usually set to the mean difficulty. Yet when different subtests are used, the test designer is faced with the problem of the comparability of different scales unless all the subtests are field-tested simultaneously with the same sample. This is what we did for the first three subtests that were calibrated with a three-parameter model. However, even if the samples that were used for the last two parts shared the same characteristics, we are not absolutely sure that the scales that were created with different models are comparable. Additional data will help us better to equate the different subtests.

Conclusion

Adaptive testing procedures have been applied in the last ten years in different domains for various purposes. As far as language testing is concerned, the constraints of the models and the technology as well as the inherent problems of natural language processing make the applications for the assessment of all the aspects of the communicative competence difficult (Meunier 1994). Despite these limitations adaptive procedures can be very useful for placement testing because it is possible to focus on aspects that can predict students' behaviours in a language class. An adaptive test is a sound alternative to large-group testing sessions where the same set of items is administered to every student—absolute beginners or almost bilingual.

During the development of a language adaptive test, important decisions must be made at different levels. Some of these decisions are based on beliefs about what a good language test should be, others on empirical analyses, others on practical considerations. The consequences of each decision at a given level must be analysed carefully in relation with other decisions to be made at other levels. The variety of choices that are available in the design of an adaptive test indicates that innovative and relevant adaptive language tests can be developed.

Acknowledgments

I am grateful to Charles Pearo for his thorough revision of this text.

References

Assessment Systems Corporation (1988) *MicroCAT* [computer software]. St. Paul, MN.

Baker, F. B. (1992) *Item Response Theory: Parameter Estimation Techniques.* New York, NY: Marcel Dekker.

Bejar, I. and Weiss, D. J. (1978) *A construct validation of adaptive achievement testing (Research Report 78–4).* Minneapolis, MN: University of Minnesota, Department of Psychology.

Birnbaum, A. (1968) Some latent-trait models and their use in inferring an examinee's ability. In Lord, F. M. and Novick, M. R. (Eds.) *Statistical Theories of Mental Test Scores.* Reading, MA: Addison-Wesley.

Blais, J. G. and Laurier, M. D. (1993) The dimensionality of a placement test from several analytical perspectives. *Language Testing* 10 (2): 72–98.

Borland International Inc. (1990) *Turbo-Pascal, version 6.0* [computer software]. Scotts Valley, CA.

Carroll, B. J. (1987) Psychometric theory and language testing. In Grotjahn, R.C., Klein-Bradley, C. and Stevenson, D. K. (Eds.) *Taking their Measure: The Validity and Validation of Language Tests,* pp. 1–40. Bochum: Studienverlag Dr N. Brockmeyer.

De Ayala, R. J. (1992) The influence of dimensionality on CAT ability estimation. *Educational and Psychological Measurement* 52 (3): 513–28.

Digvi, D. R. (1986) Does the Rasch model really work for multiple choice items? Not if you look closely. *Journal of Educational Measurement* 23 (4): 283–98.

Harrison, D. A. (1986) Robustness of IRT parameter estimation to violations of the unidimensionality assumption. *Journal of Educational Statistics* 11 (2): 91–115.

Kingsbury, G. G. and Zara, A. R. (1989) Procedures for selecting items for computerized adaptive tests. *Applied Measurement in Education* 2 (4): 359–75.

Kingsbury, G. G. and Zara, A. R. (1991). Acomparison of procedures for content sensitive item selection in computerized adaptive tests. *Applied Measurement in Education,* 4(3), 241-261.

Laurier, M. D. (1993) *L'informatisation d'un test de classement en langue seconde.* Québec: Université Laval, International Centre for Research on Language Planning.

Leblanc, R. and Painchaud, G. (1985) Self-assessment as a second language placement instrument. *TESOL Quarterly* 19 (4): 673–88.

Lord, F. (1965) *Item sampling in test theory and research design.* Princetown, NJ: Educational Testing Service.

Lord, F. M. (1980) *Applications of Item Response Theory to Practical Testing Problems.* Hillsdale, NJ: Lawrence Erlbaum Associates Publishers.

Mazzeo, J. and Harvey, A. L. (1998). The equivalance of scores from automated and conventional educational and psychological tests (college Board report No 88-8) New York, NY: College Enterance Examination Board.

Meunier, L. E. (1994) Computer adaptive language tests (CALT) offer a great potential for functional testing. Yet why don't they? *CALICO Journal* 11 (4): 23–39.

Mislevy, R. J. and Bock, R. D. (1990) *BILOG 3: Item Analysis and Test Scoring with Binary Logistic Models.* Chicago, IL: Scientific Software.

Reckase, M. D., Ackerman, T. A. and Carlson, J. E. (1988) Building a unidimensional test using multidimensional items. *Journal of Educational Measurement* 25 (3): 193–203.

Reise, S. P. and Yu, J. (1990) Parameter recovery in the graded response model using MULTILOG. *Journal of Educational Measurement* 27 (2): 133–44.

Samejima, F. (1978) The application of graded-response models: The promise for the future. In Weiss, D. J. (Ed.) *Proceedings of the 1977 Conference on Computerized Adaptive Testing*, pp. 28–37. Minneapolis, MN: University of Minnesota.

Sawyer, R. (1996) Decision theory models for validating course placement tests. *Journal of Educational Measurement* 33 (3): 271–90.

Schnipke, D. L. and Green, B. F. (1995) A comparison of item selection routines in linear and adaptive tests. *Journal of Educational Measurement* 32 (3): 227–42.

Thissen, D. (1986) *MULTILOG* [computer software]. Mooresville, IN: Scientific Software.

Traub, R. E. (1983) A priori considerations in choosing an item response model. In Hambleton, R. K. (Ed.) *Applications of Item Response Theory*, pp. 57–70. Vancouver, BC: Educational Research Institute of British Columbia.

Wainer, H. and Keily, G. L. (1987) Item clusters and computerized adaptive testing: A case for testlets. *Journal of Educational Measurement* 24 (3): 185–202.

Wall, D., Clapham, C. and Alderson, J. C. (1994) Evaluating a placement test. *Language Testing* 11 (3): 321–44.

7 Computer-adaptive testing: A view from outside

T.F. McNamara
University of Melbourne

Introduction

In some ways I feel rather an outsider in relation to the topic of computer-adaptive testing, and this is reflected in the title of my chapter, 'A view from outside'. At the Language Testing Research Centre at the University of Melbourne we have indeed had some experience with computer-adaptive testing in the development of computer-adaptive tests of grammar in French (known as The Monash/Melbourne French CAT), and in Japanese. Descriptions of the tests and reports on their development have been published, as well as reports of research conducted on them, as follows: for French: Burston *et al.* 1995; Burston and Monville-Burston, 1996; for Japanese: Brown and Iwashita 1995, 1996. For example, on the Japanese CAT, which was trialled in Korea, China, Japan and Australia, Brown and Iwashita (1995, 1996) found pronounced sub-population effects which present serious problems for the test's usability across linguistic groups. But I was not personally involved in these developments, apart from helping to initiate them and acting as a commentator on aspects of the projects involved. Instead, my own work and that of a number of colleagues in Melbourne has focused on performance assessment in adult settings, often occupation-specific ones, and the application of multi-faceted Rasch measurement within performance assessment. I therefore offer this chapter more as a generalist (if those two fields can be considered general), and to present a perspective on computer-adaptive testing in the context of wider trends in assessment, particularly performance assessment. The chapter thus does not address technical issues in CAT but rather takes a step back to view developments in perspective.

In this chapter I want to raise a number of issues relevant to the current and potential state of CAT of reading comprehension. I begin by examining the place of CAT reading comprehension testing within performance assessment more generally, discussing its limitations and potential in this regard. Secondly, I go on to talk about the issue of profiling CAT performances through content-based descriptions of achievement. Thirdly, I raise issues of the equivalence of computer-mediated and non-computer-mediated tests of reading by reporting the findings of a recent study into the equivalence of two formats of a test of speaking. I conclude with some questions about the social and ideological role of CAT. You can see then that the chapter is fairly wide-ranging, speculative and focusing on issues and potential difficulties. I do not offer it in a contentious spirit, but I hope constructively, in the interests of broadening the range of issues for debate.

CAT and current developments in performance assessment

To what extent can computer-adaptive reading tests be considered performance tests? How can we locate computer-adaptive reading tests within current frameworks of communicative testing generally and performance testing in particular? Are computer-adaptive reading tests communicative language tests, or are they restricted to measuring reading ability indirectly, or understood in a narrow sense? To what extent are they reflecting paradigms and developments in other areas of assessment?

In this section, I wish to give a brief overview of some distinguishing characteristics of performance assessments, and then to see how computer-adaptive reading tests reflect or fail to reflect these characteristics.

Fitzpatrick and Morrison (1971: 238) offer a general definition of a performance test as *'one in which some criterion situation is simulated to a much greater degree than is represented by the usual paper-and-pencil test'*. Performance assessments can cover processes (in second language reading contexts, the processes of the reader) and products (evidence of successful outcomes of the reading process, for example by the choice of a correct alternative). Fitzpatrick and Morrison (1971: 238) explain that the term performance assessment is shorthand for the fuller 'performance and product evaluation'.

Fitzpatrick and Morrison argue that the representativeness of the simulation comprises two aspects (1971: 240):

> *comprehensiveness, or the range of different aspects of the situation that are simulated, and fidelity, the degree to which each aspect approximates a fair representation of that aspect in the criterion situation.*

This raises definitional questions, of the exact degree to which the criterion situation must be simulated before the assessment becomes a performance test. Haertel (1992) contrasts narrower and broader definitions of performance test, the latter including tests where some aspect of the non-test setting are simulated, either in the stimulus, or the response, or both; he points out that high degrees of representativeness may be hard to justify on the grounds of cost and practicality.

But this question of simplification and dilution of the requirements of the criterion situation raises more than pedantic definitional questions. We need to distinguish test and criterion (cf. Figure 7.1), even when the test has simulated the criterion to a high degree. Justification for the inferences that can be drawn from performance on test tasks in terms of ability to perform in the real world remains the central issue in test validation, and empirical evidence will have to be sought.

Figure 7.1

Test and Criterion

Another aspect of the comprehensiveness of simulation is whether performance tests should also simulate the standards by which performances in the non-test situation are normally judged. Writing in relation to performance assessment in the school setting, Wiggins (1989: 704) states: '*Authentic assessments replicate the challenges and standards of performance that typically face writers, business people, scientists, community leaders, designers, or historians.*'[1] Also writing for the school context, Linn, *et al.* (1991) propose a number of terms in which the validity of performance assessments may be assessed, but none of these addresses the quality or nature of rating criteria. Instead, they focus on the cognitive dimensions of performance, which they see as central to the validity of performance assessments. In so doing they reflect the general tendency to base assessment criteria on a theoretical (usually psychological) and educationally motivated construct assumed to underlie performance.

Some writers on performance tests in second language contexts have tried to address the issue of real-world criteria more directly, although this has not necessarily led them to recommend the adoption of such criteria, whatever they might be. These attempts have however been framed within a discussion of the nature of underlying competence, and frequently revolve around the relationship of linguistic to non-linguistic factors in performance on language performance tests. In general, judgements against real-world standards are not common in performance assessments, and raise difficult issues (Elder and Brown 1997; Hamilton *et al.* 1993; Jacoby and McNamara, in press). The question of what real-world criteria might be relevant in the judging of reading skills has scarcely been addressed, although such criteria would presumably involve a focus on outcomes in relation to whole tasks, would imply an integration of both language knowledge and skill and other aspects of performance not restricted to language, and would be the same for native speakers and non-native speakers.

Authentic task stimulus, task response and task processing are all characteristics of performance assessments, then. The performance may be judged by criteria used in the real world, though this is less often done in practice. To what extent do or can computer-assisted reading comprehension tests reflect these characteristics?

Replication of task stimulus

In the most innovative kinds of reading tests, realistic simulation of reading material has long been achieved. A high-water mark in this regard was the (now sadly defunct) Royal Society of Arts Examinations in the Communicative Use of English as a Foreign Language (Morrow 1983), where candidates were given a replica of a whole section of a British Sunday newspaper as the stimulus material; the same stimulus was provided for students at all levels, with the tasks changing according to level. Students were able to and required to physically search through the material.

More conventionally, reading tests reproduce authentic texts of varying length, either in whole or in part. Non-communicative reading tests, such as the reading component of the TOEFL test, have relatively short, purpose-written texts, making little attempt to simulate the normal content, length or format of reading in the real world.

Computer-assisted reading tests which simply reproduce TOEFL-type reading tests on the computer have little claim to be communicative, and will earn the criticism that has been heaped on TOEFL for two decades and more (cf. the critical papers in Stansfield 1986). Computer-assisted reading tests which attempt to simulate the normal content, length and format of real-world reading texts run into problems in computer delivery. Text presentation and handling on computer are relatively clumsy and inauthentic, although this is improving rapidly in the area of simulation of layout and the incorporation of graphics. In terms of authenticity, computer-assisted reading tasks in fact best simulate the reading of computer text, a perfectly authentic skill in its own right, but not the same skill as reading non-computer text. A visiting colleague from Japan told me recently that he finds it difficult to read newspapers on the Web, even though Japanese papers are available to him in Melbourne in that way. He had also noticed that I was prepared to accept students' assignments by e-mail, but was reassured when I said that I printed them out before reading them! Of course this discomfort may be a generational matter but it is likely the two kinds of reading may remain distinct for many readers. One solution might be for test questions but not test stimulus materials to be delivered by computer, at least in the short term.

Replication of task demand

Item types in CAT strongly favour MCQ or other kinds of forced choice task—even when this is cleverly disguised, as in work at the Australian Council for Educational Research (ACER) in Melbourne: e.g. Logan (1992). This is clearly inauthentic in most contexts. Work at ETS on adult literacy (e.g. Mosenthal and Kirsch 1994) demonstrates in contrast how tasks can match the text, varying according to reading purpose. (This important work will be discussed further below.) Even though these authors are confident of future delivery of such tasks in conventional computer-administered format, and even anticipate computer-adaptive testing (p. 71), they speak of such developments as 'futuristic' and caution that *'task difficulty parameters will have to be recalibrated to determine the effects (if any) of this new format'*.[2] It is argued below that the format is indeed likely to influence performance.

Replication of task processing

The physical constraints of computer-presented texts mean that reading processes which involve moving rapidly over long stretches of text, as in skimming and scanning, cannot easily be replicated. (After all, this fact is recognized in computer design by the existence of the Search function; the computer does the scanning for you.) Approaches to the teaching of reading skills which emphasize metacognitive strategies (Carrell 1984, 1992) are not as readily served by CAT as by less technologically enhanced forms of testing.

The reporting of performance: Profiling the cognitive dimensions of tasks

Recent advances have been made in reporting performance in reading comprehension tests in terms of the cognitive demands of reading tasks. It is to be hoped that this progressive practice can be applied in contexts where the items are restricted to MCQ format.

The possibility of calibrating candidate ability and task difficulty on a single scale of measurement which is available in Item Response Theory approaches was first exploited for reporting purposes in the development of the TORCH reading comprehension battery in Australia in the 1980s (Mossenson *et al.* 1987), following similar work in the UK (the TELS profiles).

Figure 7.2

Reading tasks on a scale of increasing reading ability

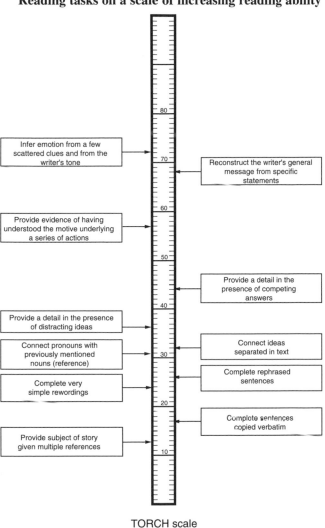

TORCH scale

The provenance of the criterion statements is an issue here. In the case of the TORCH test, the statements were developed after the fact on the basis of a casual inspection of item content by a single researcher (Geoff Masters, personal communication). Nevertheless, the approach is extremely attractive as it has the potential to provide a rational basis for reporting achievement. Other attempts to achieve the reporting of discrete reading skills by examining item content have been only partially successful, or not successful at all, and the basic approach remains controversial. Following the initial provocative study by Alderson and Lukmani (1989), which stressed the indeterminacy of what is being measured by individual items in a reading skills test, further work by Alderson (1990a, 1990b, 1995), Weir and colleagues (Weir *et al.* 1990; Weir 1994), McQueen (1992) and Lumley (1993, 1995) has clarified but not resolved the issues; see the extended discussion of the issue of reporting in McNamara (1996). An issue that emerges in this debate is that reporting in this way is made particularly difficult where (as in these studies) item types are restricted to MCQ format. One interesting attempt to provide detailed content referencing of discrete MCQ items is that of McQueen (1992), who reports on an Australian national test of elementary reading comprehension in Chinese for students in the first two years of high school language programmes. A careful analysis of task demand in relation to text content and text type provided the basis for validating sets of descriptors of reading achievement at three levels (cf. Figure 7.3).

The rather specific context of very basic reading skills in Chinese, where word and character identification were assumed to have a strong influence on task difficulty, limits the relevance of this particular study, but it does demonstrate what may be achieved in certain contexts.

Recent work at ETS on the characterization of the cognitive demands of reading tasks as part of the assessment of literacy skills represents a breakthrough in this area. This work (Mosenthal and Kirsch 1994), which was mentioned above, features a great variety of text and task type. Task demands derive naturally from reading purpose, vary considerably from text to text and may be quite complex, reflecting authentic contexts for reading. Task difficulty is carefully defined by considering the combined characteristics of the stimulus and the task demand. For example, task difficulty in the area of document literacy, one of three types of literacy, is a result of an interaction of document variables (stimulus) and process variables (task demand). The document variables refer to the structural complexity of the text. Process variables include:

1. the type of information the reader is required to identify, according to degree of abstractness;
2. the type of match required between the document and the task; and
3. the plausibility of distracting information within the text.

Figure 7.3

Ability level descriptions, Chinese elementary reading test
[McQueen 1992]

Level 1
The questions in Level 1 (starting with the easiest) were 3, 1, 4, 2, 24, 13, 25.
A typical student at this level can read Pinyin and understand some everyday words and phrases, such as names of family members, numbers and time, and pick out simple information from a short piece of writing dialogue.
Level 2
The questions in Level 2 were 20, 12, 14, 7, 18, 10, 6, 8, 17, 23.
A student at this level can read Pinyin and some Chinese characters covering everyday words and phrases such as time, dates and the location of people and objects, and pick out a piece of information from a dialogue or advertisement.
Level 3
The questions in Level 3 were 21, 16, 5, 9, 19, 15, 22, 11.
A student at this level can understand a range of everyday words and expressions written in Pinyin or Chinese characters, pick out information from a piece of writing and make inferences from the information given.

Figure 7.4

Constructs of document literacy by level of task difficulty
[adapted from Mosenthal and Kirsch 1994]

Level 1	Most of the tasks in this level require readers to identify information which is quite concrete ... Moreover, to complete these tasks, readers must process relatively brief documents to locate a single piece of information given in the question or directive. In some cases, readers must enter personal information (e.g. their name and age) onto a document. If distractors appear in the document, they tend to be representative of either given or new information but not both.
Level 2	Like tasks in Level 1, most task in Level 2 ask readers to complete information which is quite concrete. However, in Level 2, we find some tasks which also require readers to identify 'condition' information. Moreover, tasks at Level 2 often require readers to make a two-feature match or a low-level inference to relate given information to information in a document. Other tasks require readers to make two or more independent cycle matches between a legend and a graph, or between two documents. In other instances, tasks may require readers to integrate information within a document. Finally, tasks at this Level tend to have a distractor for both given and new information present but not in the same mode as the answer

The descriptions of task difficulty are then used as the basis for producing criterion-referenced statements of achievement directly from the task specifications; tasks deemed to be at certain levels of difficulty on a priori grounds are then validated in terms of their assumed difficulty by empirical data from test administrations. The resulting rating scale descriptors are as in Figure 7.4. Levels 1 and 2 of five levels are shown.

This work is a great step forward, and the authors express hope that it can be delivered in a computer-mediated and even computer-adaptive format.

CAT and test method effects

We know that there is considerable variation in personal comfort and familiarity with computers. There is the strong possibility of a method effect in computer-adaptive reading tests, and careful studies will have to be undertaken of the equivalence of the computer-mediated and non-computer-mediated reading tests. I say 'careful' because the nature and precise sources of such method effects if they are found may not be obvious. I wish to draw a parallel with recent work in the area of the assessment of speaking, and will report on a study by O'Loughlin (1995, 1997) which illustrates the point. I will give some detail of this study as the non-obviousness of the findings, and the methodological complexity of the study, suggest both the need for the equivalent research on different formats of reading test, and how this might proceed.

O'Loughlin has studied the equivalence of two formats (direct and semi-direct) of the Speaking subtest of the Access test (Brindley and Wigglesworth 1997), an Australian government test of ESL. The direct format involves live interlocutors; in the indirect format the stimulus for the speaking task is presented on tape, and the candidates response is recorded directly onto a tape. An attempt was made at the design stage to make the formats closely parallel, with mostly very similar tasks on each, and a deliberate attempt to constrain the degree of interactivity of the live version by scripting the contribution of the live interlocutor to mirror the input from the tape in the tape-based version. Standard correlational analyses suggested that scores from the two formats were broadly equivalent. O'Loughlin has used a number of approaches to investigate the equivalence of the two formats more closely. First, using Rasch-based measures of candidate ability for candidates taking the test under both conditions, careful tests of equivalence fail, indicating a significant method effect; this was confirmed in Rasch bias studies. Second, lexical density measures on candidate output under the two conditions reveal significant differences even where the behaviour of the interlocutor is highly constrained. If we take lexical density as a measure of interactivity, it seems that the attempt to suppress interaction in the live version has failed, as we might have predicted—this despite the fact that the interlocutors do on the whole keep to their script. Interactivity is not only a question of the verbal stream. Finally, ethnographic studies of raters, and of candidates actually taking both formats of the test, revealed that interactivity was indeed a key issue. In a case study of individual candidate behaviour, one candidate in fact did better on the tape-based version, being less fazed by the interlocutor factor. So it is not simply as if one format is superior to another, rather that they are different, elicit potentially different kinds of performance, and end up measuring different things. I very much suspect this will be true of computer-adaptive reading tests versus more traditional equivalents. We must commit ourselves to the needed research—but do the glamour and the funding potential associated with the technological wizardry of the CAT actually permit such a study to be carried out, and its findings implemented if it is?

CAT as a conservative force in language testing

We have spoken above about the way in which the typical item format of computer-adaptive tests may be a constraint on the new and promising approaches to reporting performance on reading tests in terms of the cognitive demands of tasks. There are other ways in which CAT may represent a conservative force in language testing. Spolsky in *Measured Words* (1995) has shown us in his careful analysis of the history of TOEFL the danger of institutions testing only what can be tested cheaply. CAT's very efficiency may act as a conservative force in our field. Its commitment to MCQ format questions will have negative implications for washback (assuming we believe in such a phenomenon: cf. Alderson and Wall 1993). The focus of research in CAT is on psychometric and technological issues, rather than on fundamental questions of the nature of the communicative abilities which are the supposed target of assessment and the nature of performance and of the assessment process in performance assessment.

The development of CAT is a social fact which requires social analysis

The main disciplinary influence on language testing, apart from psychometrics, has been psychology; we see the enterprise as focusing the measurement of cognitive traits in the individual candidate. But we need to reorient ourselves to language assessment as a social activity; in Spolsky's words (1995: 351–2) we need to 're-embody' our notions of language proficiency. We must correct our view of the candidate as an isolated figure, who bears the entire brunt of the performance; this abstraction from reality conceals a potentially Kafkaesque world of others whose behaviour and interpretation shapes the perceived significance of the candidates efforts but is removed from focus. We who sit in judgement must come to recognize the way in which our perceptions of candidates' performances are generated by things other than what is in the candidates head.

The current emphasis on the behaviour of the individual candidate in a social and interactional vacuum blinds us to the way in which the act of judgement in language testing involves an inevitable process of idealization and generalization on the part of the tester in making inferences from test performance to criterion behaviour. This process of generalization and idealization is itself a social action, social in genesis, by actors with socially derived motivations and agendas; in this sense the eliciting and the interpretation of the performance (the latter reflected in the score) is a socially constructed activity in which the candidate is only one, and not necessarily even the most important, player. The technically impersonal environment of CAT is perhaps particularly effective in disguising its inherently social nature, as the co-participant is invisible or is represented by a gleaming machine, enhancing the impression of the candidate as an individual involved in a technical, impersonal process. We need a social analysis of the meaning of CAT. Themes of such an analysis would include the way in which the candidates performance is constrained and co-constructed by the technology of CAT and by the test developer's views of language and language performance embodied in the procedures of CAT. Other targets of such analysis would include the deeper social meaning of the technology of CAT, the way in which resources devoted to the expensive technology of CAT could have alternative uses (cf. the largely futile expense in building language laboratories in the 1960s), its restriction to resource-rich settings, and so on.

Conclusion

History has shown that technological fixes are no solution to complex problems in language learning and teaching. One does not have to be a Luddite to recognize that CAT needs the same kind of critical scrutiny as is given to other forms of assessment. CAT is an exciting innovation and the technical and psychometric challenges it presents are fascinating. Nevertheless it must also be considered in a broader context if it is to be answerable to the genuine needs of our field.

Notes

1. Wiggins, writing in an educational rather than an employment context, claims that school-based performances and real-world performances are identical. This suggests that he may be more interested in standards than criteria, as clearly the two contexts differ substantially in the criteria that are applied to performance. Haertel (1992) also insufficiently distinguishes the two settings.

2. In fact, significant advances have been made since the time of writing, and are likely to be reflected in future test formats, for example in the TOEFL 2000 test.

References

Alderson, J. C. (1990a) Testing reading comprehension skills (Part 1). *Reading in a Foreign Language* 6: 425–38.

Alderson, J. C. (1990b) Testing reading comprehension skills (Part 2). *Reading in a Foreign Language* 7: 465–503.

Alderson, J. C. (1995) Response to Lumley. *Language Testing* 12 (1): 122–5.

Alderson, J. C. and Lukmani, Y. (1989) Cognition and levels of comprehension as embodied in the test question. *Reading in a Foreign Language* 5 (2): 253—70.

Alderson, J. C. and Wall, D. (1993) Does washback exist? *Applied Linguistics* 14 (2): 115–29

Brindley, G. and Wigglesworth, G. (Eds.) (1997) *Access: Issues in English Language Test Design and Delivery.* Macquarie University, Sydney National Centre for English Language Teaching and Research:

Brown, A. and Iwashita, N. (1995) *The role of language background in the validation of a computer-adaptive test.* Paper presented at the Language Testing Research Colloquium. Long Beach, CA.

Brown, A. and Iwashita, N. (1996) Language background and item difficulty: The development of a computer-adaptive test of Japanese. *System* 24 (2): 199–206.

Burston, J., Harfouch, J. and Monville-Burston, M. (1995) The French CAT: An assessment of its empirical validity. *Australian Review of Applied Linguistics* 18 (1): 52–68.

Burston, J. and Monville-Burston, M. (1996) Practical design and implementation considerations of a computer-adaptive foreign language test: The Monash/Melbourne French CAT. *CALICO Journal* 13 (1): 23–43.

Carrell, P. L. (1984) The effects of rhetorical organization on ESL readers. *TESOL Quarterly* 18: 441–69.

Carrell, P. L. (1992) Awareness of text structure: Effects on recall. *Language Learning* 42: 1–20.

Elder, C. and Brown, A. (1997) Performance testing for the professions: Language proficiency or strategic competence? *Melbourne Papers in Language Testing* 6 (1): 68–78.

Fitzpatrick, R. and Morrison, E. J. (1971) Performance and product evaluation. In Thorndike, R. L. (Ed.) *Educational Measurement* (2nd ed.), pp. 237–70. American Council on Education, Washington, DC. Reprinted in Finch, F. L. (Ed.) (1991) *Educational Performance Assessment*, pp. 89–138. Chicago, IL: The Riverside Publishing Company.

Haertel, E. (1992) Performance measurement. In Alkin, M. C. (Ed.) *Encyclopedia of Educational Research* (6th edition), New York, NY: Maxwell Macmillian International pp. 984–9.

Hamilton, J., Lopes, M., McNamara, T. F. and Sheridan, E. (1993) Rating scales and native speaker performance on a communicatively oriented EAP test. *Language Testing* 10 (3): 337–53.

Jacoby, S. and McNamara, T. F. (in press). Locating competence. *English for Specific Purposes* 18 (2).

Linn, R. L., Baker, E. L. and Dunbar, S. B. (1991) Complex, performance-based assessment: Expectations and validation criteria. *Educational Researcher* 20 (8): 15–21.

Logan, J. (1992) *Beyond the MCQ jail.* Paper presented at the NCME/ American Educational Research Association Conference. San Francisco, CA.

Lumley, T. (1993) The notion of subskills in reading comprehension tests: An EAP example. *Language Testing* 10 (3): 211–34.

Lumley, T. (1995) Response to Alderson. *Language Testing* 12 (1): 125–30.

McNamara, T. F. (1996) *Measuring Second Language Performance.* London and New York, NY: Addison-Wesley Longman.

McQueen, M. J. (1992) *Item difficulty and Rasch scaling in a test of foreign language reading.* Unpublished MA thesis, University of Melbourne.

Morrow, K. (1983) The Royal Society of Arts Examinations in the Communicative Use of English as a Foreign Language. In Jordan, R. R. (Ed.) *Case Studies in ELT*, pp. 102–7. London and Glasgow: Collins ELT.

Mosenthal, P. B. and Kirsch, I. S. (1994) *Defining the proficiency standards of adult literacy in the U.S.: A profile approach.* Paper presented at the National Reading Conference. San Diego, CA. 4 [Eric Document Reproduction Service ED 379 531].

Mossenson, L., Hill, P. and Masters, G. (1987) *TORCH: Tests of Reading Comprehension. Manual.* Australian Council for Educational Research. Hawthorns Victoria.

O'Loughlin, K. (1995) Lexical density in candidate output on direct and semi-direct versions of an oral proficiency test. *Language Testing* 12 (2): 217–37.

O'Loughlin, K. (1997) *The comparability of direct and semi-direct speaking tests: A case study.* Unpublished PhD thesis, University of Melbourne.

Spolsky, B. (1995) *Measured Words.* Oxford: Oxford University Press.

Stansfield, C. W. (Ed.) (1986) *Toward Communicative Competence Testing: Proceedings of the Second TOEFL Invitational Conference.* Princeton, NJ: Educational Testing Service.

Weir, C. J. (1994) *Reading as multidivisible or unitary: Between Scylla and Charybdis*. Paper presented at RELC Seminar. SEAMEO Regional Language Centre, Singapore.

Weir, C. J., Hughes, A. and Porter, D. (1990) Reading skills: Hierarchies, implicational relationships and identifiability. *Reading in a Foreign Language* 7: 505–10.

Wiggins, G. 1989. A true test: Toward more authentic and equitable assessment. *Phi Delta Kappan* 70 (9): 703–13.

8 From reading theory to testing practice

Carol Chapelle
Iowa State University

Introduction

This chapter acts as a link between the theoretical concerns laid out in the previous section and the computer-adaptive L2 testing issues and practices discussed in this part. It defines and situates critical testing concepts used by authors in this section—*test purpose, inference* and *construct definition*—to show potential connections of theory and research in L2 reading to design and development of computer-adaptive reading tests.

In the previous section, William Grabe and Elizabeth Bernhardt raised a range of theoretical and research concerns that are relevant for advancing a theory of L2 reading, developing pedagogical approaches and laying the foundation for computer-adaptive reading tests. Despite the fact that theory and research on reading are expected to inform decisions about the design of reading tests, as Grabe pointed out, *'the impact of research on reading assessment does not seem to have been very prominent'* (page 35). In other words, as Figure 8.1 illustrates, the link of theory and research on L2 reading to design and development of L2 reading tests appears to be missing. In Figure 8.1, the arrows should be read as 'informs' or 'influences'.

Figure 8.1

The missing link of theory and research on L2 reading to design and development of L2 reading tests

Grabe suggests that the missing link between reading research and assessment practice is due at least in part to the psychometric criteria used to evaluate reading tests. Because reading assessment succeeds by traditional standards, he questions the role that results of reading research can play in the evolution of reading assessment. If research on reading and technology is to *improve* reading assessment, current methods must first be seen by some criteria to be *lacking*.[1] Bernhardt also questions the usability of L2 reading research for practical assessment concerns but on different grounds. She suggests that test developers cannot ignore pressing needs for 'useful, convenient and friendly' tests despite unresolved theoretical issues in L2 reading.

These two impediments against linking theory and research with practice are strengthened by the fact that issues explored in L2 reading research do not appear to address directly the concerns of test construction. The theoretical papers raise questions about stages of development, strategies for lexical recognition and other areas of interest to researchers, whereas the papers in this section exemplify factors of concern to test developers such as test use, psychometric models and software for test delivery. If theory and research are to be included among those factors, the conceptual gap which exists between theory/research and design/development needs to be filled. The papers in the first section take the first step toward filling the gap by identifying what is known—and not known—about L2 reading. The four papers in this section take the next step by addressing practical issues of design and development of computer-adaptive second language tests. With issues laid out on both sides, we can begin to construct some links.

The focal topic in the papers in this section is the design and development of L2 reading tests as they are influenced by a particular *test purpose* and by the *available resources*, as shown in Figure 8.2. The test purpose plays an important role in justifying the choices that are made in test design. For example, Michael Laurier explains how users' wishes for a single score for making placement decisions in French immersion programs influenced the design of his scoring rubric. Design choices are also influenced by available resources including computer hardware and software, time, personnel and their knowledge. In Laurier's French project, test developers had both the time and knowledge to write their own software rather than relying on a pre-packaged template system. In the Hausa listening project that Pat Dunkel describes the availability of resources for a two-year period resulted in particular decisions being made about project goals including test design.

Figure 8.2

The factors affecting test design and development in computer-adaptive language testing projects

The influences on test design decisions described in these papers substantiate Grabe's and Bernhardt's observation about the minimal impact of research on assessment. Rather, the primary influences on design and development of L2 tests are factors that are 'closer to home' for the test developers. However, in the interest of the evolution of CAT for L2 reading, it seems critical to connect these practical concerns with theory and research in L2 reading. To do so, it is necessary to take a closer look at *test purpose*.

Filling the gap through 'test purpose'

Grabe suggests that research on reading might be used to help design tests that could *'provide more accurate information for the purposes of proficiency measurement, diagnosis and performance skills'* (page 36). To take up this suggestion, we would need to explore more thoroughly what is entailed by each of these specific test purposes. In order to do so, we need clarification on what is meant by 'test purpose'. Test purpose can be defined through three interrelated concepts:

1) the *uses* made of test results;
2) the *inferences* made from test performance; and
3) the intended *impacts* of the test (Chapelle and Read 1996).[2]

The uses made of language test results include investigation of second language acquisition (e.g. L2 reading development), evaluation of language instruction and decisions about learners in an educational context. All of the testing projects described in this section have educational uses. The Russian and French tests are intended to help with placement of learners into appropriate classes. The Hausa listening test is described as a proficiency test which might be used to assess readiness for exit from a program, for example. A critical test design decision associated with test use is the method of score reporting. Laurier's decision about score reporting provides a good example. Despite the fact that their placement test at first yields five separate scores corresponding the five parts of the test, '*since the placement decision usually consists in positioning the student on a general competence continuum*', a single score indicting overall ability is desired (page 126). The part scores were therefore combined into a single one to be used for a placement decision. The cases reported in this volume reflect the uses made of other L2 CAT projects to date (e.g. Kaya-Carton *et al.* 1991; Madsen 1991; Burston and Monville-Burston 1996; Brown and Iwashita 1996; Young *et al.* 1996) although as Grabe and Larson point out, other uses might include diagnosis of particular strengths and weaknesses in reading.

Inferences refer to the conclusions drawn about language ability or subsequent language performance on the basis of evidence from test performance. For example, an inference is made about test takers' 'reading comprehension' on the basis of their responses to questions on a reading comprehension test. The term *inference* is used to indicate that the test result is not itself the object of interest to test users. Instead, test users want to know what a test taker might be expected to be capable of in non-test settings.[3] In my view, inferences are the pivotal point at which theory and research on reading might have an impact on test design, and I will therefore expand on this concept in the next section.

Impact as a component of test purpose refers to the effects that test designers intend for the test to have on individuals (e.g. students and teachers), language classes and programs and on society (Bachman and Palmer 1996). For example, Laurier uses impact on test takers as an argument for the CAT by describing it as '*a more pleasant experience for the student*' because the adaptive algorithm selects items at an appropriate level. Dunkel (page 91) introduces the listening test in Hausa as a means of remedying the social problem of a lack of externally-prepared standardized tests for the less-commonly taught languages. Part of McNamara's critical appraisal of CAT is his comment on its impact on the enterprise of language testing: '*CAT's very efficiency may act as a conservative force in our field*'. [language testing] (page 145). These observations illustrate the types of impacts that test designers might consider in constructing their tests (e.g. this test is intended to be a pleasant experience for students).

Figure 8.3 illustrates this elaborated definition of test purpose which one might use for analysis of a particular diagnostic test, for example, by detailing the uses to be made of test results (and therefore the form of the most useful results), the specific inferences to be made on the basis of performance and the intended impacts of test use. As illustrated in Figure 8.3, I suggest that theory and research on L2 reading might play a role—in conjunction with test use and impacts—in defining the inferences to be drawn from test performance. In order for theory and research to help shape the way test inferences are defined for a given test, it is necessary to be more precise about what this term means.

Figure 8.3

**The potential role for theory and research on L2 reading in design
and development of L2 reading tests**

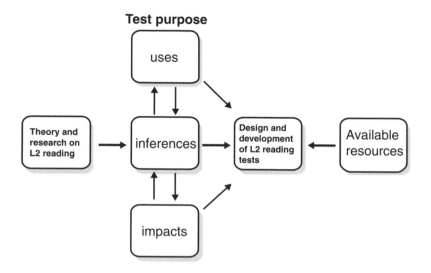

Inferences drawn from test performance

The term 'inference' is used to denote the fact that the test user does not observe directly the object of interest, but instead infers it on the basis of test performance. The object of interest is conceived in different ways depending on whether one takes an 'ability' or a 'performance' orientation to testing. Figure 8.4 illustrates the two different conceptualizations of inferences. Ability testing is based on the point of view that performance on a test is the result of some underlying capacities, which are also responsible for performance in non-test settings. The focal problem in test design is to assess accurately the ability of interest rather than other things. Performance testing, as Figure 8.4 illustrates, aims to make inferences more 'directly' about performance in non-test settings on the basis of test performance. The test design problem in performance testing therefore is constructing a test with characteristics as similar as possible to the non-test setting.

Figure 8.4

**The conceptualization of inference in ability testing vs.
performance testing**

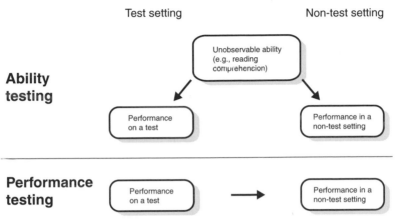

These perspectives on inference are important for the role of theory and research in CAT. Computer-adaptive L2 tests tend to work within the ability tradition, defining inferences as abilities such as 'reading comprehension' or 'overall language ability'. Theory might improve ability testing by offering more precise definitions about what comprises 'reading comprehension'. This is the approach Grabe takes in enumerating the *'the components of the reading process'* (e.g. word recognition and propositional integration). McNamara's paper offers a critical perspective on CAT in part by approaching it from a 'performance' perspective, describing the inferences to be drawn from test performance as *'future performances in a non-test setting'*. He is then able to question aspects of CAT design on the basis of their lack of 'authenticity' relative to reading in non-test settings: *'In terms of authenticity,* computer assisted *reading tasks in fact best simulate the reading of computer text, a perfectly authentic skill in its own right, but not the same skill as reading non-computer text'* (page 139). McNamara gives an anecdote to support this observation, but ideally reading theory might improve testing from the performance perspective by better defining the conditions under which similar performances can be expected. For example, one might hope for a theoretical explanation and empirical research results that substantiate or refute the assertion that reading from a computer screen is different from reading from a printed page.

In short, then, the role of theory and research on reading should be to elaborate the inference to be made on the basis of test performance—in other words, to define the construct that the test is intended to measure. The nature of the inference in turn influences test design decisions. Given the different types of inferences made through the two perspectives on testing, the nature of the construct definitions depends on whether the test developer is working within the ability or performance perspective. Because computer-adaptive reading tests work within the 'ability' tradition, I will focus on construct definition from that perspective.

Construct definition

A construct is a meaningful and useful way of interpreting test performance (Messick 1981). Table 8.1 shows the constructs, or 'meaningful interpretations', that the authors in this section have described for the performances on their tests. In each case, the meaningful interpretation is a single trait that the authors see as useful in their particular testing contexts. For example, the test users in the French immersion programs want to use the measure of 'general ability in French' to place students into levels.

Table 8.1

Examples of construct definition as the meaningful interpretation of observed performance

Author	Observed performance	Meaningful interpretation
Larson	Response to reading comprehension items representing a variety of general content areas, concrete vs. abstract vocabulary and cultural content	general reading proficiency in Russian
Dunkel	Selection of a segment of text, a graphic or a part within a larger graphic to demonstrate successful comprehension of four 'listener functions': identification/recognition, orientation, main idea comprehension and detail comprehension	listening comprehension proficiency in Hausa
Laurier	Response to items requiring 1) comprehension of approximately 30-word paragraphs, 2) sociolinguistic judgements, 3) filling in a blank with content and function words, 4) comprehension of short aural segments, self-assessment	general ability in French

The constructs in these examples illustrate the *trait*-oriented constructs endemic to classic ability testing. Trait constructs, which are defined independently of the context of language use, require that test tasks sample across contexts so that the ability can be assumed to be a 'general' one.[4] Larson's explanation of the principle underlying the Russian CAT provides a good example of the influence of the trait construct on test design decisions:

> *Government agency tests are constructed and administered in order to test consistent and sustained performance in general proficiency. These general proficiency skills are stressed by using general language contexts and topics. To accomplish this purpose, the BYU/LTD reading tests were initially designed to allow three questions in a single content area, then the computer would be instructed to select items from other content areas.* (page 86)

This trait perspective is not unique to language testing. It is also evident throughout much of the discussion in the theory papers. For example, Bernhardt identifies two types of on-line syntactic processing, assigning correct grammatical meaning to inflected words and grammatical function to sentence constituents, pointing out that if one can perform these syntactic processes efficiently during reading, '[w]*hether this happens within a friendly letter or within a magazine report is irrelevant; when it happens—that is the crucial dimension in assigning proficiency levels.*' (page 8). Similarly, Grabe's paper identifies a number of component reading processes (e.g. word recognition) which he defines in a context-independent manner. Given some consistency of perspective between construct definition in current CAT and definition of reading components by researchers, it seems, at least on the surface, that research might be able to contribute substantively to construct definition by suggesting the components that comprise the L2 reading process.

Ten years ago, I could have stopped there in the discussion of construct definition from the ability perspective. Recently, however, even within the ability perspective, test users are hoping to make inferences about more specifically-defined constructs–constructs that are defined relative to a particular context of language use. Such construct definitions include both a cognitive skill or capacity and a domain where the capacity is relevant, such as 'reading for *academic purposes*'. This more complex construct definition, which requires definition of both the trait and the context, is called an 'interactionalist' construct definition (Messick 1981, 1989; Zuroff 1986). An interactionalist approach to construct definition is consistent with current views in applied linguistics that suggest language users might be good at using the target language for some purposes but not for others.[5] This approach also evidences influences from work in both performance testing (McNamara 1996) and language for specific purposes (Douglas forthcoming). In other words, as Figure 8.5 illustrates, the interactionalist construct definition has a narrower scope than the trait-type construct definitions exemplified in Table 8.1.

Figure 8.5

Inferences made in ability testing with an interactionalist construct definition

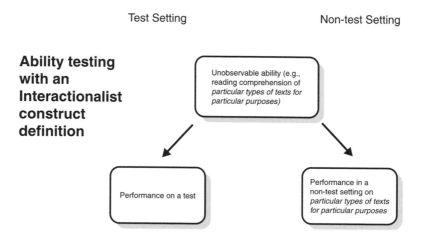

When we look at the evolutionary influence that theory and research on reading might have on CAT in the 1990s, it seems necessary to think in terms of an interactionalist construct definition. The question is the following: what specific contributions can theory and research contribute toward both the 'trait' and the 'context' side of the interactionalist construct definition to improve CAT for L2 reading?

Towards a role for theory and research

A construct was defined as a 'meaningful and useful' way of interpreting test performance. Presumably, each trait-type construct definition illustrated in Table 8.1 holds an important meaning for its respective test use. However, the question is whether or not more meanings can be derived from performance on CAT reading tests if theory and research are consulted for construct definition. I will look at this possibility from the perspective of an interactionalist construct definition. In other words, I will consider the role of theory and research for both the trait and the context aspects of the construct definition.

Moving away from monolithic trait constructs

With respect to the trait aspect of the construct definition, a large gap obviously exists between the multidimensional, process-oriented components Bernhardt and Grabe describe and the monolithic labels that CAT developers use to name the constructs their tests are intended to measure. Figure 8.6 illustrates a continuum of potential approaches to construct definitions for the trait aspect of an interactionalist construct definition. On the left-hand side is the construct definition typically used in CAT (e.g., reading comprehension or overall language proficiency). On the right-hand side is the complex processing model suggested by reading research. Bernhardt sees the definitions at the two ends of the continuum as contradictory, pointing out that her model of L2 reading is a 'multidimensional' and 'multiparameter' one. She raises the concern that has been debated repeatedly (e.g. Canale 1986; Henning 1992; Henning *et al.* 1985) about L2 CATs: '*At issue is ... how [the multidimensional model] fits with assessment models that assume unidimensionality of the data.*' (page 3). However, this concern rests on the assumption that complex models posited by reading theory should necessarily be pressed into service as construct definitions for tests. This assumption bypasses a critical step in test design: defining the construct that the test is intended to measure.[6]

Figure 8.6

The continuum of possibilities for trait-type construct definition

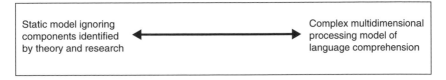

A construct definition requires a 'meaningful and useful' way of interpreting test performance, but what is meaningful and useful, of course, depends on who is doing the interpreting and what they consider useful. In the CAT projects reported in this section, the test users wanted single scores. Even the five component scores that Laurier could have interpreted as meaningful were not seen as useful by test users who wanted simple placement information. As long as test users request a single score representing static models, is there any role for theory and research on CATs?

There are at least two approaches to beginning to move from left to right along the continuum. The first, as Grabe and Larson suggest, is to consider alternative test uses (e.g. diagnosis vs. placement testing). By so doing, test developers are working for a different set of test users (i.e. teachers and learners vs. administrators) who may be prepared to find more detailed construct definitions meaningful and useful because uses might include providing evidence for what needs to be taught and learned. Second, the construct definition should serve not only the audience of the test user, but also those who design, develop and investigate the validity of the test. If we think of a construct as needing to be useful for constructing item/task specifications for the test, there is a role for the greater detail provided by theory and research on reading. If we think of a construct as useful for framing hypotheses about performance across types of items, there is a need for theory and research on reading to inform construct definition. In short, the use of information provided by complex processing models of L2 reading needs to be selectively applied to developing the trait side of a construct definition (Nichols 1994). The application involves purposefully moving from the left toward the right on the continuum. Decisions about how far to move in constructing a more detailed construct definition need to be based on its 'meaningfulness and usefulness' in view of who will interpret the meaning and what use they will make of it.

Including appropriate reading 'contexts'

The context part of the interactionalist construct definition has a similarly large gap between current testing practice and theory in applied linguistics. In the continuum shown in Figure 8.7, the left side, 'no substantive theory', represents the current CAT approaches to construct definition. Influences on test performance believed to come from the testing context are treated as error, called 'method effects' as McNamara points out in his discussion of method effects associated with live vs. taped oral interview test (page 144). From the trait perspective, 'method effects' are bad because they contaminate observed test performance with influences not associated with the trait construct. From the interactionalist perspective, however, 'method effects' can be good if they influence performance in the desired way. For example, an interactionalist construct definition would define 'live interactive spoken conversation with a person' as a different construct from 'spoken "conversation" with a machine', and, as a consequence, would predict performance in the two settings to be different.

Figure 8.7

The continuum of possibilities for inclusion of 'context' in construct definition

The interactionalist construct definition requires that the features of the

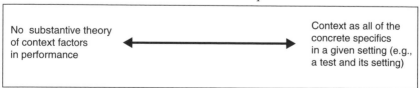

No substantive theory of context factors in performance ←——————→ Context as all of the concrete specifics in a given setting (e.g., a test and its setting)

context be included in the construct definition because the context is hypothesized to influence performance. This requirement, however, raises a problem that is analogous to the one described above. Sociolinguists will tell us that there is a complex set of specific context features which influence performance in any given setting. For example, if one were to define the complete context of the construct measured by the spoken conversation test, one would include the speaker's goals, topics, physical setting, duration of time, roles and relationship relative to the interviewer, interest and knowledge about the topic and task, the role of the language in the event, the channel (oral/written) and the time pressure for production and comprehension (e.g., Perrett 1990). If the test designer takes a sociolinguist's approach, attempting to name all of these, the risk is a construct definition that is too complex to be meaningful and useful to anyone but a sociolinguist! In language testing, it is not useful to assess ability on a construct that is defined so narrowly that it applies only to ability to complete the test. Abilities measured by tests are useful if they are expected to influence performance beyond the test—in at least some other contexts.

In language teaching and testing, the most popular alternative to expressing 'context' through excessive numbers of contextual features is to evoke the folk concept of 'authenticity'. McNamara illustrates the use of the authenticity concept in his discussion of reading tests delivered by computer:

> *Text presentation and handling on computer are relatively clumsy and inauthentic, although this is improving rapidly in the area of simulation of layout and the incorporation of graphics. In terms of authenticity, computer-assisted reading tasks in fact best simulate the reading of computer text, a perfectly authentic skill in its own right, but not the same skill as reading non-computer text. (page 139)*

Similarly, Bernhardt criticizes materials used in reading research on the basis of the fact that they are 'researcher generated' rather than 'authentic'. Despite the ease with which the term is used, 'authenticity' is a relative concept (as McNamara points out), which itself is undefined and therefore does not help in construct definition.

A more revealing approach is that initiated in language testing by Bachman's identification of 'test method facets' that are expected to influence test performance (Bachman 1990). The test method facets, or test task characteristics (Bachman and Palmer 1996), are a list of contextual features that can be used in a framework for test development of CAT (e.g. Chalhoub-Deville *et al.* 1996). They can also be used for analysis of both the testing context and the non-test setting, thereby providing a basis for defining authenticity of a test *relative* to a non-test setting because specific features can be compared across settings. Moreover, they serve as hypotheses about features which may influence performance and are therefore *relevant to construct definition*. For the purposes of construct definition, however, the many features of the test task characteristics should be placed toward the right end of the continuum: they may be too numerous to satisfy the need for a meaningful and useful definition.

To find the middle ground between too much and no context for a construct definition, it is useful to examine the approaches taken by Dunkel in her CAT listening test, and by Kirsch and Mosenthal in the research described by McNamara. In each of these testing projects, the authors attempted to identify contextual factors that they thought would influence performance in a way that was relevant to the construct definition. Dunkel identified—in addition to the 'listener functions' that would be considered as part of the trait part of ability—two 'context' variables, length of input and type of option. The 'length of input' had two levels: word or phrase and longer monologue or dialogue. The type of option could be a text choice, a graphic choice or one part of a graphic within a larger one. These variables of the test were expected to influence performance and therefore predictions of item difficulty were made on the basis of which variables were included in each item. Unfortunately, '[t]*he analysis of variance showed the absence of a statistical relationship between the full item-writing model (i.e. the dimensions of the conceptual framework used to create the item bank) and the [observed] difficulty of the items ... allowing us to tentatively reject the notion that the conceptual framework is related to item difficulty'* (page 105). One might also request a more explicit statement of how the selected context variables helped to define the construct measured. Nevertheless, this approach provides an example of how one might take a step to the right from the left end of the continuum.

McNamara describes a progressive testing project that steps even further to the right on the continuum. Attempting to assess 'document literacy' of native speakers, Kirsch and Mosenthal (1988, 1990) work with a construct defined in part by the contextual features of purpose and document text features. 'Documents' refer to written materials such as forms, charts and labels, which one might read in order to subscribe to a magazine, find which bus to take, or determine the appropriate dosage of medicine, respectively. *'Task demands derive naturally from reading purpose, vary considerably from text to text and may be quite complex, reflecting authentic contexts for reading. Task difficulty is carefully defined by considering the combined characteristics of the stimulus and the task demand'* (page 142). In this research, the defined variables were significant predictors of test difficulty, which means that these factors are the ones responsible for test takers' performance. Work remains to better understand how the purpose and text variables help to define the construct of document literacy, but this type of work makes important moves toward the right on the continuum.

Conclusion

Modern approaches to language testing presume that designing L2 tests requires input from L2 theory and research. However, when faced with specific, practical testing projects, we often find it difficult to articulate exactly what kind of input is needed and what effect it should have on test design decisions. The theory and research outlined by Grabe and Bernhardt do not transfer directly to issues in language testing; instead, they lay out the theoretical issues that may inform the definition of inferences made from test performance. The next four chapters illustrate how practical testing issues influence the inferences that they make on the basis of test performance. It is essential to examine both sides of the theory–practice dyad to begin to explore the middle ground, as I have attempted to do.

Notes

1. This observation about the mechanisms by which change can occur is developed thoroughly by Markee (1997) in relation to curricular change. Many of the points about the role of attitudes, perceptions and ideologies in classroom change are equally relevant to testing.
2. In the past, one may not have thought of intended 'impacts' as a part of test purpose, but we have included it to signify that test developers should consider impacts as part of test design. An explicit statement of impacts provides a starting point for subsequent validation work that includes analysis of consequences, or 'washback'.
3. This is an important point which is sometimes lost in part due to the use of the term 'direct' for some tests. Because test users are not interested in test takers' performance on the test alone, all tests are indirect (Bachman 1990). Performance on the test is used as an indicator of ability (which is believed to affect subsequent performance) or of subsequent performance.
4. The fact that constructs can be defined in a number of different ways is important for test design (Chapelle forthcoming). If a test's purpose is to make inferences about a general construct such as reading comprehension, language proficiency or communicative competence, test design must, for example, specify that tasks be selected systematically from a broad domain of possible tasks. On a test of general reading comprehension, test design might specify that the input for reading tasks be drawn from a variety of sources such as newspapers, magazines, advertisements, letters and stories.
5. The interactionalist construct definition is also consistent with perspectives taken by some SLA researchers who find that cognitive theories of SLA fall short in their treatment of the interplay between contextual factors and ability (e.g. Young 1989; Tarone 1988; Ellis 1989).

6. See Snow and Lohman (1989) for a thorough discussion of the difference between the types of 'models' used in educational measurement and in psychology.

Acknowledgement

I am grateful to John Read and Larry Frase for many useful conversations which helped to formulate the conception of test design influenced by test purposes and available resources.

References

Bachman, L.F. (1990) *Fundamental Considerations in Language Testing.* Oxford: Oxford University Press.

Bachman, L. F. and Palmer, A. S. (1996) *Language Testing in Practice.* Oxford: Oxford University Press.

Brown, A. and Iwashita, N. (1996) Language background and item difficulty: The development of a computer-adaptive test of Japanese. *System* 24 (2): 199–206.

Burston, J. and Monville-Burston, M. (1996) Practical design and implementation considerations of a computer-adaptive foreign language test: The Monash/Melbourne French CAT. *CALICO Journal* 13 (1): 23–43.

Canale, M. (1986) The promise and threat of computerized adaptive assessment of reading comprehension. In Stansfield, C. W. (Ed.) *Technology and Language Testing*, pp. 30–45. Washington, DC: TESOL Publications.

Chalhoub-Deville, M., Alcaya, C. and Lozier, V. M. (1996) *An operational framework for constructing a computer-adaptive test of L2 reading ability: Theoretical and practical issues. CARLA Working Paper Series #1.* Centre for the Advanced Research on Language Acquisition, University of Minnesota, Minneapolis, MN.

Chapelle, C. (forthcoming) Construct definition and validity inquiry in SLA research. In Bachman, L. F. and Cohen, A. D. (Eds.) *Second Language Acquisition and Language Testing Interfaces.* Cambridge: Cambridge University Press.

Chapelle, C. and Read, J. (1996) *Toward a framework for vocabulary assessment.* Work-in-progress presentation at the Language Testing Research Colloquium, Tampere, Finland.

Douglas, D. (forthcoming) *Testing Language for Specific Purposes.* Cambridge: Cambridge University Press.

Dunkel, P. (Ed.) (1991) Computer-assisted Language Learning and Testing: Research issues and Practice. New York, NY: Newbury House.

Ellis, R. (1989) Sources of intra-learner variability in language use and their relationship to second language acquisition. In Gass *et al.* pp. 22–45.

Gass, S., Madden, C., Preston, D. and Selinker, L. (Eds.) (1989) *Variation in Second Language Acquisition, Volume II: Psycholingustic Issues.* Philadelphia, PA: Multilingual Matters.

Henning, G. T. (1992) Dimensionality and construct validity of language tests. *Language Testing* 9 (1): 1–11.

Henning, G.T., Hudson, T. and Turner, J. (1985) Item response theory and the assumption of unidimensionality for language tests. *Language Testing* 2 (2): 141–54.

Kaya-Carton, E., Carton, A. S. and Dandonoli, P. (1991) Developing a computer-adaptive test of French reading proficiency. In Dunkel pp. 259–84.

Kirsch, I. S. and Mosenthal, P. B. (1988) *Understanding document literacy: Variables underlying the performance of young adults.* (Report no. ETS RR-88-62). Princeton, NJ: Educational Testing Service.

Kirsch, I. S. and Mosenthal, P. B. (1990) Exploring document literacy: Variables underlying performance of young adults. *Reading Research Quarterly* 25 (1): 5–30.

Linn, R. L. (Ed.) (1989) Educational Measurement (3rd ed.). New York, NY: Macmillian Publishing Co.

Madsen, H. S. (1991) Computer-adaptive testing of listening and reading comprehension: The Brigham Young University approach. In Dunkel, pp. 237–57.

Markee, N. (1997) *Managing Curricular Innovation.* Cambridge: Cambridge University Press.

McNamara, T. (1996) *Measuring Second Language Performance.* London and New York, NY: Addison-Wesley Longman.

Messick, S. (1981) Constructs and their vicissitudes in educational and psychological measurement. *Psychological Bulletin* 89: 575–88.

Messick, S. (1989) Validity. In Linn, pp. 13–103.

Nichols, P. D. (1994) A framework for developing cognitively diagnostic assessments. *Review of Educational Research* 64 (4): 575–603.

Perrett, G. (1990) The language testing interview: A reappraisal. In de Jong, J. H. A. L. and Stevenson, D. K. (Eds.) *Individualizing the Assessment of Language Abilities*, pp. 225–38. Clevedon, Avon: Multilingual Matters Ltd.

Snow, R. E. and Lohman, D. F. (1989) Implications of cognitive psychology for educational measurement. In Linn, pp. 263–331.

Tarone, E. (1988) *Variation in Interlanguage.* London: Edward Arnold.

Young, R. (1989) Ends and means: Methods for the study of interlanguage variation. In Gass *et al.* pp. 65–90.

Young, R., Shermis, M. D., Brutten, S. and Perkins, K. (1996) From conventional to computer adaptive testing of ESL reading comprehension. *System* 24 (1): 32–40.

Zuroff, D. C. (1986) Was Gordon Allport a trait theorist? *Journal of Personality and Social Psychology* 51: 933–1000.

9 Selected technical issues in the creation of computer-adaptive tests of second language reading proficiency

Daniel Eignor
Educational Testing Service

Introduction

While basic psychometric procedures for constructing computer-adaptive tests (CATs) have been in place for a number of years (see Wainer *et al.* 1990; Lord 1980; Weiss 1983), it has been only recently that a number of other important issues in the construction or creation of CATs have been addressed. This chapter will focus on three of these recently addressed issues:

1. how to deal with complex content specifications in the CAT construction process;
2. how to control item exposure in CAT administrations; and
3. if the CAT is to be set based, the level of IRT modeling, individual item or total set, that should be implemented.

Each of these CAT issues will be discussed in two CAT construction contexts, the first being the construction of large-scale, high-stakes examinations of second language reading proficiency, and the other the construction of smaller-scale, lower-stakes examinations in the field. In preparing these discussion sections, the author will draw upon his experiences while being involved in a number of CAT development projects at Educational Testing Service (ETS), including the development of a computer-based version of the Test of English as a Foreign Language (TOEFL), which was implemented operationally in July 1998.

Dealing with content specifications in the CAT construction process

In earlier discussions of CAT in books such as Lord (1980) and Weiss (1983), the role of test content in the CAT construction process was given only minimal consideration. If discussed at all, test specifications were generally viewed as simple two-way grids of the underlying content by process dimensions and the CAT procedure was set up to work systematically through the cells of the grid, selecting a prespecified number of items from each cell subject to the additional stipulation that each item typically provide maximum item response theory (IRT) information at the current estimate of ability. Kingsbury and Zara (1989) describe such a procedure in detail, referring to it as a constrained-CAT or C-CAT procedure. Early work in the implementation of computer-adaptive tests, such as the College Board Computerized Placement Tests (CPTs), made use of the C-CAT methodology (see Ward 1988), but the procedure has also been used recently in the development and implementation of the National Council of State Boards of Nursing (NCSBN) Nursing Licensure examinations (NCLEX using CAT; see Eignor, Way and Amoss 1994). If test specifications can be configured as two-way grids, the C-CAT procedure can effectively deal with content issues in the CAT construction process.

Unfortunately, test specifications for many current tests cannot be expressed as simple two-way grids. Specifications are frequently overlapping, i.e., the same item can satisfy multiple specifications (usually referred to as constraints), and specifications are often multi-level; i.e., a given constraint may contain multiple sub-constraints. See Stocking and Swanson (1993) for further discussion of these complex constraint systems.

Almost coincidental from a time perspective with the need to deal with complex specifications in the CAT construction process came a renewed interest in procedures for automated construction of paper-and-pencil test forms. These efforts began with initial work by Theunissen (1985, 1986) and have extended in a number of different yet related directions. Common to all procedures is the use of algorithmic approaches, usually based on integer linear programming techniques, and the use of a target information curve or curves (i.e., minimum and maximum target curves). Armstrong *et al.* (1996) have classified these automated test construction approaches into three categories; for purposes of this paper, it seems reasonable to group two of these categories together. These categories are then:

1) models making use of formal constraints that search for constrained-optimal solutions. Included here are models by Armstrong *et al.* (1992), the earlier mentioned Theunissen models, and a number of other related procedures developed for the most part by psychometricians in the Netherlands (see, for instance, van der Linden and Boekkooi-Timminga 1989); and
2) approaches or heuristics that do not search for constrained-optimal solutions. Included in this category are Ackerman's (1989) model, Luecht and Hirsch's (1992) average growth approximation algorithm, which extends Ackerman's model, and the weighted deviations algorithm of Swanson and Stocking (1993).

Swanson and Stocking compare in some detail these two categories of approaches.

Certain of these automated test construction procedures, namely the heuristic procedures, have provided a basis for dealing with complex content specifications or constraints in the CAT construction process. Such procedures are algorithmic in nature and it is relatively easy to replace the constraint dealing with the selection of the next item that best contributes to 'filling' a target test information curve for a paper-and-pencil form with a constraint dealing with the selection of the next item that provides maximum information at a current ability estimate for a CAT. However, only one of the procedures, the Stocking/Swanson weighted deviations approach (see Stocking and Swanson 1993), has been used to date in the development of a number of large-scale CATs having complex content specifications. These tests include the Graduate Records Examination (GRE) General CAT (see Eignor *et al.* 1993), the Praxis I CAT (see Eignor, Folk, Li and Stocking 1994), and sections of the recently implemented TOEFL computer-based test. The description of the Stocking/Swanson weighted deviations model that follows is taken from Eignor *et al.* (1993).

The Stocking/Swanson weighted deviations model

The underlying philosophy of the Stocking/Swanson weighted deviations model, which makes it ideally suited for the construction of CATs subject to a large number of constraints, is as follows: test assembly is less concerned with optimizing some function of the items selected (for example, maximizing test information or minimizing test length) or even meeting formally all constraints of interest (as is done by methods that search for constrained-optimal solutions) than it is with coming 'as close as possible' to meeting all constraints simultaneously. Thus constraints, including statistical constraints, are thought of as more like 'desired properties' than as true constraints. This approach allows for the possibility of constructing a test that may lack each of the desired properties at the expected levels while at the same time minimizing failures in the aggregate. Moreover, the model provides for the possibility that not all constraints are equally important by incorporating explicit relative weights as part of the modeling of constraints.

With this model, the constraints are formulated as bounds on the number of items having specified properties to appear on the CAT. The constraints need not, and most frequently do not, divide the item pool into mutually exclusive subsets. Rather, each item can have many different features that satisfy many different constraints. Statistical constraints on item selection are treated like the other constraints. The algorithm seeks to minimize the weighted sum of positive deviations from these constraints. It employs a successive item selection procedure that makes it especially useful for CAT construction purposes.

Through the use of constraints and item lists, the following four areas of concern are accounted for by the weighted deviations model.

Content specifications

The control of item features or properties is accomplished through the use of explicit constraints, that is, lower and upper bounds (which may be equal) on the desired number of items that possess the particular feature and that are to appear on the CAT.

Item overlap

Item overlap on a CAT is controlled by employing overlap groups. An overlap group consists of a listing of items, compiled clerically or with help of the computer, that may not appear together on the same CAT. These groups are used by the item selection algorithm to avoid the selection of an item that appears in a group with an item already administered.

Item sets

Item sets, whether based on a common stimulus or common directions, need to be administered in a fashion such that items belonging to the set are not interrupted by the administration of items not belonging to the set. Each item set is assigned a conceptual partition of the item pool (a block); items not belonging to the set are not considered to be part of the partition. The partition or block will, in most cases, contain more items than will be administered on any particular CAT.

Statistical specifications

This is controlled by a single constraint and the explicit weight is set to some relatively large number. The weighted deviations algorithm then selects the item that has the largest maximum likelihood item information at the examinee's current estimate of ability, subject to the item satisfying as many other constraints as possible.

In summary, with the weighted deviations model, the next item to be administered in a CAT is the item that simultaneously:

1. is the most informative at the examinee's current estimated ability level; and
2. contributes the most to the satisfaction of all other constraints in addition to the constraint on item information.

At the same time, it is required that the item:

3. does not appear in an overlap group containing an item already administered; and
4. is in the current block (if in a block), starts a new block, or is in no block. security.

Implications for adaptive testing of second language reading proficiency

Clearly, the amount of algorithmic development that will be needed to support an adaptive test of second language reading proficiency is a direct function of the test specifications for the test. If specifications can be kept relatively simple, as might be the case for low-stakes exams, where specifications might take the form of exclusive cells of a two-way grid, test construction procedures such as the C-CAT procedure should function well. For more complex content schemes, approaches like the weighted deviations algorithm will need to be employed. While the weighted deviations algorithm has been successfully employed in constructing a number of CAT systems, other approaches such as that of Luecht and Hirsch (1992) would also be likely to work well. It should also be noted that algorithmic approaches making use of procedures for constrained-optimal solutions may also work well in this context, and a good deal of developmental work is currently underway in this area (see van der Linden and Reese 1997; Amstrong *et al.* 1997).

As mentioned earlier, the adaptive sections of the TOEFL computer-based test (CBT) make use of the Stocking/Swanson weighted deviations algorithm for item selection purposes. This is partly because of the level of complexity of the test specifications for each section of TOEFL and partly because the algorithm had been used for a number of years in the automated construction of TOEFL paper-and-pencil forms, and a lot of hands-on experience had been accumulated.

Controlling item exposure in CAT administrations

With even the simplest CAT construction procedures, certain items in the item pool will end up being administered more frequently than others. For example, with an algorithm that selects solely based on item information, items that provide more information at selected ability levels will be chosen more often than items providing less information. Hence a number of different procedures, ranging in degree of complexity, have been developed to control the exposure rate of items in a CAT pool.

Any scheme that seeks to control the exposure of items in a CAT will employ a mechanism or mechanisms that override the item selection procedure in use, thus degrading the quality of the resulting CAT. Longer tests will therefore be required to achieve the level of efficiency obtained when only the item selection procedure in use governs the choice of the next item, but longer tests can be viewed as a reasonable exchange for greater item security.

Early attempts to control for item exposure made use of randomization or count-down randomization approaches, although such procedures are employed with a number of CATs being used operationally at this point in time. A typical count-down randomization approach might be to select the first item to be administered in a CAT randomly from a group of the five most appropriate items, the second randomly from a group of the four most appropriate, the third randomly from a group of the three most appropriate, and the fourth randomly from a group of the two most appropriate. The fifth and subsequent items would then be chosen to be optimal, given the set of other constraints to be satisfied. (See McBride and Martin 1983.) The assumption with such an approach is that after some set of initial items, examinees will be sufficiently differentiated so that the subsequent items that are selected will vary a great deal.

Eignor *et al.* (1993) describe the development of a prototype CAT version of the SAT. An eight item count-down randomization procedure was used for controlling item exposure with the SAT verbal and math prototype CATs; i.e. the first item to be administered was randomly chosen from the set of the best eight items, the second chosen from the set of the best seven, and so forth. In follow-up simulation work, Eignor *et al.* found that while overall average exposure rates across items could be kept around 10% (i.e., 10% of the simulation population on average would see an item), certain of the items in the verbal and math pools had individual exposure rates of up to 60%. While it is difficult to generalize from such results because the exposure control procedure employed interacts with the item selection procedure (Eignor *et al.* used the Stocking/Swanson weighted deviations algorithm), these results were deemed sufficiently problematic that other CATs based on the weighted deviations algorithm developed at Educational Testing Service have made use of different procedures for controlling item exposure.

One variation on the count-down randomization procedure just described involves the possibility of never choosing the next item at a particular point in the CAT in an optimal fashion; that is, the minimum set size to choose from would always be two or greater. This approach recognizes that in spite of an attempt to randomize initial items, examinees with similar abilities may still end up receiving many of the same items later in the test unless controls are placed on the exposure of these items.

The level at which this randomization factor is set will depend in part on the size and quality of the item pool. With the NCSBN NCLEX using CAT exams described earlier, this randomization factor was set at 10 (see Way, 1994). The sizes of the NCLEX item pools used when simulation work was done to support this decision were extremely large however, upwards of 1600 items. In addition, the C-CAT rather than the weighted deviations item selection procedure was implemented and the one-parameter logistic (1-PL) or Rasch model was used for calibration purposes. With the Rasch model, only item difficulty determines the information provided by an item at a particular ability level, and many more items can be considered 'statistically interchangeable' than when using the more complex IRT models.

The randomization procedures just described attempt to control item exposure in an indirect fashion. As mentioned previously, results for the SAT CAT prototype were sufficiently poor that ETS has abandoned use of these procedures with the weighted deviations algorithm. Instead, ETS now uses extensions of a probabilistic model first suggested by Sympson and Hetter (1985). This procedure, which will be briefly described next, is a good deal more complex than the randomization procedures and requires a CAT simulation system because a fairly lengthy set of simulations will need to be done. Descriptions of CAT simulations systems are beyond the scope of this chapter; see papers by Eignor *et al.* (1993) and Way (1994) for descriptions of simulation systems used at ETS.

The following description of the Sympson and Hetter procedure is taken from Eignor *et al.* (1993). The procedure distinguishes between the probability $P(S)$ that an item is selected as optimal in an adaptive test for an examinee randomly sampled from a typical group of examinees, and $P(A/S)$, the probability that an item is administered, given that it has been selected. If an item is administered every time it is selected as the optimal item, the item might become overexposed. The procedure seeks to control the overall probability that an item is administered, $P(A) = P(A/S)*P(S)$, and to insure that the maximum value over all $P(A)$s is less than some value r. This value r is the expected (not observed) maximum rate of item usage.

The conditional probability $P(A/S) = k$ is some fraction that indicates the proportion of the time an item is selected that it should actually be administered. The exposure control parameters, k, one for each item, are determined through a series of simulations (described in detail in Stocking 1993) using an already established adaptive test procedure, such as the weighted deviations algorithm, and simulees drawn from a typical distribution of ability.

Once the exposure control parameters have been established, they are used in the adaptive test as follows.

1. Select the next item for administration.
2. Generate a random number uniformly distributed between 0 and 1.
3. If the random number is less than or equal to the exposure control parameter for the selected item, administer the item.
4. If the random number is greater than the exposure control parameter for the selected item, do not administer the item, and remove it from the pool of remaining items for this examinee. Repeat this procedure for the next-most-optimal item. Continue until an item is found that can be administered.

The original Sympson/Hetter methodology was developed to control the exposure rates of discrete items only. A number of the CATs that have subsequently been built contain combinations of discrete items and sets of items based on common stimulus material, as in a set of quantitative items based on the same diagram. Stocking (1993) extended the Sympson/Hetter procedure to deal with both the stimulus material and the items. This extension follows the same logic as the original Sympson/Hetter procedure, and the stimuli have exposure control parameters along with the items. This procedure, which is referred to as the Extended Sympson/Hetter procedure, was implemented with the CATs constructed at ETS after careful study through simulations.

The Sympson/Hetter and Extended Sympson/Hetter procedures attempt to control for item exposure rates unconditional on ability. In the simulations, exposure rates with a typical distribution of examinee abilities are studied for the items. Subsequent operational experience with the GRE General CAT has suggested that it is also important to study and control exposure rates at selected ability levels and not just in some overall fashion. To accommodate this tighter level of control on exposure rates, Stocking and Lewis (1995a, 1995b) have further extended the basic Sympson/Hetter methodology to work at the conditional (on ability) level, and refer to the new procedure as the multinominal control procedure. This procedure, which is considerably more complex than the original Sympson/Hetter procedure, requires even larger item pools than the original procedure and extensive simulation work before implementation.

To date, the new Stocking/Lewis multinominal procedure has been tested via simulation work and then implemented with GRE General CAT pools, and has been shown to be an effective procedure provided the pools are both large and 'rich' enough, i.e., have sufficient numbers of items at various ability levels. The new procedure was also used with the sections of the TOEFL computer-based test that are adaptive in nature.

Implications for adaptive testing of second language reading proficiency

Regardless of whether the adaptive test to be developed is high or low stakes, any item exposure control procedure under consideration will need to be studied before it is actually implemented. The best way to do such study is via simulation techniques, and certain of the procedures will require fairly extensive computer simulation systems.

For low-stakes tests, somewhat higher exposure rates can typically be tolerated. Also, if multiple pools are available for use simultaneously, item exposure rates can be directly controlled through the process of distribution of pools to examinees. In such low-stakes situations, it seems reasonable to begin by attempting to implement one of the randomization approaches and then studying performance via simulation. As has been the experience with the NCLEX using CAT, the larger the item pool, the higher the randomization factor that can be set.

Practical experience with tests like the GRE General CAT suggests that one of the more complex procedures will need to be implemented if the second language test in question is of a high-stakes variety. Implementation of one of these procedures is clearly non-trivial, and requires extensive simulation work. The payoff is that these procedures will clearly increase the 'life' of certain items in the pool.

Modeling item sets for CATs

A number of the different CATs now being administered operationally make use of item sets, such as when a reading passage is presented on screen and then followed by a set of adaptively chosen questions based on that passage. Examples include the Verbal section of the GRE General CAT and the Praxis I Reading CAT. The IRT calibration to support these CATs was done at the individual item level, using one of the IRT models for dichotomously or right/wrong scored data. The three-parameter logistic (3-PL) model has been used, for instance, with both the GRE General and Praxis I CATs. Typically, item sets are pretested in an intact fashion and then calibrated and placed in the pool. Items for a CAT are then selected on an item-by-item basis from the complete set of items related to the passage, making use of individual item information in the process. For instance, for the GRE General Verbal CAT discussed in Eignor *et al.* (1993), the pool of reading comprehension passages contains 31 passages having from five to ten items per passage. (The pool also contains discrete antonym, analogy and sentence completion items which also appear on the CATs.) Any CAT constructed from the pool then contains three passages, with two of the passages having two items each and the other having four items, along with the other item types mentioned above.

Wainer and Kiely (1987) were the first to introduce the notion of a testlet in the IRT calibration context. A testlet is a group or set of items to be treated as an intact unit for calibration purposes. Wainer and Kiely felt that the use of testlets would help overcome difficulties experienced with item parameter estimates for individual items caused by context and item positions effects. Within a testlet, items maintain their positions with respect to the other items. Wainer and Kiely were also aware, however, of the relevance of the testlet notion to sets of items related to the same stimulus material. Such sets of items are likely to demonstrate considerable 'interrelatedness' or local dependence (see Yen 1993), thereby violating the IRT assumption of local independence if each item is treated separately. If the set of items is treated as a single polytomously scored 'macro-item', this local dependence can adequately be accounted for. Thissen *et al.* (1989) argue persuasively for such an approach, using reading comprehension passages and item sets as examples, and clearly demonstrate how it is misleading to treat each of the items in an item set on an individual basis. Wainer and Lewis (1990) develop similar arguments.

When a set of items related to a common stimulus is treated as a unit, the set can be viewed as a single polytomously scored item with as many score categories as there are items in the set. For instance, if there are five items in the set, the individual who gets none correct would get a score of zero on the polytomously scored item and the individual who got all five correct would receive a score of five. A number of different IRT models for polytomously scored items can then be used to calibrate the data. Thissen *et al.* (1989) made use of the nominal IRT model for polytomous items (see Bock 1972) in calibrating their testlet data. Tang and Eignor (1996) made use of the polytomous generalized partial credit model (see Muraki 1992) and the graded response model (see Samejima 1969, 1972) in calibrating testlets made up of TOEFL reading and listening comprehension item sets. Still other researchers have made use of the partial credit model (see Masters 1982), which is a simpler Rasch-like version of the generalized partial credit model. Andrich (1995) compares and contrasts the polytomous models just mentioned. Regardless of the specific polytomous IRT model used, the testlet or item set can be characterized by a testlet information function in a way analogous to how individual items calibrated using one of the dichotomous IRT models can be characterized by item information functions.

The existence of testlet information functions suggests the possibility of a CAT procedure similar to that used with individual items, whereby a testlet, or item set, could be chosen next in a CAT that provides maximum information at the examinee's current estimate of ability. For a variety of reasons, such a procedure has yet to be implemented operationally. First, based on the original conceptualization of testlets, the item sets would need to be given in an intact fashion each time the testlet was chosen by the algorithm. This would place considerably greater demand on the sizes of the pools to avoid overexposure of items than is presently the case for passage-based CATs where only a subset of the total set of items is typically chosen for administration. Second, item sets constructed for many of today's large-scale tests are often extremely heterogeneous with respect to item difficulty. Hence, selecting a set of items based on an overall testlet information function would in no way ensure that the individual items constituting the set are 'tailored' to the examinee.

Two suggestions have been made that might improve matters, so that testlet-level CAT might become a reality. One obvious way of dealing with problems is to attempt to write item sets of relatively homogeneous difficulty. If this were the case, then selection of an item set based on testlet information (sort of an 'average' information) would ensure the administration of items that are tailored to the examinee.

The other suggestion involves the formation of a set of 'sub-testlets' and then administering one of these adaptively, rather than the full testlet. The passage and related set of items would be pretested in an intact fashion. Based on pretest data, various sub-combinations of items would be calibrated as testlets. For instance, a reading comprehension set of eight items could be broken up into sets of four-item testlets, using all possible combinations of four-items chosen from the eight. If item order matters, then only the sets of four -item testlets where items maintain the same relative order as in the total set could be created and calibrated. For CAT administration purposes, the four-item testlet that provided maximum testlet information at the examinee's current estimate of ability would be chosen from the total set. It should be noted that such a procedure disregards effects due to item context, which was one of the reasons why Wainer and Kiely (1987) suggested the use of testlets in the first place. Empirical study of this second suggested procedure would be needed before it were implemented operationally. Of particular interest would be whether such a procedure results in appreciably different quality CATs over the procedure when the four items are each selected individually using item information functions.

Implications for adaptive testing of second language reading proficiency

For low-stakes examinations of second language reading proficiency, where potential decision errors do not have grave implications, the use of an individual item item selection procedure with item sets for CAT construction purposes seems reasonable. While the IRT modeling is not being done in a strictly appropriate fashion, the consequences of improper item selection seem relatively minor.

For high-stakes examinations, consequences of improper IRT modeling are likely to be greater, but these consequences are a function of the size of the item sets to be used for the CAT. It can be argued that improper modeling will - likely to be less of a problem for a five-item set than it would be for a ten be item set. The lower the total number of items in the set, the more probable it is that a small degree of local dependence will be present, thereby increasing the viability of a CAT procedure where modeling and selection are done on an individual item basis.

For this reason, the Listening Comprehension section of the TOEFL CBT was constructed to be adaptive in nature, with IRT modeling done at the individual item level. The Listening Comprehension CAT is made up of a combination of discrete items and item sets. The item sets are relatively small in size, five to six items, so that the effects of using an IRT model where assumptions are violated was considered to be relatively minor.

The TOEFL Reading Comprehension section of the CBT, however, does not call for administration of a CAT, but rather a linear computer section constructed 'on the fly'. Reasons for this decision are discussed below. In this case, examinees are administered linear sections, with each examinee receiving his/her own specific combination of reading passages and intact sets. (Note that this section is completely set-based.) The Stocking/Swanson weighted deviations procedure is employed, and item selection is done as it currently is done in constructing paper-and-pencil forms, with the additional stipulation that construction be done on an individual examinee basis.

Besides the item sets to be pretested for Reading Comprehension being quite large (10–13 items), construction of the Reading Comprehension pool has depended greatly on the pretesting of these item sets via paper-and-pencil. TOEFL Reading Comprehension item sets have traditionally been pretested in paper-and-pencil mode with the items sequenced in the same way as the examinee encounters the relevant content when reading through the text. The concern is that such a structure is likely to introduce even more local dependence among the items in a set than the fact that all items are related to a single passage. In addition, the positioning of the items is likely to affect the parameter estimates. The concern is that item parameters for items administered in a particular sequence are likely to be inappropriate when the sequence is altered, as would be the case with an individual item-based adaptive test. For these reasons, the Reading Comprehension Section of the TOEFL computer-based test has been constructed to be 'linear on the fly' rather as a CAT. Issues of this sort need to be confronted when deciding how to construct high-stakes examinations of second language reading proficiency.

References

Ackerman, T. (1989) *An alternative methodology for creating test forms using the IRT information function.* Paper presented at the annual meeting of National Council on Measurement in Education, San Francisco, CA.

Andrich, D. (1995) Distinctive and incompatible properties of two common choices of IRT models for graded responses. *Applied Psychological Measurement*, 19: 101–19.

Armstrong, R. D., Jones, D. H. and Cordova, M. (1997) Mathematical programming approaches to computerized adaptive testing. Paper presented at the annual meeting at National Council on Measurement in Education, Chicago, IL.

Armstrong, R. D., Jones, D. H., Li, X. and Wu., I.-L. (1996) A study of a network-flow algorithm and a noncorrecting algorithm for test assembly. *Applied Psychological Measurement* 20: 89–98.

Armstrong, R. D., Jones, D. H. and Wu., I.-L. (1992) An automated procedure for development of tests parallel to a seed test. *Psychometrika* 57: 256–71.

Bock, R. D. (1972) Estimating item parameters and latent ability when responses are scored in two or more nominal categories. *Psychometrika* 37: 29–51.

Eignor, D. R., Folk, V. G., Li, M. and Stocking, M. L. (1994) *Pinpointing Praxis I CAT characteristics through simulation procedures.* Paper presented at the annual meeting of National Council on Measurement in Education, New Orleans, LA.

Eignor, D. R., Stocking, M. L., Way, W. D. and Steffen, M. (1993) *Case studies in computer-adaptive test design through simulation.* Research Report 93-56. Princeton, NJ: Educational Testing Service.

Eignor, D. R., Way, W. D. and Amoss, K. E. (1994) *Establishing the comparability of the NCLEX using CAT with traditional NCLEX examinations.* Paper presented at the annual meeting of National Council on Measurement in Education, New Orleans, LA.

Kingsbury, G. G. and Zara, A. R. (1989) Procedures for selecting items for computerized adaptive tests. *Applied Measurement in Education* 2 (4): 359–75.

Lord, F. M. (1980) *Applications of Item Response Theory to Practical Testing Problems.* Hillsdale, NJ: Lawrence Erlbaum Associates Publishers.

Luecht, R. M. and Hirsch, T. M. (1992) Item selection using an average growth approximation of target information functions. *Applied Psychological Measurement* 16: 41–51.

Masters, G. N. (1982) A Rasch model for partial credit scoring. *Psychometrika* 47: 149–74.

McBride, J. R. and Martin, J. T. (1983) Reliability and validity of adaptive ability tests in a military setting. In Weiss.

Muraki, E. (1992) A generalized partial credit model. Arbitration of an EM algorithm. *Applied Psychological Measurement* 16: 159–76.

Samejima, F. (1969) Estimation of latent ability using a response pattern of graded scores. *Psychometrika, Monograph Supplement* No. 17.

Samejima, F. (1972) A general model for free-response data. *Psychometrika, Monograph Supplement* No. 18.

Stocking, M. L. (1993) *Controlling item exposure rates in a realistic adaptive testing paradigm.* Research Report 93-2. Princeton, NJ: Educational Testing Service.

Stocking, M. L. and Lewis, C. (1995a) *Controlling item exposure on ability in computerized adaptive testing.* Research Report 95-24. Princeton, NJ: Educational Testing Service.

Stocking, M. L. and Lewis, C. (1995b) *A new method of controlling item exposure in computerized adaptive testing.* Research Report 95-25. Princeton, NJ: Educational Testing Service.

Stocking, M. L., Swanson, L. (1993) A method for severely constrained item selection in adaptive testing. *Applied Psychological Measurement* 17: 277–92.

Swanson, L., Stocking M. L. (1993) A model and heuristic for solving very large item selection problems. *Applied Psychological Measurement* 17: 151–66.

Sympson, J. B., Hetter, R. D. (1985) *Controlling item exposure rates in computerized adaptive testing.* Proceedings of the 27th annual meeting of the Military Testing Association. San Diego, CA: Naval Personnel Research and Development Centre.

Tang, K. L., Eignor, D. R. (1996) *Concurrent calibration of dichotomously and polytomously scored TOEFL items using IRT models.* TOEFL Research Report. Princeton, NJ: Educational Testing Service.

Theunissen, T. J. J. M. (1985) Binary programming and test design. *Psychometrika* 50: 411–20.

Theunissen, T. J. J. M. (1986) Some applications of optimization algorithms in test design and adaptive testing. *Applied Psychological Measurement* 10: 381–89.

Thissen, D., Steinberg, L., Mooney, J. (1989) Trace lines for testlets: A use of multiple-categorical-response models. *Journal of Educational Measurement* 26: 247–60.

van der Linden, W. J., Boekkooi-Timminga, E. (1989) A maximin model for test design with practical constraints. *Psychometrika* 54: 237–48.

van der Linden, W. J., Reese, L. M. (March 1997) *A model for optimal constrained adaptive testing.* Paper presented at the annual meeting at National Council on Measurement in Education, Chicago, IL.

Wainer, H., Dorans, N. J., Flaugher, R., Green, B. F., Mislevy, R. J., Steinberg, L. and Thissen, D. (1990) *Computerized Adaptive Testing: A Primer.* Hillsdale, NJ: Lawrence Erlbaum Associates Publishers.

Wainer, H. and Kiely, G. L. (1987) Item clusters and computerized adaptive testing: A case for testlets. *Journal of Educational Measurement* 24: 195–201.

Wainer, H., Lewis, C. (1990) Towards a psychometrics for testlets. *Journal of Educational Measurement* 27: 1–14.

Ward, W. C. (1988) The College Board computerized placement tests: An application of computerized adaptive testing. *Machine-Mediated Learning* 2: 217–82.

Way, W. D. (April 1994) *Psychometric results of the NCLEX Beta Test.* Paper presented at the annual meeting of American Educational Research Association, New Orleans, LA.

Weiss, D. J. (Ed.) (1983) *New horizons in testing.* New York, NY: Academic Press.

Wright, B. D., Stone, M. H. (1979). Best Test Design Chicago, IL: MESA Press

Yen, W. M. (1993) Scaling performance assessments: Strategies for managing local item dependence. *Journal of Educational Measurement* 30: 187–213.

10 A measurement approach to computer-adaptive testing of reading comprehension

John M. Linacre
MESA Psychometric Laboratory
University of Chicago

Introduction

Science advances when complex situations are summarized into simple regularities. These regularities are expressed as Laws. Laws are always simplifications, but they permit the regularity to be used for inference into situations beyond the original knowledge base that induced the Law.

Examples of such simplifications include Mendeleev's periodic table and Newton's laws of motion. The periodic table does not explain every property of every element, but it does provide a mechanism for predicting properties of unexamined and undiscovered elements from known properties of known elements. Newton's laws of motion, when first proposed, did not describe the motion of the planets as precisely as the Ptolemaic system. Newton's laws, however, could be used to predict motion in terrestrial as well as astronomical situations, which Ptolemy could not. Further, apparently anomalous motion could be used to predict the locations of undiscovered planets, rather than merely to construct further epicycles.

Reading comprehension is complex and idiosyncratic. Each reader brings to a text different education and experience. Further, each reader provides a unique cognitive and affective context for each word. To discover exactly what each reader understands a particular word to mean would be Herculean. To discover exactly what a paragraph means would be overwhelming. Further, since the understanding itself would generally have to be expressed as text, the solution to one reading comprehension problem would become the next reading comprehension problem.

Yet we do use text to communicate. We become adept at approximating and guessing at an author's message. We are skilled at adjusting and improving our understanding of earlier text based on later text. In fact, we enjoy doing it. The basic mechanism of many jokes is deliberately to mislead the reader (or hearer) to guess the wrong meaning, only to discover that the wrong meaning is in humorous contradiction to the correct meaning.

Thus the scientific challenge in the measurement of reading comprehension is to invent simplifications that usefully discriminate between different levels of text understanding. Failure of readers and texts to behave exactly according to these predictions is expected, but the simplifications provide a regular framework. This framework is designed to subsume most manifestations of text difficulty and reader comprehension. Small departures, though frequent, are expected to be generally inconsequential. Major departures, such as the idiosyncratic way in which first language knowledge affects understanding of second language texts, appear as anomalies. These anomalies can be diagnosed, and, when regular enough, can lead to refinement of the original laws or become the basis for further laws. This is how science advances.

Useful or perfect?

What degree of perfection is required when testing an individual's reading comprehension? First, the fact that we are willing to base our evaluation on a 'test' shows that we are prepared to accept the individual's behaviour on a small sample of text as representing that individual's behaviour on all text. Second, we know the individual's performance levels vary from minute to minute based on level of concentration, and from day to day as the individual is exposed to new text and forgets earlier texts. We further know, for second language readers, that we can construct texts that are easy or hard merely by choice of vocabulary that has little effect on the comprehension levels of first language readers.

Our aim, therefore, in constructing a reading comprehension test, is to put together the shortest, simplest test which will give us 'good enough' information to facilitate the decision for which the test is intended. The question is 'Can the individual read well enough to ...?'. The obvious test of this is to give individuals a sample piece of relevant text (instruction manual, newspaper article, passage out of a textbook) and see whether they can make sense of it or, at an advanced level, read it fluently.

Simplification in the measurement of reading comprehension

Readability formulae are widely used to assess text difficulty. Though not perfect, they have proven useful. For the purposes of the measurement of text difficulty, a formula (or suite of formulae) is required which is simple to implement and fast to apply to natural text entered into a computer data base. The formula, however, must also produce linear numbers.

A common misconception involves the identification of numerosity with measurement. The cardinal numbers necessarily have equal-interval properties, but measures expressed as cardinal numbers are not forced into substantive linearity. Conspicuously non-linear numbering systems for measurements include the Richter scale for earthquakes, the Beaufort scale of wind strength and the Rockwell scale for hardness. For the measures produced by a computer-adaptive testing system to be comprehensible, it is necessary that the measurement system provide numerical values with substantively linear properties and clearly defined meaning.

At least one readability formula, the Lexile system (Stenner 1995a), has been developed which produces measures that can be shown to have linear properties.

A model for producing linear measurement properties

A test of reading comprehension produces qualitative indicators of performance. In their simplest form, these indicators are successes and failures on dichotomous test items probing text comprehension. From such dichotomous observations linear measures of text difficulty and reading comprehension ability are to be inferred. The necessary and sufficient model expressing the relationship between dichotomous observations and linear measures is the Rasch model (Rasch 1960). This model expresses an ideal relationship, it does not describe a cognitive operation. Empirical data always fall short of the ideal, but it is only to the extent that the data approximate to the ideal that linear measures can be constructed.

In physical measurement, it is understood that a measuring instrument, such as a yardstick, is not perfect. It is only required to be good enough for practical use under certain conditions. The same rule applies to the estimation of measures using the Rasch model. It is expected that reasonable test items are to be posed about reasonable pieces of text in order to obtain meaningful measures.

Over the past 30 years, the Rasch model has been applied to data collected using many tests of reading comprehension (e.g. Woodcock 1973). Consequently, many reading comprehension test items have been calibrated onto linear frames of reference.

The Lexile readability formula

Reading comprehension test item calibrations provide a context within which to examine the linearity of readability formulae. A readability formula producing linear measures of text difficulty would produce numbers which plot a straight line with item calibrations.

In constructing a readability formula, there are many possible indicators of text difficulty: word length, sentence length, sentence complexity, word familiarity. A. J. Stenner (1995a) constructed a simple readability formula which usefully predicts the Rasch difficulty measures of reading comprehension test items. He found that most of the variability in reading comprehension difficulty for *natural text* read by a fluent reader could be modelled with:

text difficulty = recall effort + decoding load

This is equivalent to

text difficulty = word unfamiliarity + sentence complexity

Stenner found that the more frequently a word occurs in natural language the easier it is to recall its meaning and so the easier it is to understand. Thus word unfamiliarity is equivalent to word frequency in a broad corpus of written text.

Though it is easy to construct complex short sentences, e.g., 'To be or not to be?', and simple long sentences, e.g. 'John threw the ball and the dog caught the ball and the dog ran with the ball and ...', these occur rarely in natural text. Stenner found that sentence length is a useful proxy for sentence complexity.

The desired readability formula, however, must do more than rank text in difficulty order. It must predict linear measures of text difficulty. Linearization of Stenner's model is feasible because both word frequency and sentence length can be considered to be outcomes of Poisson processes. Each additional occurrence of a word contributes to its familiarity, but in such a way that the impact of each additional occurrence is less, in general, than that of the immediately previous occurrence. Similarly, each extra word added to a sentence contributes to sentence complexity, but with an impact that is less, in general, than the previously added word. These phenomena are conveniently linearized with logarithmic transformations. In a given piece of text, the transformation is averaged across all words (for word familiarity) and all sentences (for sentence complexity).

Stenner's Lexile readability formula (Stenner 1995b) becomes:

text difficulty in Lexiles = 582 − 386 × mean (ln (word frequency))
+ 1768 × ln (mean (sentence length))

This formula produces text readability measures, called *Lexiles*, that are usefully collinear with empirically-based Rasch linear measure estimates for the difficulty of items on standardized tests. Word frequency is the raw count of how often a given word appeared in a corpus of 5,088,721 words sampled from school materials (Carroll, Davies and Richman 1971).

Using the Lexile formula, it is possible to predict the empirical difficulty of a typical reading comprehension test item, provided that the item formulation itself does not add noticeably to the difficulty of the text (e.g. no 'trick' questions, or test items with complex response mechanisms).

Pragmatic item difficulty calibration

Stenner provides the Lexile calibrations for many texts and widely-used standardized tests in a convenient chart (Stenner 1995a). A selection of these texts are shown in Table 10.1. These texts provide a useful basis for calibrating new test items. After reading the 15 passages on the chart in their Lexile difficulty order, the approximate difficulty of any other natural language prose is evident.

Table 10.1

Lexile difficulties of selected natural text passages

Text title	Example text	Lexile difficulty
Ivanhoe. Sir Walter Scott.	These knights, therefore, their aim being thus eluded, rushed from the opposite sides betwixt the object of their attack and the Templar ...	1400 Lexiles (reading level of College Senior texts)
David Copperfield. Charles Dickens.	Ham was quite as earnest as he. I dare say they would have said much more about her, if they ...	1200 Lexiles (reading level of 11th Grade texts)
Twenty Thousand Leagues Under The Sea. Jules Verne.	I discussed the question in all its forms, politically and scientifically; and ...	1000 Lexiles (reading level of 7th Grade texts)
Encyclopedia Brown, Boy Detective. Duncan Searl.	'Aar,' Encyclopedia answered after a moment. He always waited a moment. He wanted to be helpful.	600 Lexiles (reading level of 3rd Grade texts)

These approximate 'guessed' Lexile difficulties for additional texts are good enough for most test applications. Wright and Panchapakesan (1969) demonstrate mathematically that small random errors in item calibration have no meaningful impact on person measurement for tests of any reasonable length. This was confirmed in a computer-adaptive test of comprehension of Chinese street signs (Yao 1991). Accordingly, items calibrated by rough correspondence with Stenner's (1995a) chart provide a useful basis for measurement. In due course, these calibrations can be refined either by application of Stenner's Lexile theory (based on sentence length and word frequency for the particular passage) or by recalibration based on examinees' actual responses.

Item bank construction

The test item format that best operationalizes the Lexile approach presents an additional sentence added to the end of the paragraph of natural language text (e.g. a paragraph excerpted from Hemingway's *For Whom the Bell Tolls*). This additional sentence continues the paragraph or some major theme in it, but is missing one pivotal word. The reader is presented with a list of words. The words have distinctly different meanings, but are of lesser difficulty than the text itself. Each word makes sense when placed in the blank in the final sentence, when the sentence is read by itself. Only one word follows a central idea in the paragraph. Fluent readers would select that one word. Figure 10.1 shows test items excerpted from a bank of items (MetaMetrics 1993-1995). The Lexile difficulties shown are not those of the publisher but were obtained pragmatically as described above.

Figure 10.1.
Sample items from Lexile Item Bank (Metametrics Inc. 1993–5)

1. The giant was mean. He was very ugly, too. We all ran away. We were   .
 	
     A.   afraid
     B.   done
     C.   quiet   _____
     D.   tired
 	
 Correct response: A.
 Lexile difficulty: 100 lexiles
 	
 2. The baby was very young. He was in a little bed. He had little hands. He had little feet. He was   .
 	
     A.   gone
     B.   right
     C.   sad_____
     D.   tiny
 	
 Correct response: D.
 Lexile difficulty: 150 lexiles

The underlying item construction rationale is that the test item itself should not add noticeably to the reading comprehension difficulty of the whole passage. The intention is not to investigate test-taking skills for multiple-choice items, but to measure reading comprehension of the base passage. Readers with low comprehension or second language readers might select familiar words or words at random. Though this guessing gives rise to occasional 'success', it is not frequent enough to prevent the reader failing difficult texts on average, and so being administered easier and easier texts until the he or she can maintain a consistently high success rate on the presented simpler texts.

Computer-adaptive administration of Lexile test items

Computer-adaptive testing (CAT) can be complex. Apart from hardware and programming considerations, there are comprehension-related issues such as how to deliver the text (e.g. as screen 'pages', or by scrolling one long page, with or without a split-screen horizontally or vertically to display the text and the text item). Reader-related issues are also important, such as the stress of reading text in an unfamiliar medium with time constraints. The CAT literature contains investigations and recommendations concerning these concerns and many more (e.g. Schoonman 1989). Again, to make progress, simplification is required.

In principle, computer-adaptive testing of reading comprehension is simple. Many Lexile-format test items are arranged in Lexile difficulty order to comprise the item bank. An item is selected from the bank, perhaps because it is close to some important cut-point, and administered to the examinee. If the examinee succeeds, a more difficult item is administered. If the examinee fails, an easier item is administered. This process continues until the examinee ability–item difficulty match is such that the examinee is succeeding consistently at the target success rate. A success rate of 50% is most informative psychometrically, but promotes 'problem-solving' rather than fluent reading. A success rate of 70%-80% is more satisfactory psychologically and corresponds to the administration of prose text which the respondent could be reading fluently.

After administering a few items, the approximate general reading comprehension level, the 'ability', of the examinee is identified. Administering more items enables a more precise determination to be made. Perfect precision is never obtained. In principle, perfection would require the administration of an infinite number of items. Even high precision is unlikely. First, the relevant items in the bank (i.e. those with difficulty near the examinee's reading level) become exhausted. Second, the examinee's performance is inevitably irregular and unstable. The examinee is more or less alert. The examinee is more or less familiar with particular words or sentence constructions than the bulk of the population with that reading comprehension level. Nevertheless, useful results can be obtained.

Figure 10.2.
Example of CAT administered Lexile item

Question Identifier: 30

Please select the best answer to the following question:

The most famous black bear was Smokey the Bear. He was saved by forest rangers from a forest fire. He became a national symbol for fire prevention. Many people _____ him.

The answer is one of:

A. called
B. chased
C. forget
D. know

Type the number of your selection here:___

(program control information – not yet seen by examinee:)

Item Information			Examination Information		
Sequence Number	Lexile Difficulty	Correct Answer	Score so far	Ability Measure	Standard Error
7	250	4	3 out of 6	197	186

Figure 10. 2 illustrates an item administered during a CAT. The examinee is not informed of item difficulty, nor of success so far on the test. This information, shown towards the bottom of the figure, is used by the computer to select which item to administer next, and also to decide when to stop the test.

A useful flow for a CAT is shown in Figure 10.3 (after Halkitis 1993). To begin CAT using this approach, a Bayesian ability estimate is provided by awarding each student one success and one failure on two dummy items, say, at the mean Lexile difficulty, D0, of the reading comprehension item bank or at the student's expected performance level. Thus each student is provided with an initial transient ability estimate.

John M. Linacre

Figure 10.3.
Flowchart of procticle CAT test (after Halkitis 1993)

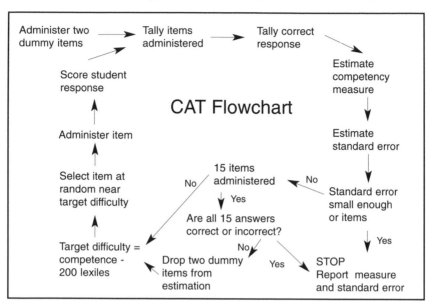

The first item a student sees is selected at random from those near 200 lexiles less than the initial estimated ability. Since 200 lexiles is equivalent to 1.1 logits, this yields a putative 75% chance of success for a student whose actual ability corresponds to 200 lexiles above the item's difficulty (see Wright and Stone 1979; 36). This provides such a student the opportunity to read the passage fluently and to succeed in answering the item correctly. Items are deliberately selected *at random* from the target range of item difficulties, usually around 200 lexiles below the student's ability, because randomization improves test security by preventing students from experiencing very similar tests. It also equalizes bank item use.

After the student responds to the first item, a revised competency measure and standard error are estimated. Again, an item is chosen from those about 200 lexiles easier (lower) than the estimated competency. After the student responds, the competency is again revised and a further item selected and administered, and so on.

Ability estimation

At any given point, say just after the administration of the mth item, the examinee has an ability measure of B_m lexiles (m includes the two dummy items, when indicated). An examinee of ability B_m has predicted success on item i of difficulty D_i amounting to P_{mi} which would be, according to the Rasch model:

$$P_m = \frac{e^{\frac{1.1}{200}\left(B_m - D_i\right)}}{1 + e^{\frac{1.1}{200}\left(B_m - D_i\right)}}$$

The examinee's expected score on the m items so far would be:

$$S_m = \sum_{i=1}^{m} P_{mi}$$

After the m responses have been scored with R_m successes, a revised competency measure, B_{m+1}, is obtained from the previous competency estimate, B_m, by:

$$B_{m+1} = B_m + \frac{200 \cdot \left(R_m - S_m\right)}{1.1 \sum_{i=1}^{m} P_{mi}\left(1 - P_{mi}\right)}$$

The logit standard error of this estimate, SE_{m+1}, is:

$$SE_{m+1} = \frac{200}{1.1} \sqrt{\frac{1}{\sum_{i=1}^{m} P_{mi}\left(1 - P_{mi}\right)}}$$

The initial two dummy items (one success and one failure on items of difficulty D_0) can be included in the summations. This will reduce the size of the change in the ability estimate, lessening the effect on the test of early nervousness or luck.

If, after 15 responses, the student has succeeded (or failed) on every administered item, testing ceases. The student is awarded a maximum (or minimum) measure. Otherwise, the two dummy items are dropped from the estimation process, because guesses or mistakes are now overwhelmed by valid responses.

Figure 10.4.
Example of ability estimation during a CAT test

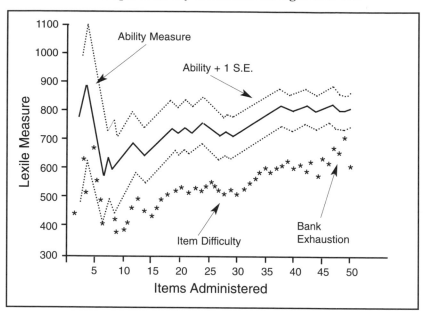

Figure 10.4 shows the progress of the updated ability measures during the course of a CAT. The items are targeted about 200 lexiles below the respondent's estimated ability level. Success raises the ability estimate, failure lowers it. Towards the end of the test, the supply of items close to the desired difficulty level becomes depleted. The bank becomes exhausted, so somewhat off-target items must be administered. This common situation reinforces the fact that there is no advantage to being extremely precise in selecting the 'best' items according to their difficulty levels at the start of the test.

Stopping the computer-adaptive testing test

In one practical application, there are two stopping rules. All tests cease when 30 items have been administered. Then the measures have standard errors of about 100 lexiles. Some tests may end sooner, because the examinee's ability is far above or far below the criterion cut-points. The examinee's lexile ability and standard error (precision) are reported for statistical decision making.

The computed ability level corresponds to a 50% chance of success on an item of matching difficulty. This corresponds to 'problem-solving' rather than fluent reading. Fluent reading is possible on passages up to about 200 lexiles less than the reported lexile ability level.

Examinees have clearly passed (or clearly failed) a criterion level when their estimated ability level is more than one or two standard errors away from the cut-point. If efficient testing is required, the CAT can stop when this occurs. In high-stakes testing, however, two other concerns come into play:

1. examinees who take short tests, and fail, may claim that if they had taken as many items as the other candidates they would have passed, because, by chance, they were first asked only those questions they didn't know; and
2. examinees who take short tests and pass cannot later be failed if, on review of their test performance, some unexpected feature of the testing situation is noted.

Thus, for high-stakes testing, it has been found expedient for all candidates to take a standard minimum number of items. The CAT method, however, still has the virtue that they all take different, targeted tests, increasing ability estimation accuracy and reducing test security issues.

A computer program, UCAT (Linacre 1987), is available which performs similar functions to those shown in Figure 10.3, and also re-estimates item difficulties based on the actual responses of examinees, when desired.

Validating lexile ability estimates by reading aloud

A quick check of reported ability levels can be made to confirm CAT results, using an approach similar to that of Gray (1915). The examinee can be requested to read aloud paragraphs of ascending lexile difficulty, such as the passages in Stenner (1995a). A fluent reader can read a passage aloud at a natural pace, and automatically incorporate natural intonation. The most difficult piece read fluently (without hesitation and with obvious understanding, based on phrasing and intonation) will be about 200 lexiles below that person's estimated ability level. A 'problem-solving' reader stumbles through the passage. Problem-solving can be performed successfully on texts with difficulty in the range from 200 lexiles below the reader's ability level up to the reader's level. A problem-solver may be able to discover the meaning of every word, but cannot communicate meaning while reading aloud in the instantaneous way a fluent reader can. When the text difficulty is above the reader's ability level, it is clearly too difficult. Then the reader produces such a garbled version of the text that no coherent meaning is communicated to the listener or to the reader. In fact, the reader is likely to stop reading before the end of the passage in frustration. This suggests that reading aloud may be a quick testing and validating mechanism for native language speakers.

For second language speakers, however, the problems of pronunciation and intonation must be addressed. Many languages are taught only as written languages, not spoken (e.g. 'dead' languages). Others may be taught only to be read and heard, not spoken (e.g. liturgical Latin for the laity). Modern languages may also be taught only as literary languages (e.g. 'classical' method of teaching French). For these languages and approaches, reading aloud may not be satisfactory.

Conclusion

Both the reading comprehension assessment methodology and the computer-adaptive testing technology described here are relatively unsophisticated and easy to implement. If these approaches are successful, then the investment in more sophisticated methods may produce more accurate and precise ability estimates. The improvements, however, are unlikely to make much practical difference.

Failure of these simple methods, however, would indicate that the concepts of better and poorer reader, and harder and easier passages are so obscure and context-bound that no generalizations are possible. If so, the only sure test of whether an individual can read a particular text is to administer that text to the individual. Fifty years of large-scale reading comprehension testing (e.g. Gates 1943), however, indicate that reading comprehension is a generalizable and measurable trait.

References

Carroll, J. B., Davies, P. and Richman, B. (1971) *Word Frequency Book.* Boston, MA: Hougton Mifflin.

Gates, A. I. (1943) *Gates Basic Reading Tests.* New York, NY: Teacher's College, Columbia University

Gray, W. S. (1915) *Standardized Oral Reading Paragraphs.* Bloomington, IL: Public School Publishing Company.

Halkitis, P. N. (1993) Computer-adaptive testing algorithm. *Rasch Measurement Transactions* 6 (4): 245–55.

Linacre, J. M. (1987) *UCAT: A BASIC computer-adaptive testing program.* MESA Memorandum number 40, MESA Psychometric Laboratory, University of Chicago, IL. (ERIC ED 280 895).

Metametrics Inc. (1993–95) *Early Learning Inventory.* Durham, NC: Author.

Rasch, G. (1960, 1992) *Probabilistic Models for Some Intelligence and Attainment Tests.* (p.20) Chicago, IL: MESA Press.

Schoonman, W. (1989) *An Applied Study on Computerized Adaptive Testing.* Rockland, MA: Swets & Zeitlinger.

Stenner, A. J. (1995a) *The Lexile Framework for Reading.* Durham, NC: Metametrics Inc.

Stenner, A. J. (1995b) *The objective measurement of reading comprehension.* Paper presented at the Eighth International Objective Measurement Workshop, Berkeley, CA.

Woodcock, R. W. (1973) *Woodcock Reading Mastery Tests.* Circle Pines, MN: American Guidance Service.

Wright, B. D. and Panchapakesan, N. A. (1969) A procedure for sample-free item analysis. *Educational and Psychological Measurement* 29: 23–48.

Yao, T. (1991) CAT with a poorly calibrated item bank. *Rasch Measurement Transactions* 5 (2): 141.

11 The practical utility of Rasch measurement models

Richard Luecht
National Board of Medical Examiners

Introduction

Item response theory (IRT) provides a powerful set of inferential statistical tools for analyzing the characteristics of items and examinees, if the observed data fit a particular IRT model. IRT makes use of mathematical models to describe the statistical characteristics of items and examinees relative to one or more latent traits or abilities assumed to underly the responses. A particular IRT mathematical model is numerically fit to raw response data. Some IRT models are relatively simple, others are more complex. For example, the Rasch model or RM (Rasch 1960) has a single parameter denoting the difficulty of each item and a single parameter denoting the ability or latent trait score for each examinee. The Rasch model for dichotomous data can be expressed as:

$$\text{Prob}\left(u_{ij} = 1 \middle| b_i, \theta_j\right) \equiv P_{ij} = \frac{\exp\left(\theta_j - b_i\right)}{1 + \exp\left(\theta_j - b_i\right)}$$

where: u_{ij} is a scored response to item i by examinee j (i.e. $u_{ij} = 1$ if correct, otherwise $u_{ij} = 0$);

b_i is an item 'location' denoting the difficulty of item i; and

θ_j is the latent trait score for examinee j.

Other models for the same type of data can contain more than one parameter for each item and/or examinee. For example, the three-parameter logistic model or 3PLM (Birnbaum 1968; Lord 1980) can be written as:

$$\text{Prob}\left(u_{ij} = 1 \middle| a_i, b_i, c_i; \theta_j\right) \equiv P_{ij} = c_i + \left(1 - c_i\right)\frac{\exp\left[a_i\left(\theta_j - b_i\right)\right]}{1 + \exp\left[a_i\left(\theta_j - b_i\right)\right]}$$

where:

u_{ij} is again a dichotomously scored response to item i by examinee j;

a_i is an item discrimination parameter denoting the sensitivity or loading of item i on the latent trait, θ;

b_i is the item difficulty or location parameter;

c_i is a lower asymptote parameter that acts as a scoring penalty function for low ability examinees who randomly guess; and

θ_j is the latent trait score for examinee j.

There are many other variations of IRT models. Unfortunately, most mathematical IRT models are usually wrong or incomplete representations of real data (Goldstein and Wood 1989; Goldstein 1994)—i.e. they almost always misfit the data to some extent. IRT is not a psychological theory about item responses; it is a collection of fallible, mathemathical models for fitting data to one or more underlying score scales.

Misfit usually implies errors with the mathematical model used, not the data (i.e. the data are real, the model is a fabrication). Of course, there are nuisance or extraneous factors unrelated to the assessment which can sometimes lead to aberrant response patterns (e.g. a noisy or disruptive testing environment). We usually attribute such factors to 'random error'. However, we would like our models to explain as much as possible, recognizing that some amount of misfit or error in the measurements is inevitable.

There are causes of misfit which are not necessarily due to random error. Sometimes misfit occurs because the assumed latent trait(s), θ, are insufficient in number to explain the residual covariances among responses (e.g. McDonald 1967). It may be the case that there are multivariate person or examinee traits, i.e. $\underline{\theta} = \theta_1, ..., \theta_m$. Multidimensional IRT models have been developed to deal with multiple traits (Reckase 1985; Reckase *et al.* 1988; Reckase and McKinley 1991).

This same multidimensionality issue relates to items that exhibit local item dependence, or LID (Yen 1993); there is 'something else', not included in the model—another valid trait or even a nuisance factor—which differentially affects the likelihood of performance for some examinees on some items, but not necessarily all items. The misfit issue is likewise closely related to DIF (differential item functioning) studies. DIF studies are usually performed to show differential performance on particular items among various subgroups within the examinee population (male versus female, ethnic group differences, etc.). However, strong rationale has been offered (e.g. Mellenbergh 1995) suggesting that DIF is little more than model misfit due to potential violations of the unidimensionality assumption so common to IRT models. Van der Linden (1995) has offered a similar rationale. Essentially, the message is that multidimensionality, LID, and/or DIF in the data will be improperly represented by a faulty or incomplete IRT model.

There are also IRT models that attempt to fit 'aberrant' data by assuming that the latent trait is unidimensional and simply adding more item parameters (i.e. structural parameters) to the mathematical model function to adjust for certain types of noise in the data. The 3PLM shown earlier in Equation 2 is a good example. The 3PLM attempts to correct for assumed guessing on difficult items by low ability examinees by explicitly including a 'guessing' parameter in the model (i.e. the c_i parameter in Equation 2). Adding this type of lower asymptote parameter to the model effectively makes the assumption that most or all of the random noise or misfit error should be attributed to the lower ability examinees near the tail of that θ distribution (Luecht 1995). However, adding this type of guessing correction factor is only valid if the low ability examinees actually do randomly guess on the difficult items. If they do not guess—e.g. if they are warned of a penalty for guessing and simply skip the more difficult items or if they are responding based on partial knowledge of the correct response—the 3PLM could be improperly parameterized and might actually lead to undesired measurement outcomes—e.g. increasing measurement precision for the supposedly high ability examinees at the expense of sacrificing precision for the lower ability examinees (Luecht 1995).

This chapter ultimately demonstrates that one of the simplest IRT models, the Rasch model from Equation 1, is a highly practical and useful model for detecting and understanding misfit and is actually quite robust when there is misfit arising from multidimensionality or guessing. The 3PLM from Equation 2 was chosen as a competing model because of its popularity for calibrating dichotomously-scored multiple choice data.

This chapter presents a rather specific context of computer-adaptive testing (CAT) involving subgroups who may not all fit a particular idealized population model. The examples used in this chapter focus on administering a multiple choice CAT in reading to different subgroups of examinees who vary systematically from the 'normal' population. This somewhat specific context does not limit generalization; it highlights some of the all too common flaws in IRT model selection or specification which can be magnified in CAT.

Methods

Two computer-adaptive testing (CAT) simulation studies were conducted to compare the practical utility of the Rasch model (RM) with the three-parameter logistic model (3PLM) under realistic conditions of model misfit.

The outcomes from the two studies highlight their similarities and differences in the face of model misfit. In the first study, multidimensionality was introduced into the simulations so that the data explicitly violated the unidimensionality assumption of both the RM and the 3PLM. Guessing was introduced in the second study.

Methods of simulation, item pools and data generation

Both studies simulated giving a computerized-adaptive reading test to a large sample of examinees where items associated with four content-balanced reading passages were seen by each examinee. The data used in this study were based on unidimensional and multidimensional IRT calibrated item statistics obtained from the ACT Assessment Reading Testing (ACT 1992). In paper-and-pencil format, the ACT Assessment Reading Test forms consist of 40 items. There are ten items associated with each of four content-based reading passages: social sciences (SS); humanities (HU); prose fiction (PF); and natural science (NS). Under the adaptive framework, the number of items was reduced; however, the passage content requirements were retained as constraints during the CAT item selection process. Two separate pools of ACT Assessment Reading Test items were used, one for each study.

There were two independent samples of simulated examinees generated for each study. One sample was designated as the calibration sample; the other was called the experimental sample. The calibration sample was considered to be a 'normal' sample of examinees (examinees having about average abilities when compared to the total examinee population). The calibration samples had a singular purpose—to provide response data that were used to obtain the RM and 3PLM item parameter estimates (i.e. calibrated item statistics) for the item pools. Those calibrated item statistics were subsequently used to carry out the CAT simulations with the other examinee samples. The calibration samples were purposely kept relatively small. In a real CAT, item exposure concerns related to examinees memorizing and collaborating to share information or answers from an active item pool often restrict the number of examinees in the population allowed to see the items prior to and after calibration. A maximum 'pre-calibration' exposure of 500 examinee responses per item is quite realistic for any type of real adaptive testing program where there are serious concerns about item exposure security risks.

The experimental samples were the focal groups in each study. These experimental samples were drawn from the lower ability tail of the assumed examinee population(s) and administered the simulated computer-adaptive reading tests. Each experimental sample comprised 1000 examinees of significantly lower ability than the calibration sample. Low ability groups are often of focal interest in certification or licensure contexts, where a pass/fail decision must be made for 'minimally compentent' examinees, or in educational settings involving placement decisions for remedial programs or when investigating DIF, where certain population subgroups might systematically perform worse than other subgroups.

The experimental samples of examinees were administered the simulated computer-adaptive tests, using the item statistics estimated from the corresponding calibration sample for each study. Each of the 1000 simulated examinees in each of the experimental samples was administered a CAT from the available pool of reading test items, based on model-generated item responses. No exposure controls were used; i.e. the items were selected with replacement of items across examinees. The CAT item selection mechanism did require that a specific number of items be selected from each of the four content areas for that examination—i.e. one and only one passage in social science, humanities, prose fiction and natural science. Therefore, the simulations modeled each examinee seeing exactly four reading passages (one SS passage, one HU passage, one PF passage and one NS passage), with a specific number of items selected per passage.

The initial items/passages were selected using uniform random selections of:

1. one of the four passage content areas;
2. a passage within that area; and
3, a randomized folding method of selecting the most informative items in the selected passage (Kingsbury and Zara 1989).

This approach to initial passage and item selection precluded the same passages and items from always being chosen first for examinees of similar abilities. The adaptive selection process also mimicked reality so that once a passage was selected, all of the required items for that passage had to be administered before moving on to the next passage.

The CAT item selection mechanism used in both studies employed a standard 'maximum information criterion' (e.g. Birnbaum 1968; Kingsbury and Zara 1989) where the item selected from the pool is the one that contributes most to the score precision at the current estimated value of θ, the examinee's score (subject to the passage-based content constraints). The passage-based content balancing imposed through the simulation mitigated the maximum information criterion. For example, all of the items selected for SS had to come from the same passage. The same was true for the HU, PF and NS passage topic areas.

Table 11.1 summarizes the major design aspects for the two studies. More complete details for each study are provided below.

Table 11.1

Design parameters for Studies I and II

Description of data		Study I	Study II
Underlying data generation model		Multivariate	Unidimensional 3PLM
Item pool:	Number of items	400	360
	Number of reading passages	10	9
	Mean item pool difficulty	0.0 (regular)	-1.0 (easy)
Calibration sample:	Number of examinees	500	500
	Mean ability	$\mu(\theta) = 0$	$\mu(\theta) = 0$
	Variance-covariance	$\Sigma = \rho$ (see below)	$\sigma(\theta) = 1.0$
CAT sample:	Number of examinees	1000	2000
	Mean abilities	$\mu(\theta) = (-1, -1, -.75, -.5, -.25)$	$\mu(\theta) = -1.0$
	Covariance matrix	$\Sigma = \rho$ (see below)	$\sigma(\theta) = -1.0$
CAT administration:	Content balancing	By passage type	By passage type
	Test lengths	Test A=20;B=28	Test C=12;D=24
	Items per passage	Test A=5; B=7	Test C=12;D=24

Study I design

The item pool for Study I consisted of 400 items from the ACT Assessment Reading Test. There were 40 reading passages each covering one of four content topic areas: social studies (SS), humanities (HU), prose fiction (PF) and natural sciences (NS) and each item was associated with a particular reading passage.

These same 400 items were used to generate multidimensional response data for the calibration sample and for the experimental sample. The multidimensional response data were generated using calibrated item statistics produced by NOHARM (Fraser 1986) for approximately 2000 real ACT Assessment examinees. Gessaroli (1995) demonstrated that a nonlinear common factor model provided a reasonable fit to this particular ACT Assessment Reading Test. His model consisted of one common factor and four oblique passage factors (each orthogonal to the common factor). The factor correlation matrix from Gessaroli's study was

$$\rho= \begin{matrix} 1.0 & & & & \\ 0.0 & 1.0 & & & \\ 0.0 & 0.4 & 1.0 & & \\ 0.0 & 0.5 & 0.4 & 1.0 & \\ 0.0 & 0.1 & -0.1 & 0.1 & 1.0 \end{matrix}$$

The common factor (total test) is represented by the first column. The passage factors (i.e. the unique factors) are shown in columns 2 to 5, with moderate to low correlations between the passage factors: SS, HU, PF and NS, respectively. This multivariate, common factor structure was used to induce a type of local item dependence (LID) into the data.

Using the above structure, normally distributed values of θ(Total), θ(SS), θ(HU), θ(PF) and θ(NS) were generated to simulate the examinees' abilities, using a modification of a multivariate random normal data generation program developed by Aquinis (1994). As noted earlier, two samples of data were produced: a calibration sample and an experimental sample. The calibration sample consisted of 500 examinees. The number of examinees for the calibration sample was deliberately kept small to simulate the typical size of calibration sample for items used in a moderate-stakes CAT, where item exposure might be limited within the population of test takers.

The five abilities for each examinee were randomly drawn from a multivariate normal distribution with a mean vector of $\mu(\theta) = (0, 0, 0, 0, 0)$ and a covariance matrix, $\Sigma = \rho$, from the Gessaroli study. The ability vectors, θ_j, j=1,....,500, were then used in conjunction with the five dimensional NOHARM item parameter estimates from Gessaroli's study for all 400 items in the CAT item pool to generate the scored item responses. Specifically, a true response function for each examinee x item interaction was generated using a multidimensional model.

$$\text{Prob}\left(u_{ij} = 1 \middle| a_i, d_i; \theta_j\right) \equiv P_{ij} = \Phi\left(a_i^T \theta_j + d_i\right)$$

given a vector of abilities, θ_j a vector of item discrimination parameters for the a_i, and a threshold parameter, d_i. The function F( ) is the normal cumulative density function. This type of nonlinear factor analysis model (e.g. Bock et al. 1988) is merely a different way of expressing the IRT response probability function for multidimensional data and, except for a constant change in the variance of the scale, is closely related to the logistic IRT models shown in Equations 1 and 2.

Given the generated response function, P_{ij} for examinee j on item i, a corresponding uniform random probability was computed for each examinee x item interaction, π_{ij}. A dichotomous item score of $u_{ij} = 1$ (correct) was assigned if P_{ij} was greater than or equal to π_{ij} or $u_{ij} = 0$ (incorrect), otherwise.

The response data for the calibration sample (i.e. the matrix of 500 examinees x 400 item dichotomous responses) were calibrated using BILOG (Mislevy and Bock 1990) to obtain 3PLM estimates of the a_i, b_i and c_i parameters, i=1,...,400. The logistic model option was set in BILOG to remain consistent with the model shown in Equation 2. The item parameter estimates for the i=1,...,400 items became 'known' statistics in the item pool used in the

CAT simulation conducted for the experimental sample. The unidimensional calibrations did converge for all items, even though the data were generated to be multidimensional. Standard errors and other relevant indices suggested that the calibrations were reasonable for most of the items. The same response data were also calibrated using the one-parameter model in BILOG, which is closely related to the RM shown in Equation 1. Under the one-parameter model, a_i is estimated as a constant for all items and c_i (the pseudo-guessing parameter in Equation 2) is set to zero. A third calibration was performed on the data using BIGSTEPS (Linacre and Wright 1995) which estimates the item difficulty and examinee abilities under the formal Rasch model (RM) shown in Equation 1. The BIGSTEPS solution was found to be somewhat more stable than the one-parameter BILOG solution; the item difficulties from BIGSTEPS were therefore used for the RM CAT item pool.

The experimental sample consisted of 1000 simulated examinees generated by the modified version of Aquinis' (1994) multivariate random normal data generation program. The means, standard deviations and the product–moment correlation coefficients between the ability parameters for this sample of 1000 examinees are shown in Table 11.2. In addition to representing the population correlation matrix reasonably well, Table 11.2 also documents how the abilities were varied within the common factor model framework. That is, for the total test and for social sciences (SS) the mean abilities were forced to be approximately -1.0. For humanities (HU), prose fiction (PF) and natural science (NS), the means were systematically increased in increments of 0.25. The standard deviations, however, were held constant at approximately 0.75, for the common and unique factor scores (the multidimensional θ).

Table 11.2

Descriptive statistics for Study I multivariate abilities (N=1000)

	Total test	SS	HU	PF	NS
Mean	-1.01	-0.99	-0.75	-0.49	-0.23
SD	0.72	0.73	0.74	0.75	0.77
Correlations					
Total test	1.00				
SS	-0.03	1.00			
HU	0.03	0.40	1.00		
PF	-0.01	0.51	0.41	1.00	
NS	-0.01	0.11	-0.09	0.07	1.00

The experimental sample was therefore modeled using a somewhat different pattern of means for the examinees' multivariate abilities than in the 'normal' population (i.e. compared to the calibration sample). A systematic change was induced for the vector of means used in the data generation, across the unique factors, so that, on average;

$$\mu(\theta)= (-1.00,-1.00,-0.750,-0.50,-0.25).$$

The serial positions in $\mu(\theta)$ correspond to the common factor total test and unique factors: social science, humanities, prose fiction and natural science abilities. This structure simulates the type of pattern of means which might occur if a subgroup of the examinee population had varied amounts of training or instruction within specific content areas. For example, these examinees were not only low in ability, but may have also had very little experience reading social science and humanities materials (or proportionally more experience reading prose fiction and natural science).

Each of the 1000 simulated examinees was administered two CATs from the available pool of 400 items, with replacement of items between each CAT. (This was the same as drawing two independent experimental samples. The same sample was used twice only as a convenience for subsequent analyses.) Each CAT required that a specific number of items be selected from each of the four content areas (SS, HU, PF and NS) where the items were further linked to reading passages. Therefore, the simulations modeled each examinee seeing exactly four reading passages. For one of the two CATs, five items were administered for each of the selected four reading passages (20 items in total); for the second CAT, eight items were administered for each of the selected four reading passages (32 items in total). The two CATs were considered as independent events. The same examinees were used in both parts of Study I only as a convenience. The two test lengths used in Study I represented reductions of 50 per cent and 20 per cent, respectively, from the standard 40-item test length of the paper-and-pencil ACT Assessment Reading Test.

Study II

Study II assumed that a 3PLM model was the correct model for the data, but manipulated the test characteristics and conditions of estimation somewhat. In this study, an item pool of 360 items from the ACT Assessment Reading Test was used. Each item was again associated with a particular reading passage; there were ten items per reading passage and 36 reading passages represented by the pool. The reading passages each covered one of the four content topic areas (SS, HU, PF and NS).

Item parameters calibrated under the 3PLM using real ACT Assessment Reading Test data were obtained for each of the 360 items. The original item parameter estimates are summarized in Table 11.3. Note that the parameters are scaled using the logistic model. For purposes of the simulation the item difficulty parameter estimates were then modified by adding -1.0 to each of the b_i (i.e. computing a new difficulty, $b_i^*=b_i$ -1.0, i=1,...,360). This rather simple modification therefore made the item pool easier and somewhat optimal for examinees at an average θ score near to -1.0. This type of situation might occur if the test were designed for the purpose of making remedial reading placement decisions or similar mastery decisions in the lower region of the ability scale. In those cases, we would probably want the test to have an average difficulty near to the decision point of the θ scale.

Table 11.3

**Original 3PLM parameter estimates for Study II item pool
(logistic scaling used)**

Statistic	a-parameters	b-parameters	c-parameters
Mean	0.448	0.116	0.218
Std. deviation	0.183	2.009	0.072
Minimum	0.129	-8.331	0.078
Maximum	1.602	5.645	0.496

Response data for a 'normal' calibration sample and for a separate, lower-ability experimental CAT sample were generated. The calibration sample comprised 500 examinee abilities drawn randomly from a unit normal distribution, i.e. $\theta \sim [\mu(\theta)=0.0, \sigma(\theta)=1.0]$. Responses were generated by computing an item response function (Equation 2), denoted P_{ij}, for the items, i=1,...,360, and for the examinees, j=1,...,500. A corresponding uniform random probability, π_{ij}, was generated for each examinee x item interaction. An item score of u_{ij} = 1 (correct) was assigned if P_{ij} was greater than or equal to π_{ij} or u_{ij} = 0 (incorrect).

The dichotomous response data matrix (500 examinees x 360 items) was calibrated under the 3PLM using BILOG (Mislevy and Bock 1990), with the logistic scaling option set. This calibration provided the 3PLM item pool estimates for the item a-, b- and c-parameters. The same response data were also calibrated using BIGSTEPS (Linacre and Wright 1995) to obtain the RM item difficulty estimates (the b_i from Equation 1, i=1,...,360).

The modified 3PLM item parameters that had been used to generate the calibration sample were also used to generate the experimental CAT sample response data. This data set included generated dichotomous responses for all

1000 examinees to all 360 items. The abilities for the examinees in the CAT sample examinees were drawn randomly from a distribution, $\theta \sim [\mu(\theta)=-1.0, \sigma(\theta)=0.75]$. Accordingly, the items in the pool were not necessarily optimally informative for examinees in the calibration sample; however, they were somewhat optimal for the examinees in the experimental sample (on average).

In addition, a second set of responses were generated for another sample of 1000 low-ability examinees—i.e., $\mu(\theta)=-1.0$—but with all the c_i, i=1,...,360 item parameters (i.e., the pseudo-guessing parameters) set to zero. The CAT simulation program was again used on these data where, according to the generating function underlying the responses, there was no guessing present. However, the same item pools containing the 3PLM and RM item statistics from the calibration sample were used for the adaptive tests run using this 'no guessing'.

Each examinee in the two experimental samples was administered 32 items, with replacement of items between each CAT. For each CAT, four passages were selected (one SS, one HU, one PF and one NS passage) along with eight items of the ten items associated with each of those passages. The RM and 3PLM CAT simulations were done twice; once using the 3PLM data with guessing and the second time using the 3PLM data without guessing.

Results

The majority of the CAT results are based on expected a posteriori (EAP) ability estimates (Bock and Mislevy 1982). These EAP estimated abilities were calculated from the observed CAT responses and the item statistics obtained from the corresponding calibration sample data. A normally-distributed prior (i.e., $\theta \sim [0,1]$) was employed to match the assumed density for the 'normal' population. This choice of a population prior to distribution may have produced a slight regression bias effect for the lower-ability experiment samples involved. Maximum likelihood estimates of ability were also computed but were discarded in favor of the more stable EAPs.

Study I

The Study I data were generated according to a true underlying multidimensional structure. This approach complicated comparisons between the unidimensional RM and 3PLM CAT results, since neither IRT calibration model was correct. However, there was a way to circumvent the problem.

One advantage of doing this type of CAT simulation is that item responses can be (and were) generated for the entire item pool so that the same data for each examinee are available across the CAT simulations. The observed number correct scores to 400 items represent stable estimates of the examinees' total test true ability. Using the pool-level raw scores also avoids the complication of needing to make any comparisons between the unidimensional EAPs and the 'true' multidimensional abilities underlying the data. The results from Study I are based directly on comparisons of the observed pool-level raw scores to the model-based predicted pool-level scores (the latter are based on the EAP ability estimates for each of the 1000 simulated examinees). The pool-level observed number correct scores and predicted scores were converted to percentage correct scale to facilitate interpretation.

The model-based predicted scores were computed as follows. Using each examinee's EAP (i.e., estimated θ under either the 3PLM or the RM), a predicted raw score was computed by plugging that estimate respectively into Equation 1 (for the RM) or Equation 2 (for the 3PLM), using the corresponding item statistics obtained for the 400-item pool from the calibration sample. This 'domain scoring' approach was suggested by Yen (1993). As noted above, since response data had been generated for each simulated examinee in the experimental sample to all the items in the pool, this domain score analysis provided a very robust view of misfit using all of the available observed raw data. It is also possible to compare the 3PLM and RM model fit within each of the passage content areas, without the complication of dealing with multivariate ability estimates.

Table 11.4 shows the product–moment correlations between the observed item pool percentage correct scores–i.e. $100(\Sigma_i u_{ij} \div n)$ as the number correct score for examinee j on $i=1,...,n$ items—and the expected percentage correct 'domain scores'—i.e., $100(\Sigma_i P_{ij} \div n)$, where P_{ij} is defined by Equations 1 or 2, using the item statistics from the corresponding calibration sample and the estimated value of q_j under the appropriate IRT model. These correlations coefficients were computed for the total pool of n=400 items and for the respective blocks of 100 items in each of the four content areas (SS, HU, PF and NS).

Table 11.4

Product–moment correlations between number correct scores and

CAT length	Total	SS	HU	PF	NS
RM 20 items	0.78	0.67	0.71	0.60	0.66
RM 32 items	0.84	0.75	0.78	0.64	0.73
3PLM 20 items	0.76	0.66	0.73	0.58	0.63
3PLM 32 items	0.84	0.71	0.77	0.63	0.74

expected scores for Study I examinees (N=1000)

Clearly, increasing the length of the test from 20 to 32 items (i.e. from five to eight items per passage) improves the fit of the model-based domain scores to the number of correct scores for each examinee. For example, the correlation coefficient between the 'total' number correct score and the 'total' domain score is 0.78 for the Rasch model (RM) estimates at 20 items, and increases to 0.84 at 32 items. For the 3PLM, the change is from 0.76 to 0.84. These results are not surprising; it is well known that increasing test length will usually improve the accuracy of the test scores. Note that, with the exception of the humanities scores for a 20-items total CAT, the Rasch model nominally fits the raw data equal to or better than the 3PLM. Given the 'sufficient statistics' property of the Rasch model (see Rasch 1960), this would not be surprising had just the items actually seen by each examinee been used in the ability estimation calculations; however, these domain scores were based on abilities estimated from as few as 20 items for the total scores or as few as only five items within any single topic area (SS, HU, PS or NS).

Figure 11.1 shows a scatter plot of the predicted domain percentage correct scores—i.e. $100(\Sigma_i P_{ij} \div 360)$, $i=1,...,360$, for each examinee j—plotted against the observed item pool percentage correct scores, $100(\Sigma_i u_{ij} \div 360)$. The four regression lines, each corresponding to one of the four adaptive tests, are also shown. This figure indicates, to some extent, the amount of bias present in the EAP estimated abilities. If there were no bias present, the regression lines would fall along the identify line (lower-left to upper-right, on the diagonal). In general, however, all of the predicted domain percentage scores underestimate the observed item pool percentage correct scores.

Figure 11.1

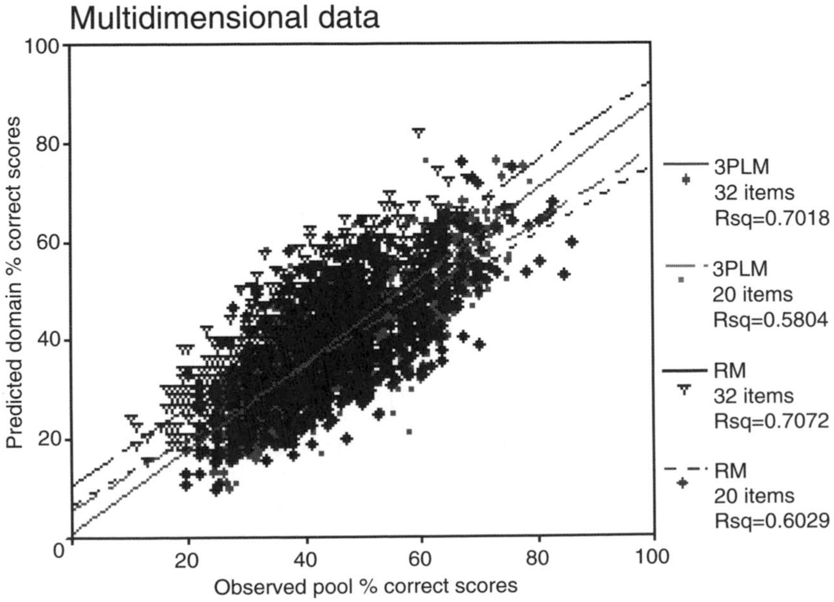

Multidimensional data

Since the domain scores are functions of the EAPs that were calculated at 20 and 32 items, an explanation of the bias is that the ability estimates may simply be overestimates. It is entirely possible that the choice of prior—i.e., assuming $\theta \sim N(\mu=0.0,\ \sigma=1)$ for the lower-ability experimental sample may have regressed the EAPs toward the mean. This is a fairly well-known phenomenon (e.g. Bock and Mislevy 1982). The fact that the apparent estimation bias diminishes by increasing the length of each CAT from 20 to 32 items is consistent with that regression effect explanation of the observed bias.

Study II

In Study II, the simulation scenario was one of administering an adaptive reading test to lower-ability examinees, where the item parameters had been estimated from a higher ability, albeit 'normal' examinee sample. Since the data were generated from a unidimensional three-parameter logistic model (3PLM), with and without guessing, the 'true' ability for each examinee was known. It was therefore possible to compare directly the RM and 3PLM EAPs for the 32-item CATs (with and without guessing) to the known values.

Table 11.5 summarizes the various fit indices for EAP ability estimates from both the 'guessing' and 'no guessing' data in Study II. In each case, the estimated EAPs are compared to the 'true' θ values which generated the data. First, considering the Pearson product-moment correlation, $\rho(\theta,\text{EAP})$ and the mean square error between the θs and EAPs, the Rasch model actually fits slightly better for both the 'guessing' and 'no guessing' data. Because the calibration sample had a mean ability near to zero—while the mean item pool difficulty was nearer to -1.0—the 3PLM a-, b- and c-parameter estimates were potentially quite biased since there was insufficient good 'person information' to stabilize the solutions (Luecht 1995). That potential problem would imply that any estimation bias in the CAT ability estimates (EAPs) under the 3PLM could be almost entirely the fault of poor quality estimation of the item pool parameters. The Rasch model item difficulty estimates were less demanding in terms of 'person information' and therefore were not as susceptible to this problem.

The rightmost column in Table 11.5 shows the mean and standard deviation of the mean square person misfit. This person misfit statistic was computed as

$$\varepsilon_j = \frac{\sum\limits_{i=1}^{n}\left(u_{ij} - P_{ij}\right)^2}{\sum\limits_{i=1}^{n} P_{ij}\left(1 - P_{ij}\right)}$$

where u_{ij} is the observed dichotomous item response, $i=1,....,n$ items, seen by examinee j, and P_{ij} is the model-based response probability computed from

Equations 1 or 2, using the calibration sample item parameter estimates and replacing θ in those equations with the corresponding EAP from the CAT simulation. If the model properly fits the data, this person fit statistic should approach unity (i.e. is distributed as a non-central χ^2 with one degree of freedom, (See Kendall and Stuart 1969.) The mean fit statistic for the Rasch model consistently approaches 1, whether or not there is 'guessing' present. The same cannot be said for the 3PLM. When there is 'guessing', the mean person fit moves near to the expected value of 1; when there is no 'guessing', the 3PLM overfits the data. This finding is consistent with overcorrecting for assumed guessing by effectively lowering the scores of already low-ability examinees who did not guess. One could make the case that any such adjustment in the face of no guessing (or at least not random guessing) represents an unfair scoring penalty for low-ability examinees.

Table 11.5

Descriptive summary of EAP ability estimate for Study II

Data source	Calibration	Correlation $r(\theta, EAP)$	MS-Error $Err(\theta, EAP)^2$	Person Fit (MS)
3PLM data with model-based guessing	Rashmodel	0.899	0.192	0.981 (0.106)
	3PLM	0.887	0.213	0.963 (0.115)
3PLM data without guessing	Rasch model	0.932	0.131	0.958 (0.117)
	3PLM	0.925	0.144	0.873 (0.111)

( ) denotes standard deviation of fit statistic

Figures 11.2 and 11.3 respectively show the observed minus expected domain scores as 95 per cent confidence interval error bands about the mean score differences, conditional on the examinees' 'true' abilities, θ. The computed intervals are equally spaced. Sample sizes per interval are shown along the abscissa. The deviations are shown in percentage correct score units to facilitate interpretation. (See the Study I results for a description of how the domain scores were computed.)

In Figure 11.2, the 'guessing' data seem to be better represented by the 3PLM, at least $\theta > -0.50$. Below that point, there is a tendency for the 3PLM to overfit the scored, observed item pool response data. In contrast, the Rasch model predictions tend to underfit the raw data. However, the magnitude of the misfit for the RM is only about 5 per cent, on average, and never higher than 10 per cent.

Figures 11.2 and 11.3 show the fit for the 'no guessing' data. Here, we begin to see more directly the impact of applying a 3PLM random guessing correction factor (the c-parameters) to lower-ability examinees who do not guess. The expected percentage correct domain scores for the item pool overpredict the examinees' actual performance by as much as 10 to 20 percentage points. If we mapped an examinee's observed percentage correct score to the predicted response function for the items that examinee saw, the lower-than-predicted observed score would result in a lower score on the ability scale, θ.

Figure 11.2

Model fit to data without guessing

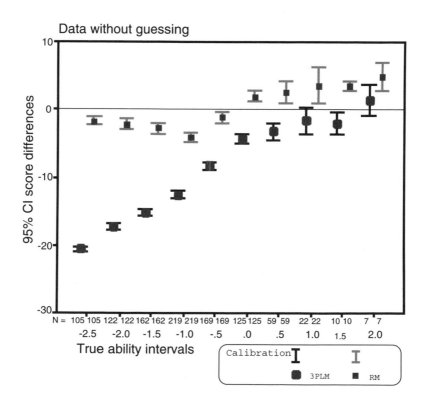

Figure 11.3

Model fit to data without guessing

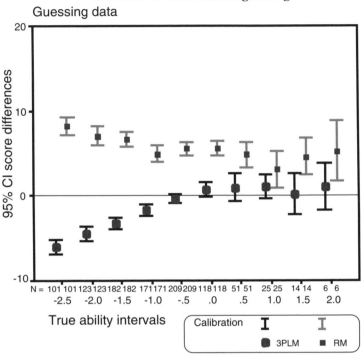

Guessing data

Summary and conclusions

These studies looked at the performance of two common unidimensional IRT models—the Rasch model (RM) and the three-parameter logistic model (3PLM)—in the face of potential misfit. Misfit was operationally induced by using a multidimensional model for the data in Study I and the 3PLM to create the data with and without guessing for Study II. The computer-adaptive simulations employed in these studies further introduced some realistic factors including the restriction of using small 'normal' calibration samples to obtain the item statistics for the CAT simulation and then administering the CATs to lower-ability samples who might not behave the way the RM or 3PLM calibration models would predict. Finally, by focusing on a reading test, realistic passage and content constraints were introduced during the CAT item selections, thus avoiding a strictly psychometric treatment of the latent trait(s) of interest.

Study I demonstrated that the RM worked as well as if not slightly better than the 3PLM (in the presence of multidimensionality) to predict the observed domain scores for the item pools. There was some bias present under both IRT models; that bias was attributed to possible regression bias in the EAP ability estimates. Perhaps the most important finding of this simulation is that the two models were more or less of equivalent utility. All things being equal, it certainly appears as if the RM, as the simpler model, is a reasonable starting point. It might be possible to achieve a better fit to these multidimensional data by using a multidimensional extension of the RM. (See Glas 1992.) Under a multidimensional Rasch model framework, the typical demands for extremely large samples to obtain stable estimates of multidimensional parameters can be avoided. However, to date no multidimensional models have been successfully implemented by any testing programs for use in scaling operational test data.

In any event, this type of analysis demonstrates the capability of the RM to fit a particular type of multidimensional data at least as well as the 3PLM. If a more complicated model than the RM is needed to improve the fit, these results suggest that moving to a multidimensional RM or some other multidimensional model might be better advised than simply opting for a more complicated model and selecting the 3PLM.

Study II simulated an adaptive reading test where the item pool was well targeted for low ability examinees, but calibrated using 'normal' examinees (i.e., higher-ability examinees who fit the data generation model). Correcting for guessing using the 3PLM did no better than the RM and overfit the data when there was no guessing. Even when there was guessing, the 3PLM did not perform all that well; the reduced quality of the item statistics in the item pool (based on the 'normal' calibration sample data) was offered as an explanation.

In conclusion, these simulations demonstrate that the Rasch model (RM) is a robust starting point for analyzing the nature of any misfit and selecting or building an appropriate IRT calibration model. The model has straight - forward mathematics (i.e., belongs to the exponential family of models) and raw scores are sufficient statistics for estimating the item and examinee parameters. Furthermore, the data demands for estimating the RM item statistics are fairly minimal (e.g., 300 responses per item can yield reasonable estimates of the RM item difficulties: Lord 1980). This low data demand can be important in CAT situations where item exposure concerns and other logistical issues limit the amount of data obtained for all items, prior to initial or 'on-line' calibration. Many operational, high-stakes testing programs use the RM because of its robust estimation properties.

Perhaps most importantly, fit can be readily evaluated under the Rasch model, without complicating the model by adding arbitrary parameters that may or may not be appropriate. Understanding in depth the nature of the fit of the data to the most parsimonious model, before opting for something more complicated, would seem to be a recommended practice.

References

ACT (1992) *ACT Assessment Reading Test*. Iowa City, IA: ACT.

Aquinis, H. (1994) A QuickBasic program for generating correlated multivariate random normal scores. *Educational and Psychological Measurement* 54 (3): 687–90.

Birnbaum, A. (1968) Test scores, sufficient statistics, and the information structure of tests. In Lord, F. M. and Novick, M. R (Eds.) *Statistical Theories of Mental Test Scores*. Reading, MA: Addison-Wesley.

Bock, R. D., Gibbons, R. and Muraki, E. (1988) Full-information factor analysis. *Applied Psychological Measurement* 12 (3): 261–80.

Bock, R. D. and Mislevy, R. J. (1982) Adaptive EAP estimation of ability in a microcomputer environment. *Applied Psychological Measurement* 6 (4): 431–44.

Fraser, C. (1986) *NOHARM: An IBM PC computer program for fitting both unidimensional and multidimensional normal ogive models of latent trait theory*. Armidale, New South Wales, Australia: The University of New England.

Gessaroli, M. (1995) *Assessing dimensionality using nonlinear factor analysis*. Paper presented at the annual meeting of the American Educational Research Association, San Francisco, CA.

Glas, C. A. W. (1992) A Rasch model with a multivariate distribution of ability. In Wilson, M. (Ed.) *Objective Measurement: Theory into Practice*. Norwood, NJ: Ablex.

Goldstein, H. (1994) Mathematical and ideological assumptions in the modeling of test item responses. In Laveault, D., Zumbo, B. D., Gessaroli, M. and Boss, M. *Modern Theories of Measurement: Problems & Issues*. Ottawa: University of Ottawa, Faculty of Education.

Goldstein, H. and Wood, R. (1989) Five decades of item response modeling. *British Journal of Mathematical Statistical Psychology* 42: 139–67.

Kingsbury, G. G. and Zara, A. R. (1989) Procedures for selecting items for computerized adaptive tests. *Applied Measurement in Education* 2 (4): 359–75.

Kendall, M. G. and Stuart, A. (1969). *The Advanced theory of statistics*. 3rd Edition. London: Griffin.

Linacre, J. M. and Wright, B. D. (1995) *BIGSTEPS: Rasch Model Computer Program*. Chicago, IL: MESA Press.

Lord, F. M. (1980) *Applications of Item Response Theory to Practical Testing Problems*. Hillsdale, NJ: Lawrence Erlbaum Associates Publishers.

Luecht, R. M. (1995) *A conceptual twist on the parameterization of IRT models*. Paper presented at the Annual Meeting of the Psychometric Society. Minneapolis, MN.

McDonald, R. P. (1967) Nonlinear factor analysis. *Psychometrika*, Monograph No. 15, 32 (4).

Mellenbergh, G. J. (1995) Conceptual notes on models for discrete polytomous item responses. *Applied Psychological Measurement* 19 (1): 91–100.

Mislevy, R. J. and Bock, R. D. (1990) *BILOG 3: Item Analysis and Test Scoring with Binary Logistic Models*. Chicago, IL: Scientific Software.

Rasch, G. (1960) *Probabilistic Models for Some Intelligence and Attainment Tests*. Chicago, IL: MESA Press.

Reckase, M. D. (1985) The difficulty of test items that measure more than one dimension. *Applied Psychological Measurement* 9: 401–12.

Reckase, M. D., Ackerman, T. A. and Carlson, J. E. (1988) Building a unidimensional test using multidimensional items. *Journal of Educational Measurement* 25 (3): 193–203.

Reckase, M. D. and McKinley, R. L. (1991) The discriminating power of test items that measure more than one dimension. *Applied Psychological Measurement* 15 (4): 361–73.

van der Linden, W. J. (1995) *Test score and prediction bias: Artefacts due to the use of incomplete regression models*. Paper presented at the annual meeting of the American Educational Research Association. San Francisco, CA.

Yen, W. M. (1993) Scaling performance assessments: Strategies for managing local item dependence. *Journal of Educational Measurement* 30 (3): 187–213.

12

An overview and some observations on the psychometric models used in computer-adaptive language testing

Bruno D. Zumbo
University of Northern British Columbia and
Carleton University

Peter D. MacMillan
University of Northern British Columbia

Introduction

This chapter has two aims, one fairly general and the other fairly specific. The general aim is to provide some observations and comments on the variety of psychometric models currently at our disposal, whether for computer-adaptive testing or more generally in the wide-sense application of measurement. With this general aim we intend to go beyond a simple discussion of the preceding chapters and draw on our experiences and knowledge in philosophies of science, educational measurement, psychometrics, pure and applied mathematics and statistical science to shed some light on the on-going debate regarding which psychometric models are most appropriate and when. To place psychometric models into a particular camp or box in some classification scheme invites criticism, often rather facile. Nevertheless, if someone does not attempt to identify similarities among apparently different psychometric views and to synthesize the results of various analyses, we would probably find ourselves overwhelmed by a mass of independent models and investigations with little hope of communicating with anyone who does not happen to be specializing on 'our' problem or techniques. Hence, in the interest of avoiding the monotony of the latter state of affairs, even thoroughly committed measurement specialists must welcome occasional attempts to compare, contrast and wrest the kernels of truth from disparate positions. However, while we are welcoming such attempts, we must also guard against oversimplifications and confusions and it is in the interest of the latter responsibility that we write to the more general aim.

The more specific aim of this chapter is to discuss the three previous chapters in this section: those by Eignor, Linacre and Leucht. In order to do these chapters justice, it was necessary for us to be familiar with them. The reading of the entire set of chapters leaves us with an impression that we wish to comment on. As our section marks the end of the reading construct and CAT sections and the beginning of the measurement section, it seems appropriate to do so. The reading of individual chapters leaves us with the impression that the specialists in their respective fields are 'talking past' each other. This is perhaps inevitable; hopefully this volume will reduce the degree to which this continues to occur.

While it is helpful for reading specialists and particularly for CAT specialists to have some knowledge of measurement, especially item response modeling (IRM), it is not necessary that these specialists be experts in this area, nor is it reasonable for them to be expected to make measurement decisions and/or derive new models.

Problems were most evident in the attempts of the CAT chapters to justify the use of the Rasch model (RM) over the three-parameter logistic model (3PLM) or vice versa. This has been an on-going debate, even argument, since the inception of IRM. Considerable writing and reading could have been saved if the CAT writers had merely chosen their preferred model and, at most, provided the readers with evidence that the model worked in the given situation. Discussion of Luecht's chapter is the more logical place to continue this debate although no one chapter, even Luecht's, will be likely to convince the adherents of one model that the other is superior.

Likewise, the measurement specialists cannot and should not be expected to be reading specialists. However, it is reasonable to expect the measurement specialist to demonstrate sufficient background knowledge in the area to be measured in order to know that the model on which the measurement is based is judged sound in the light of present day reading comprehension theory. We discuss reading comprehension because it is necessary to do so in order to discuss the Linacre chapter. It is not our intention to promote one reading comprehension model over another nor is it our intention to pass ourselves off as particularly knowledgeable in this field.

The varieties of 'model'

'Model' is a favourite word of measurement specialists. Sometimes it is unwittingly/unintentionally used with various shades of meaning. Often we use it to convey the sense of:

1. a mathematical model;
2. a model in the wider philosophic sense;
3. an explanatory model;
4. a descriptive model;
5. a stochastic or random variable model;
6. a logical model; and
7. a computational model, to list but a few.

What complicates matters is that these uses of 'model' are not mutually exclusive (nor exhaustive) but they do have essential but subtle distinctions that we will attempt to elucidate. We have found it incredible that a word that is so commonly used and is the source of so much tension has yet, to our knowledge, to be adequately defined and discussed in the psychometric literature. After defining various features of models we will return to shed some light on psychometric models and the on-going battles over their use.

In the technical philosophy of science literature there are two distinct meanings of 'model': postulational or axiomatic and iconic.

Logic and mathematical logic (postulational or axiomatic)

In certain formal disciplines such as logic and mathematics a model (for or of a theory) has its roots in the axiomatic or postulational method of deductive systems including some branches of modern mathematics. This method can be seen in the early work of scholars such as Thales, Pythagoras, and later in the logical format of Euclid's classics. The basic idea of the axiomatic method is that the content of a scientific subject should consist of a set of assumed propositions, called axioms or postulates, and that other propositions, called theorems, should be derived from the basic assumptions by applying the rules of deductive logic. Note that the axioms must be accepted without proof. However, if the scientific subject under construction in this axiomatic or postulational-deductive fashion is to be practical, realistic and purposeful, the axioms are usually selected so as to approximate or idealize actual experience. Even Euclid, in many senses the major protagonist of axiomatic method, did not conceive of his postulates as mere assumptions. Instead he described them as common notions or what was later described as self-evident truths or empirical fact, and Euclid's axioms about points and lines, for example, do actually appear to correspond with the drawings we make by use of a pencil and ruler.

The attitude of pure or abstract modern mathematics is quite different from the one just described. In it one has the right to choose the content of axioms somewhat arbitrarily (often allowing for undefined terms or empty symbols), subject only to certain logical criteria such as consistency. A set of postulates is said to be consistent if there exists an interpretation of the undefined terms which converts all the postulates into true statements. In mathematical logic the result of such interpretation, that is, the concrete set of true statements, is called a 'model' of the abstract postulate system. In so doing the abstract deductive system is said to be transformed from an abstract theory into a concrete theory.

Therefore, two models, in this mathematical sense, can then be quite different. For example, Kolmogorov laid the set-theoretic foundation for a probability theory for which there are two interpretations (or models) of probability. These two models, Bayesian and Frequentist, have at times led to debates that make the Rasch versus 2-parameter or 3-parameter debate appear cordial. Similarly, quantum and relativistic physics have a variety of interpretations. Finally, as these two examples may imply, most but not all axiomatic models are deterministic rather than stochastic (or statistical/probabilistic).

Analogues of things or processes (iconic)

The second meaning of 'model' in the technical philosophy of science literature involves analogues of things and/or processes. Some real or imagined thing, or process, behaves similarly to some other thing or process. In this sense a mathematical model is an abstract idealization of various features of a real situation in the same sense that pure Euclidean plane geometry is the abstract counterpart of the surveyors concept of physical points, lines, polygons, circles, etc. and their properties.

Note that although we consistently refer to mathematical models, the term 'model' has a wider-sense meaning in the philosophies of science. For example, we have the molecule model of gas or the computer model of human cognition or memory.

Before we turn back to psychometric models it is important to highlight that models are used for certain definite purposes in the sciences:

1. they enable certain inferences to be made which would not otherwise be possible: a logical purpose; and
2. they express our knowledge of the world, and they enable us to delineate and extend our knowledge of the world: an epistemological purpose allowing us to reflect on the standards to which genuine knowledge should conform.

To fully appreciate these purposes for models it is instructive to note that models can be homeomorphs or paramorphs. The essential difference between these is the source of a model and the subject of a model. For example, a model airplane has as its source the real thing, the airplane, while its subject is the airplane—a homeomorph. However, when one is using the computer as the model for cognition, the computer is not modeled on cognition in any way at all. The computer is modeled on something quite different, namely principles in logic and solid state physics.

Bruno D. Zumbo & Peter D. MacMillan

Therefore, the two main uses of models in science are:

1. heuristic, to simplify a phenomenon; or
2. explanatory, to describe the causal mechanism which produces the phenomena.

It is often argued in the literature on philosophies of science that explanatory models (or theories) are (use) paramorphic models.

What do the various meanings of 'model' tell us about psychometric models?

First, all measurement models known to us are paramorphic but heuristic. This lack of explanatory focus has been the root of a long-standing *Angst* among some measurement specialists. The most recent attempt at relieving this *Angst* has been to prevail on cognitive theory to lend an explanatory hand. Our only observation on this front is that not all cognitive theories are explanatory so that we need to be careful that in our quest for explanatory power we do not inadvertently supplant one heuristic model with another while deluding ourselves that our new model is explanatory. Furthermore, these cognitive theories need to be empirically tested—see, for example, Zumbo *et al.* (1997) wherein we test a social-cognition theory of item discrimination.

Second, most measurement models vary on the degree of iconic and/or axiomatic or postulational focus. For example, there exists an extensive literature on purely axiomatic measurement with key figures such as S. S. Stevens, Duncan Luce, Louis Narens, Patrick Suppes, Fred Suppe, and other mathematicians, philosophers of science and mathematical psychologists. Such models of measurement have been used almost exclusively in psychophysics, decision sciences and mathematical social/behavioural sciences. These models, however, are not used in the everyday practice of psychometrics, nor were they necessarily intended to—the major cause of this lack of use of the models inspired by psychophysics is that they are mostly deterministic models so that one is left asking how many axioms need to be false before a model is not useable. The most common result discussed outside of the fields of psychophysics and decision sciences is that of scaling theory and scales of measurement. In this light, the Rasch model has some kinship with this axiomatic approach—one could argue that the Rasch model is a probabilistic/stochastic variant on these traditional deterministic models. Yet another axiomatic-like model or characterization is that of Don Zimmerman's (Hilbert Space or conditional probability) abstractions of test theory. Zimmerman's model is distinct in purpose in psychometrics because its level of abstraction is deliberately chosen so as to weed out contradiction and apparent paradoxes and to provide an over-arching framework in test theory.

Most of the psychometric models in practice today have both a deterministic (or structural) component and a stochastic component, and most are of the iconic variety — IRM, generalizability theory and some results in test theory. The purpose of these models is to allow us to make certain inferences about test scores. In this light, the Rasch model has an essential difference (and one that distinguishes it from the one-parameter logistic model: 1PLM) in that it also has an epistemological purpose. However, for simple inferential purposes the Rasch model has much in common with the 1PLM (or, in fact, the 2- or 3PLM) IRM, but its epistemological purpose sets it aside. This is a subtle but essential point that is seldom appreciated outside the Rasch camp. This epistemological purpose is, beyond a doubt, controversial because some psychometricians may argue that psychometric models should not serve epistemological purposes but rather should only aid in inference.

As the first author has noted previously (Zumbo 1992; 1996), axiomatic models in broad strokes do not rely on validity theory for buttressing their score inferences but rather on proofs of uniqueness and representational theorems. The iconic models, on the other hand, like classical test theory, IRM and generalizability theory, rely on validity theory for validating their inferences. Again, in this light the Rasch model relies on its axiomatic and epistemological kinship to aid in its interpretational framework (interval scale measurement).

Our last word on model theory is a point that Estes (1975) highlights. He describes a useful model as one needing sharpness. That is, the model must capture aspects of a phenomenon that are believed to be important in a simple enough form that unambiguous empirical implications can be derived and so that disparities between predictions and observations will be informative and instructive. Without intending to advocate that our models be all-encompassing, complex and hence almost irrefutable, the practitioner of psychometrics cannot shirk the question of the realism of the model used, except on pain of failure.

The on-going psychometric battles regarding models

RM vs. 3PLM

We wish to add a fundamental point on the Rasch (RM) versus three-parameter logistic model (3PLM) debate that was either missed or glossed over in the various chapters of this book. While this point is primarily aimed at the non-IRM specialists, we hope it will be useful to all.

Proponents of RM appear to differ in a very fundamental way from the conventional view of modeling data (e.g. the proponents of the 3PLM). The conventional view is that the models adequacy is determined by how well the model fits the data for which the model is being proposed for use. RM proponents talk of the data fitting the model. This contrasting view arises because for RM proponents the Rasch model is axiomatic (in the sense of the propositional tradition described above so that the axioms are 'given' and the data are made to fit) and derived so that it has properties of sample-free item difficulties and person ability estimates (Rasch 1992/1960). There must be fit of individual persons and individual items to the Rasch model in order to make use of the models property of 'specific or local objectivity'; that is, the measurement result is not dependent on the items used or the persons being measured.

From our model theory framework described above, then, because the Rasch model is an axiomatic model, the mathematical function that the data must fit is determined by the model itself. Unlike 2PLM and 3PLM, or even 1PLM practitioners, the RM proponent is not free to shop around for the function that best fits the data of interest at the time; rather he/she must shop around for the data that fit the model. If particular persons or items do not behave in a way compatible with the Rasch model, the persons or items are discarded.

This seemingly radical view is not really different from everyday expectations. A nurse would not use a weighing scale that was known to give inaccurate readings, nor would she/he retain a patient's reading if the patient misbehaved by bouncing up and down on the scales when the measurement was being taken. This lack of recognition of a difference in outlook is not noted throughout the chapters, even during comparisons between the RM and the 3PLM. We believe 3PLM proponents act in the same fashion as the RM proponents. What researcher would not remove an outlier from the data when it could be demonstrated that the measurement was the result of misbehaviour rather than merely exceptional behaviour? Removal of faulty test items after item analysis is standard practice.

Specific comments on the chapters

Lurking in all of these chapters is the long-standing psychometric debate over Rasch versus non-Rasch models. Although we comment on the differences, we will try to avoid being drawn into this debate and taking sides but even among us there are lurking (and not so lurking) affinities.

Discussion of Eignor

Eignor raises important practical issues related to the necessity of an examinee responding to multiple items based on a single piece of text, that is, a testlet. Concerns are expressed in relation to item independence and the inefficiency of being required to use items that are not maximally matched to the examinee's ability level.

Furthermore, the chapter thoroughly discusses issues and approaches to deal with item exposure. Item exposure is a fundamental concern of CAT. In fact, item exposure and/or curricular and other external changes may result in item parameter drift—change in item parameters over time. Uncontrolled high exposure can result in an item becoming easier and/or less discriminating over time. Of course, item parameter drift is not exclusive to CAT but rather is a common issue with maintaining any item pool over time.

Within the Eignor chapter, the preference for the 3PLM over the RM leads to the statement that if the Rasch model is chosen more items are statistically interchangeable as items need only be matched on the difficulty parameter value. Although Eignor does not directly make the claim, the reader might assume that the RM selection would retain items that were unsuitable by more rigorous 3PLM criteria of discrimination and pseudo-guessing parameter matches in addition to the difficulty parameter matching. A proponent of the RM would quickly dismiss these additional parameters as being sample-dependent artefacts and thus not appropriate for matching at all. To match on irrelevant and unstable characteristics would not be considered an improvement in measurement. More is not necessarily better. Wright (1997) reminds us of the Hambleton and Mortois results in which the RM demonstrated better fit between data and model than the 3PLM model across a variety of data sets. Luecht's chapter (this volume) supports this earlier study.

Discussion of Linacre

Linacre presents us with a good lucid reminder of the scientific (reductionist) view of research and measurement. In fact, given our delineation of the type of model that the RM is, Linacre's chapter could be re-titled *An **Axiomatic** Measurement Approach* ... Several of the points are summarized here as they set the stage not only for CAT for reading comprehension but for measurement in general. In order to measure reading comprehension, simplifications must be developed that allow for the discrimination among different levels of text understanding. Linacre describes Stenner's (1995) model for text difficulty as being a combination of recall effort and decoding load, that is:

text difficulty = recall effort + decoding load

yet offers little rationale for Stenner's choice of this model. Recall effort is equated with word unfamiliarity and decoding load with sentence complexity.

This results in the equation:

text difficulty = word unfamiliarity + sentence complexity

Word familiarity, the reverse of word unfamiliarity, is directly related to word frequency, whereas sentence length is described as a useful measure of sentence complexity. This results in Stenner's Lexile measure of text difficulty:

text difficulty (measured in Lexiles, a logit transformation)
= 582 – 386 x mean(ln(word frequency)) + 1768xln(mean(sentence length))

As presented, the Stenner model appears to be pure empiricism until 'The Simple View of Reading' as described in the Grabe chapter (this volume) is re-examined. This model, which is represented as:

reading comprehension = decoding * comprehension,

begins to be seen as the Stenner model when reading comprehension is described as a combination of word recognition abilities and general comprehension abilities. The multiplicative model is converted to an additive model by taking the logarithm of the equation:

ln(reading comprehension) = ln(word recognition) + ln(comprehension)

The establishment of the equivalence of text difficulty, or item difficulty for the items associated with the text, and reading comprehension ability, requires an understanding of a property of Rasch measurement and IRMs in general. These models place both the characteristic of the person, generally called ability, and the characteristic of the item, generally called difficulty, on the same scale of measurement. Thus, a person's ability can be determined to be greater than, equal to, or less than the difficulty of the item. In this specific case, the reading comprehension ability of the individual is compared to the reading comprehension difficulty of the text. Now it is clear that the simple view of reading is embodied in Stenner's model when Stenner's measures of word recognition and comprehension are employed.

Returning to the comparison of text difficulty and reading comprehension ability, a person's reading ability would be said to equal to the text's difficulty when the probability of the of the person answering a comprehension item correctly is .5. Within the CAT chapters, much discussion is directed at this desirability, even necessity, of matching person ability with item difficulty. Notice that text difficulty and difficulty of the items associated with that text become synonymous. In short, maximum information is obtained when an examinee is presented with an item equal in difficulty to the examinee's ability. As previously mentioned, the inability of all items within a testlet to optimally match the estimated ability of the examinee is discussed by Eignor. Yet, as Linacre points out, Stenner rejected this optimal 0.5 probability level for a level of 0.7. The level of 0.7 is linked to a pragmatic view that the reader has to be relatively successful if reading comprehension is indeed being measured. Again Stenner's (1995) view is congruent with the views of the reading specialists and the CAT specialists. For instance, Grabe's description of a good reader as being both fluent and automatic, and reading as being a rapid process, supports Stenner. The 'inefficient' 0.7 level also must be quite acceptable to anyone in agreement with Larson's (this volume) suggested testing routine of warm-up, testing at level, then wind-down. The importance of the 'feel' of the testing is more strongly stated by Bernhardt (this volume), who believes that tests must be friendly to test takers and that the process must not be paralyzed by theoretical issues. Returning to Stenner, his choice of 0.7 is more than pragmatic; if the reader cannot read the text fluently, then comprehension is not being measured. Text less difficult than the reader is able is a necessity, not a nicety, for measurement of reading comprehension.

Discussion of Luecht

This chapter focuses on model choice, model fit and modeling of item responses. Data were simulated based on Gessaroli's (1995) model consisting of one common factor and four oblique factors (each orthogonal to the common factor). Given that the model is based on an analysis of ACT assessment data, it is depicting a realistic situation.

We wonder, however, what the results would be if the local item dependence (LID) structure was such that the four oblique factors were not orthogonal to the common factor. This is not an entirely nonsensical model because it simply implies that the degree of LID is correlated with the level of the latent variable—there is no reason to assume that the degree of LID need be constant across the continuum of variation. It is certainly possible that the degree of LID would be, for example, greater for individuals scoring high on the common factor. Part of the reason why they score higher may be because they understand the contextual nature (i.e. LID) of the questions.

The issue of guessing

Within a CAT environment, particularly for reading comprehension, the issue of guessing seems less of an issue than in other testing situations. The examinee must be presented with text and items that are of a difficulty level that is lower than the examinee's ability. Even in the certification and licensure situation, does not CAT establish the examinee's ability as being above or below a cut-score, all the while employing items that efficiently measure examinee ability? Or does certification CAT take a non-CAT approach and present the inadequate examinee with a set of items that are more difficult than the examinee is able? Guessing should not be an issue for CAT.

Luecht's chapter brings to mind the commonly read phrase (attributable to George Box) that no model is correct but that nonetheless some models are still useful. This highlights for us that in an empirical context a 'best' model is nearly impossible to ascertain and that a model need only be useful for the purpose at hand.

If however, one combines Box's sentiments with our previous review of philosophical model theory, several interesting observations arise. First, all modeling eventually prompts a reality or truthfulness question. Even models in modern pure mathematics eventually lead to a question of the 'truth' of the model. Second, as we noted above, consistency is the only essential property of a set of axioms. However, a pure mathematician may also ask a question of economy. Has she assumed too much? Can she dispense with one or two axioms? Finally, this highlights the fact that more economical models which assume less are more attractive, given that consistency is still met. In an important sense a simpler model that can achieve its ends with fewer assumptions is more powerful.

Does this sense of economy of assumptions exist in iconic (and more specifically psychometric) models? We would argue that it does and that the tradition for such comes from statistical science. In empirical modeling, reliance on models that are relatively non-committal is preferred, so as to reduce liability to gross error. In general, the less one is certain of the generating process (i.e., the factors contributing to the score variability) the more attractive noncommittal formulations become. By noncommittal formulations we are referring to methods that make few assumptions about the generating process of the data and sometimes go under the title of 'nonparametric' models—the best examples of which are Ramsey's (1991: 1995) approaches to item analysis which are embodied in his program TESTGRAF.

The future

Measurement of writing ability

While CAT related to reading comprehension has been discussed in this book, the issues of writing ability and listening comprehension have not, except in the chapter by Dunkel. We have chosen to speculate on the possibilities for the use of CAT techniques in these two areas. First, the possibility of computerized measurement of writing ability is addressed, followed by discussions of measurement of listening comprehension. Stenner's Windows-based software program Lexile Analyzer, see http://www.lexile.com, is capable of analyzing the difficulty level of any text. Rather than employ standard texts for an examinee to read as in a measure of reading comprehension, the examinee could instead be prompted to produce text under some standardized testing conditions. The difficulty level of the text could be determined; this level would correspond to the writing ability level of the examinee. Quite apart from the expected rules of testing time and topic choice, computer spell checks would be required as misspelled words would appear to be novel words and, as such, artificially drive up the difficulty level of the text produced by the examinee. The issue of computerized grammar checks might also be required in order to avoid the appearance of incredibly long sentences that in reality are due to flawed sentence construction or even a lack of punctuation. Again this error would artificially inflate the text difficulty estimate. Yet are not these flaws that must be corrected for indicative of the examinee's ability? How might we account for these flaws as indicators of examinee ability?

A CAT might be especially necessary if writing prompts are found to elicit differing levels of text difficulty, that is, too complex or simple to elicit text production that is representative of the best efforts of an individual. While differing reading comprehension difficulty among samples of text that appear to be of equal difficulty might be expected, the thought that writing probes might vary in difficulty is less intuitive. Examination of the results of a norming study that involved both text prompts for measurement of reading fluency and writing prompts designed for measurement of writing fluency indicates that both types of prompt display some differences in difficulty (MacMillan 1997).

Listening comprehension

Tapes of spoken dialogue have been used to measure listening comprehension. In a CAT situation, this would require: quick selection of a segment of tape (chosen on the basis of the difficulty of the new piece being matched with the updated ability estimate for the examinee), playing of the tape, followed by presentations of written items for the subject to respond to according to typical CAT practice. Computer programs that can scan text and 'read out loud' are already available. Refinement of these programs could result in computer-generated speech prompts followed by questions in either, or both, written or spoken format. This would result in increased authenticity for listening comprehension, particularly second language comprehension measurement.

Authors' note

We consider the relative contribution of the authors to be equal. Order of authorship was decided by a random process.

References

Estes, W. K. (1975) Some targets for mathematical psychology. *Journal of Mathematical Psychology* 12: 263–82.

Gesaroli, M. (1995) *Assessing Dimensionality using nonlinear factor analysis.* Paper presented at the annual meeting of the american Education Research Association, San Francisco, CA.

MacMillan, P. D. (1997) *Rasch solutions to curriculum based measurement problems.* Paper presented at the Ninth International Objective Measurement Workshop, Chicago, IL.

Ramsey, J. O. (1991) Kernel smoothing approaches to nonparametric item characteristic curve estimation. *Psychometrika* 56: 611–30.

Ramsey, J. O. (1995) A similarity-based smoothing approach to nondimensional item analysis. *Psychometrika* 60: 323–39.

Rasch, G. (1960, 1992) *Probabilistic Models for Some Intelligence and Attainment Tests.* Chicago, IL: MESA Press.

Stenner, A. J. (1995) *The objective measurement of reading comprehension.* Paper presented at the Eighth International Objective Measurement Workshop, Berkeley, CA

Wright, B. D. (1997) A history of social science measurement. *Educational Measurement: Issues and Practice* 16 (4): 33–45.

Zumbo, B. D. (1992) Statistics and research design in the behavioral sciences—A review. *Educational and Psychological Measurement* 52: 787–94.

Zumbo, B. D. (1996) Discussion on statistics and the theory of measurement (by D. J. Hand 1996). *Journal of the Royal Statistical Society, Series A* 159: 488.

Zumbo, B. D., Pope, G. A., Watson, J. E. and Hubley, A. M. (1997) An empirical test of Roskam's conjecture about the interpretation of an ICC parameter in personality inventories. *Educational and Psychological Measurement* 57: 963–9.

Subject index

A

B

background   2, 5, 6, 17, 18, 19, 20, 24, 25, 43, 45, 50, 51, 53, 55, 61, 63, 69, 114, 116, 127, 147, 164, 213

background knowledge   2, 5, 17, 18, 19, 20, 24, 25, 45, 50, 53, 55, 61, 69, 213

BIGSTEPS   199, 201, 213, 215

BILOG   128, 129, 135, 196, 199, 201, 212, 213, 215

C

calibration   64, 103, 104, 105, 107, 108, 110, 111, 114, 121, 128, 129, 172, 175, 180, 185, 191, 196, 197, 198, 199, 200, 201, 202, 203, 205, 206, 208, 209

cloze   58, 59, 68, 78

cognitive   2, 10, 11, 12, 14, 21, 23, 27, 39, 40, 41, 43, 46, 47, 54, 60, 70, 77, 116, 138, 140, 143, 146, 157, 163, 165, 181, 183, 216

cohesion   51

comprehension   1, 7, 9, 10, 11, 12, 13, 14, 15, 16, 17, 18, 19, 20, 21, 22, 23, 24, 25, 26, 27, 28, 29, 30, 31, 32, 33, 34, 35, 37, 39, 40, 41, 42, 43, 44, 45, 46, 47, 48, 50, 52, 56, 65, 66, 67, 68, 69, 70, 78, 84, 91, 93, 94, 95, 96, 97, 98, 99, 105, 108, 110, 111, 117, 118, 119, 120, 121, 128, 130, 132, 137, 139, 140, 142, 147, 148, 151, 155, 156, 159, 161, 163, 164, 165, 166, 175, 176, 177, 178, 181, 182, 183, 184, 185, 186, 187, 190, 191, 213, 219, 220, 221, 222, 223, 224

computer   2, 16, 36, 37, 51, 54, 55, 57, 58, 60, 62, 64, 67, 68, 71, 72, 73, 76, 78, 79, 80, 81, 82, 83, 84, 85, 86, 87, 88, 89, 90, 91, 92, 93, 94, 95, 99, 101, 102, 110, 111, 115, 120, 121, 130, 131, 132, 133, 135, 136, 138, 139, 140, 142, 144, 145, 146, 148, 149, 150, 155, 160, 164, 166, 167, 168, 170, 174, 177, 179, 182, 187, 190, 195, 196, 208, 210, 215, 218, 223

computer-adaptive   2, 37, 51, 55, 60, 64, 71, 72, 73, 78, 79, 82, 83, 84, 88, 89, 93, 135, 136, 138, 140, 142, 144, 145, 146, 148, 164, 165, 166, 177, 193, 196, 197, 208, 218, 226

computer-based   58, 64

connectionist   31

constraints   11, 26, 31, 40, 45, 49, 64, 90, 106, 116, 117, 133, 140, 166, 167, 168, 170, 178, 184, 196, 197, 208

construct definition   148, 150, 154, 155, 156, 157, 158, 159, 160, 161, 162

S

TOEFL   25, 43, 56, 62, 65, 139, 145, 147, 148, 167, 169, 171, 174, 176, 177, 178, 180

trial/trialing   91, 93, 94, 100, 101, 102, 103, 108, 109, 110

true–false items/questions

U

unidimensionality   3, 54, 104, 105, 106, 107, 114, 118, 119, 120, 121, 126, 129, 134, 159, 165, 195, 196

V

validity   35, 36, 57, 58, 59, 60, 62, 69, 76, 77, 79, 80, 83, 93, 104, 116, 121, 134, 185, 147, 160, 164, 165, 179, 217

- **concurrent**   180
- **construct**   164, 165
- **predictive**   116

visual   2, 14, 19, 26, 29, 39, 44, 98

vocabulary   2, 4, 5, 11, 15, 22, 31, 32, 34, 35, 36, 41, 42, 43, 45, 48, 50, 65, 75, 78, 79, 86, 98, 101, 111, 125, 128, 156, 164, 182

W

wind-down   74, 80, 83, 84, 85, 86, 215, 235

word recognition   2, 5, 11, 13, 14, 15, 16, 19, 22, 23, 24, 26, 29, 31, 32, 33, 34, 36, 37, 39, 42, 44, 45, 46, 47, 50, 60, 62, 64, 65, 155, 157, 220

writing   4, 5, 35, 37, 41, 43, 45, 59, 64, 69, 73, 78, 87, 96, 97, 102, 106, 107, 117, 138, 143, 146, 147, 2013 222, 223